D1233294

EDRA

Frederick Law Olmsted and the City Planning Movement in the United States

Architecture and Urban Design, No. 15

Stephen C. Foster, Series Editor

Associate Professor of Art History
University of Iowa

Other Titles in This Series

Frederick Law Olmsted and the City Planning Movement in the United States

by
Irving D. Fisher

UMI RESEARCH PRESS
Ann Arbor, Michigan

Produced and distributed by
UMI Research Press
an imprint of
University Microfilms, Inc.
Ann Arbor, Michigan 48106

Library of Congress Cataloging in Publication Data

Fisher, Irving D.
  Frederick Law Olmsted and the city planning
movement in the United States.

  (Architecture and urban design ; no. 15)
  Revision of Thesis (Ph.D.)—Columbia University,
1976.
  Bibliography: p.
  Includes index.
  1. Olmsted, Frederick Law, 1822-1903—Contributions
in city planning.   2. City planning—United States—
History—19th century.   3. Parks—United States—
History—19th century.   I. Title.   II. Series.
NA9085.056F57   1986   711'.4'0924   85-31588
ISBN 0-8357-1685-6 (alk. paper)

To the memory of
Nathan and Clara Fisher

Frederick Law Olmsted, ca. 1890
*(Courtesy National Park Service
Frederick Law Olmsted National Historic Site)*

Contents

Figures

Acknowledgments

In my long preoccupation with this study I have become indebted to only a few, but to them I am deeply grateful. Through their aid and patience they have tried to keep me from error; where error remains the fault is mine.

Julian Franklin read and reread the entire manuscript in its early and late stages. His critical appraisal and encouragement have buoyed me over the years. Herbert Deane kindly and diligently read the entire manuscript for my benefit. Martin Fleisher deserves my thanks for his critique of the early portion of my study. Augusta Siegel selflessly gave me the invaluable opportunity to find my direction when she first typed my notes into coherent form. Virginia Emery merits my deep appreciation for her commitment to excellence in typing the final version of my manuscript. To Drusilla Fielding Stemper I owe a profound debt; she gave me a quiet place to work and her intelligence and discerning eye have refined the entire manuscript.

I am happy to acknowledge the cheerful aid of Casandra Fitzherbert, Gerald Banner, James Brady, and the library staff at the University of Southern Maine. I gratefully acknowledge my debt to the staff at the Hawthorne-Longfellow Library at Bowdoin College. Over the years their facilities have always been available to me. Thanks are due to Anne E. Jordan of the Frederick Law Olmsted National Historic Site in Brookline, Massachusetts for her assistance.

Finally, to my wife Janice and my children, Nathaniel, Elizabeth, Mark, Claire, and Dan, for their loyal support and patient impatience over the years, thanks and peace.

1

Introduction

Plans for early towns and cities, drawn to meet the needs of a limited population in a subsistence-agricultural economy, were static in conception. Rapid urban growth that accompanied the industrial society of the nineteenth century taxed the adequacy of these plans. Rural migrants and European immigrants, seeking jobs and housing along with the social amenities of education, culture, and comfort, surged into cities. The influx brought problems that city administrations found difficult to solve. The plans of the city founders proved inadequate to handle the rapid development and growth. In some cities, such as New York and Chicago, where attempts were made to extend the original city plans, the results proved ungratifying.[1] Moreover, the municipal governmental structures of nineteenth-century American cities were not suited to deliver the services that the agglomerated cities required. Faced with the problem of servicing a rapidly increasing, heterogeneous population—economically, socially, and culturally diverse, and attempting to accommodate to an urban environment—the political administrators were incapacitated by the traditional forms of municipal government. The city governments were administratively fragmented and limited in their decision-making capacities by the constitutional and statutory restrictions of the states. To adequately handle the physical and social needs of congested urban aggregates there was need for comprehensive city planning. But to make the planning effective there was the additional need to establish unified municipal structures possessing adequate political powers. Urban expansion had been largely unplanned and haphazard, as was the delivery of services, where any existed. There was neither an ideological doctrine nor a political theory which was acceptable as a basis for an institutional approach to deal with social problems. The pervading ideology was that of laissez-faire—"the least government is the best." This ideological residue of the Adam Smith and the Jeffersonian traditions was reinforced by the doctrines of the Social Darwinists and the philosophy of Herbert Spencer. Even the Americans who were influenced by British and German transcendental idealism were uncompromising in their belief in individualism and in their rejection of governmental intervention. The New England Transcendentalists aimed at a thorough reform of society. But they approached the reform of society by means of individual awakening and regeneration rather than the use of the apparatus of the state. The Transcendentalist of New England "was less a reformer of human circumstance than a regenerator of the human spirit."[2]

For the romantic idealists of the Concord circle it was not institutional mechanisms but individual self-improvement that afforded the basis for the betterment of society. Emerson reflected this view in his essay on "Self-Reliance": "Reformers summon conventions and vote and resolve in multitude. Not so, O friends! will the God deign to enter and inhabit you, but by a method precisely the reverse. It is only as a man puts off all foreign support and stands alone that I see him to be strong and to prevail."[3] In his essay "Politics," Emerson rejected the state as an instrumentality of reform. He explicitly stated, "the less government we have the better,—the fewer laws, and the less confided power. The antidote to this abuse of formal government is the influence of private character, the growth of the Individual."[4] For Emerson the "State must follow and not lead the character and progress of the citizen. . . . the appearance of character makes the State unnecessary."[5] The negative view of government was stated in its most extreme form by Henry Thoreau in his *Civil Disobedience*. Orestes A. Brownson, a sometime member of the Transcendentalist group, attributed "the poverty around him to the absence of true *laissez-faire* and demanded that free competition be restored."[6]

A rationale for governmental intervention was needed, but such use of governmental power as an instrument of social reform was so negatively regarded that it was hardly considered. However, the problems were apparent and pressing. The moral impulse to correct them stimulated a host of private activists, many motivated by religious principles, to engage in reform schemes. But governments, especially municipal administrations, were negligent in taking requisite action.

In 1870 an early advocate of city planning, Frederick Law Olmsted, urged the importance of a comprehensive city plan that would make provision for physical and mental health, safety and transportation needs in commercial and residential districts, proper housing and recreation, and even the aesthetic proclivities of the people. But Olmsted's farsighted thinking found little active response among municipal administrators. In the nineteenth century there was indifference, if not antagonism, to attempts to correct the disparities of the cities through planning. Since the correctives frequently concerned private property, landlords were quick to invoke the rights of private property to resist the intervention of planners. Supported by the courts, individual property rights were accorded primacy over governmental attempts to regulate property for reasons of public welfare or aesthetic considerations. Such decisions authoritatively demonstrated the opposition to governmental planning. Judicial constraints upon the governmental regulation of property, however, were but one manifestation of what Erber calls an "anti-planning culture."[7]

The population influx into nineteenth-century American industrial cities resulted in agglomerations of displaced, isolated individuals, united by an impersonal market economy, and living under inhospitable conditions. The dysfunctions were so acute that municipal leaders were forced to consider governmental action through city planning.

A leading example of city planning for social welfare was the effort of the municipal administration of New York City to provide a public park for the population of the city. Though the park was intended to benefit all classes, of particular concern was the desire to make available to the poorer classes a place to escape the onerous conditions of the city and thus to improve their moral posture. In his message to the Common Council of the city of New York in 1851, Mayor Kingsland urged support for the park to improve the moral fiber of New York's inhabitants: "There are thousands who pass the day of rest among the idle and dissolute, in porter-houses, or in places more objectionable, who would rejoice in being enabled to breathe the pure air in such a place."[8]

The creation of New York's municipal park was a minimal and, at best, an indirect means of improving the social and physical conditions of the city residents. But the creation of the park became the vehicle that launched the career of Frederick Law Olmsted as a landscape architect. By virtue of his award-winning design for the new park, in collaboration with his partner, Calvert Vaux, Olmsted became the architect-in-chief of Central Park in 1858.

The park movement came at a time of transition; the United States was changing from an agrarian to an industrial society. The park movement was partly conditioned by the nostalgia for a departing manner of life, recalling an age of innocence, childhood, and virtue that was receding into history. While Olmsted and the park movement capitalized on this sentiment, Olmsted did not use it to support his basis for designing parks. He was deeply influenced by the literature of the romantic idealists and he derived his aesthetic theory for park design and city planning from the philosophy of German idealism. He believed that society could be reformed through the aesthetic impulse. Moreover, he was, for his time, one of the rare advocates of city life. Olmsted regarded the city as a manifestation of the progress of civilization. When changes to the city were left to the haphazard thrusts of disparate social forces, Olmsted asserted that there was a habitual lag between the form of the city and the functions it was expected to perform. To correct this Olmsted urged the unity of art and science to form a comprehensive city plan for the welfare of the community.

This study will show that the modern city planning movement was a manifestation of a social reform that had its inception in the 1850s and in the efforts of Frederick Law Olmsted. Through his comprehensive planning of space in the metropolitan area, Olmsted demonstrated that the form of the city could be rationally reconstructed to meet the social and aesthetic needs of society.

Olmsted was one of the first Americans to arrive at such a conceptualization and bring it to fruition. He accepted the city as a valuable and rational structure in the evolution of man. The city, he held, provided culture, refinement, wealth, sociability, and progress. The problem which he faced was to preserve the city but, at the same time, to reform it. To carry out his purpose Olmsted derived an aesthetic theory from German romantic idealism. He believed that man's achievement in progress, morality, and unity could be achieved only through and with nature, not in antagonism to it. Olmsted had no fundamental quarrel with man-made civilization (i.e., the city). He did not doubt that the quality of life could be improved. The method he used was to combine the beauty to be found in nature with the suspect city as a means of reforming the city. Thus there would be no need to resort to rural living to escape from the disadvantages of the city. Underlying all Olmsted's park and city planning was the assumption that man was capable of reform and improvement. In this notion he followed Emerson's teaching that

> The whole secret of the teacher's force lies in the conviction that men are convertible. . . . They want awakening. Get the soul out of bed, out of her deep habitual sleep, out into God's universe, to a perception of its beauty, and hearing of its call, and your vulgar man, your prosy, selfish sensualist awakes, a god, and is conscious of force to shake the world.[9]

In this way the basic element of the agrarian myth, the wholesome relationship of man to nature, was reconstituted in a new and rational form and enters into the planning of cities.

Olmsted's creative genius, manifesting itself in the planning of Central Park, signaled the beginning of the city planning movement in the United States. It was an important step in the development of the park movement, and the park movement became the basis which led to the conception that the entire city could be conceived and planned as an organic work of art.

In this way city planning entered the orbit of the aesthetic theory of romantic philosophy. Combining the elements of beauty, function, and morality, intrinsic to the aesthetic theories of German romanticism and American Transcendentalism, the creation of parks and city planning emerged as part of the reform movement of the latter nineteenth century. And the city planner became the artistic genius who, by the infusion of his thought into nature, recreates nature at a higher level of organic unity.

Frederick Law Olmsted: The Formative Years

" 'I want to make myself useful in the world, to make others happy, to help advance the condition of Society and hasten the preparation of the Millenium, as well as other things too numerous to mention.' " It is with this obscure letter written by Frederick Law Olmsted to his friend Frederick Kingsbury in 1846 that Henry James described the social and intellectual atmosphere of the pre-Civil War nineteenth century. "There spoke not only the spirit of generous youth, but the moral buoyancy of the time. Altruisms were too numerous to mention. The millenium was not enough."[1]

Nineteenth-century antebellum America, the period in which Olmsted was reared, was undergoing rapid changes. The social institutions were being subjected to critical evaluation. The dysfunctions evoked by the shift from a homogeneous, agricultural society to a heterogeneous, industrial, urban society gave rise to a proliferation of social reformers. There was little doubt among them that the besetting problems could be solved.

What gave the reformers a buoyancy and zeal in their activities was a pervasive conviction that the millenium would be achieved. The millenium seemed so close to some expectant Americans that only the precise date for its inception seemed to elude them.[2]

An amalgam of diverse elements—belief in the perfectibility of man and his institutions, the idealism of romantic philosophy, and the Calvinist striving for the holy community—animated the religious zealots and the reformers of the nineteenth century.

Childhood Enjoyment of Natural Scenery

Frederick Law Olmsted came to manhood during this epoch of restless ferment and experiment in America. Olmsted was born in Hartford, Connecticut in 1822 and was reared in its Puritan, Yankee, small-town environment. The Connecticut towns had changed very little from the days of their early settlement. Following the usual New England pattern, the houses were compactly grouped on town lots about a common with church, town hall, and school standing in the center of the community. (Even today, the basic structure of some of these early Connecticut towns is still visible.) The impact upon Olmsted of these early town designs was strong and the pattern always remained with him. Later in his life, during his career as a city planner, the large municipal park took on for Olmsted the nature of a city commons. In suburban communities he clearly identified the old New England community farming village as the prototype of the suburban towns developing at the periphery of the urban centers.

Appreciation of nature was a strong element in Olmsted's early life. In autobiographical fragments he revealed that his father and his stepmother had a strong love of nature. His father, John Olmsted, a prosperous Hartford dry goods merchant, displayed a sensitivity to the beauty of nature which was "extraordinary, judging from the degree in which his habits were affected by it, for he gave more time and thought to the pursuit of this means of enjoyment than to all other luxuries."[3] Not content with the scenic beauty of central Connecticut, Olmsted's parents took him "in search of the picturesque" on numerous extended tours through the Connecticut Valley, the White Hills, upper New York and Canada, and along most of the New England coast from Connecticut to Maine. These walks and drives in search of natural beauty Olmsted recollected as the happiest memories of his early life.[4]

Availing themselves of the improved network of turnpikes, public roads, and canals which veined New England by the 1820s, the Olmsted family toured the New England and New York countryside in their own coach.[5] Years before such places had become the popular meccas of curious tourists, the Olmsteds had visited the White Hills, Trenton Falls, Niagara, and Lake George. In 1838, when Frederick was sixteen, his father recorded in his diary a journey to the White Mountains which he made with his wife and their two sons. They enjoyed visiting scenes which had been painted by the landscape painter, Thomas Cole, in 1836, and which were later to be celebrated in painting by Doughty, Durand, and Kensett, and in verse and prose by Thoreau, Hawthorne, and Whittier.[6]

It seems that the Olmsteds were not satisfied only to visit the places of scenic beauty; they sought out and read some of the earliest travel books describing America's scenic beauty and grandeur written by American and European visitors. Olmsted later acknowledged the influence of these early writers upon his artistic development: "I had heard my father reading the books of travel in New England of President Dwight, Professor Silliman and Miss Martineau, in all of which the observations on scenery with which I was familiar had helped to make me think that the love of nature, not simply as a naturalist but as a poet loves it, was respectable."[7]

Impelled by the delight to be found in natural scenery, the Olmsteds in their extensive tours travelled the scenic routes and visited the natural wonders described by the well-known travelers. But aesthetic satisfaction was not enough for American tourists. The sheer enjoyment in the observation of the beauty of natural scenery seemed suspect to the Puritanic sensibilities of Dwight, Silliman, and the Olmsteds. To assuage the guilt that the observation of natural beauty might be only a sensuous gratification, they found it necessary to defend their pleasure on the grounds of morality and utility. Silliman, for example, took the trouble to justify his delightful tour between Hartford and Quebec by observing that "natural scenery is intimately connected with taste, moral feeling, utility, and instruction."[8]

The interest which the Olmsteds displayed in America's visible nature—the configuration of its landscapes—was but a manifestation of the growing interest of the American people in the physical and aesthetic attributes of their natural environment. In the ensuing cultural development, the literature and painting of America were absorbed with American scenes. With Washington Irving and James Fenimore Cooper in literature, and the Hudson River School of painters, American artistic genius had flowered into an indigenous artistry in which the wonders of nature were celebrated. In the 1820s, American literature and art were emerging.

Farming as a Vocation

His love of the outdoors and nature gave the young Olmsted an abiding interest in the cultivation of the land and the resolution to turn to farming as a vocation. While Olmsted had every intention of attending college, he was advised to give up the academic because of partial blindness brought on by sumac poisoning when he was fourteen years old. The disorder did not permanently disable him, but gave him an excuse "to indulge [his] strong natural propensity for roaming afield and day dreaming under a tree" while his friends prepared for college.[9] Later, Olmsted "attended" Yale informally with his friends. Though the temporary impairment of his sight did not prevent him later from engaging in extensive reading, studying, and editing, the accident to his eyes may have turned him away from a profession requiring rigorous study to farming.

Having made his vocational choice, Olmsted was not content to train himself to be an ordinary farmer. He felt that farming must be "an honorable and learned profession" based upon science in order that the drudgery and meanness of "old-fashioned" farming "might be dispensed with to advantage." If farming was to be his calling then it must be the vehicle through which Olmsted would participate in the reformation of society. Writing in 1846 to his friend Frederick Kingsbury, he wondered:

> Now, how shall I prepare myself to exercise the greatest and best influence in the situation of life I am likely to be placed in. You know perhaps as well as I what that is—I suppose it's no very great stretch of ambition to anticipate my being a Country Squire in Old Connecticut in the course of fifteen years. I should like to help then as far as I could [to foster] in the popular mind generosity, charity, taste, and etc.,— independence of thought of voting and of acting. The education of the *ignoble vulgus* ought to be much improved and extended.
>
> The Agricultural Interest greatly preponderates in number and wealth in the state, but perhaps has the least influence in Legislation. . . . Now the people-farmers and mechanics—the producing classes that the rest live on—want to think and judge for themselves, to cultivate the intellectual.[10]

Olmsted's letter reveals the confluence of factors which were to control his vocation—whether farmer, writer, landscape architect, or city planner. At the same time it reveals the essence of the American *Zeitgeist* in the thirty years prior to the Civil War. The Calvinist preoccupation with usefulness through one's calling, the optimism that the American experiment in a democratic society will be fulfilled, the potentiality of human perfectionism through reform of institutional practices, the attainment of the ideal society, the reliance upon the farmer as the pivot of the society—these elements of an ideology, reinforced by the romantic philosophy, had already filtered into Olmsted's thinking. They motivated Olmsted to "exercise the greatest and best influence in the situation of life" in which he was likely to be placed.

The conditions which evoked Olmsted's ardor for reformation involved the long-term disintegrating tendencies in Connecticut's predominantly agrarian society. As early as 1750 people had begun to leave Connecticut in search of more fertile lands to the north or west. This westward movement had increased steadily from the latter part of the eighteenth century, and it continued without abatement beyond the year 1840. The flight of emigrants from the rural districts of Connecticut to the West and to the cities (particularly Boston and New York) mirrored a general dissatisfaction with conditions in Connecticut and left in its wake a "great number of dilapidated chimneys and weed-grown cellar holes which mark the sites of once prosperous farm houses."[11]

In choosing to make scientific farming his profession, Olmsted launched himself into the mainstream of America's economy. The period 1815–1860 was, as Paul Gates states, the farmer's age. But at the same time it was a period of accelerating growth in the nonrural population. In the North, particularly, the growth of commercial and industrial cities produced an increasing demand for agricultural products. To adjust to these demands the farmers of the Northeast had not only to meet these demands, but had also to meet the competition of the cheaper products of the western farmers. New England's, and especially Connecticut's, conservative "drudge" farmers (as Bushnell called them) were "obstinately perverse [in hesitating to take] advantage of new machines, tools, and cropping methods." They hesitated to buy even the simplest labor-saving and money-making instruments.[12]

Even as late as 1858 Emerson was admonishing the farmers of New England, whose ways he so much admired, to give up their narrow "petty economics" for the new scientific and mechanical farming methods. In his oration before the Middlesex Agricultural Society Emerson urged the farmers to give up their ox-paced farming economy for scientific methods, machines, chemical fertilizers, and tile drainage.

> I congratulate you at being born at a happy time, when the old slow ways of culture must go out with the sharp stick and the bow and arrow, when the steam engine is in full use, and new plants and new culture are daily brought forward. I congratulate you on the fact that the new year that has just witnessed the successful employment of new machines, of the mower and reaper, on the plains and prairies, has also witnessed the laying of the Atlantic Cable.[13]

But what was characteristic of New England's farmers was not true for the whole of the agricultural community. As Gates states, "The quarter century before the Civil War was a period of continuous agricultural experimentation."[14] The results of research and experiment by European scientists were imported to America and utilized and developed to suit the conditions of the farmers of the United States. New crops or varieties of crops were introduced along with the collection of foreign seeds, plants, and trees. During this period the government itself stimulated the agricultural revolution by financing scientific expeditions in the search for new specimens, seeds, and plants. It was also an era in which the use of mechanized farm machinery was becoming widespread. By 1860 the manufacture of agricultural implements and machines had become a major industry.[15]

In addition to the scientific and mechanical advances during the first half of the nineteenth century, agricultural societies were developing at the local and national levels, as were farm journals and newspapers, and agricultural experts to advise the farmer on crops and methods.

In all these developments Olmsted became deeply involved, determined to become a leader among farmers in a period of agricultural revolution. He wrote,

> I had several years of training on widely separated farms, then bought a small farm [at Guilford, Connecticut] for myself which I afterwards sold in order to buy a larger, and upon this I lived ten years [on Staten Island, New York]. I was a good farmer and a good neighbor, served on the school committee, improved the highways, was secretary of a local farmer's club and of the County Agricultural Society, took prizes for the best crops of wheat and turnips and the best assortment of fruits, imported an English machine, and in partnership with a friend established the first cylindrical drainage tile works in America.[16]

Olmsted's letters in the years 1844–1851 show him to be an avid subscriber and reader of numerous farm journals and publications relating to scientific agriculture and horticulture by American and English scientists and farming experts.[17]

Olmsted explained that while his rural tastes turned him towards farming, it was not only in the technical and scientific aspects of farming that he hoped to exert his influence. The goals which loomed important in Olmsted's idealism were widely encompassing. Taste, political awareness and participation, education—a cultivation of the intellectual—must be introduced and developed. Connecticut's rural society was characterized by individual physical and social isolation, nativism, a stern, orthodox Congregationalism, a dilapidated school system (run mainly by Calvinist ministers), and a state constitution which permitted the control of the state legislature by the small, often depopulated towns. In addition, as the Reverend Horace Bushnell, Olmsted's friend and religious mentor, warned, the emigration of the young people to the more fertile and tractable western lands and to the urban centers was depopulating the state and undermining its social and religious institutions. To curb the trend Bushnell urged that the crude methods of Connecticut farmers could be overcome with the unity of science, experience, formal education, and ingenuity to create what must become the art of farming. Thus achieved, Connecticut agriculture would become an "attractive hope to our sons and daughters . . . [and] enrich both them and the great and respectable class to which they belong."[18]

Olmsted echoed these notions a few years later. A farm owner on Staten Island, and corresponding secretary of the Richmond County Agricultural Society in 1850, Olmsted issued an "Appeal to the Citizens of Staten Island." It was a challenge to adopt the "very best method of Farming," to understand agriculture as a science, to recognize the need for beauty, a seemly architecture, refined rural tastes, and a congeniality within and unity of the farming community.[19]

Notwithstanding his affinity for the rural, Olmsted and his family were of the town, and the development of his interests led him to interpret his rural tastes from the point of view of the townsman. Though he sincerely attempted to train himself for a profession and a life which he respected highly, as a farmer he was a failure. To make it pay Olmsted recognized that his Staten Island farm required intensive farming. Except for the first two years, his attention to the farm was sporadic. He much preferred travel to farming. And when the accounts of his travels were published, he was increasingly attracted to writing, to the detriment of his farming. Even when he took the time to farm the results were often disappointing. It seems his cabbage crops froze too frequently. In the seven years in which he held title to his farm Olmsted was able to sustain himself only by calling upon his father to provide a thousand dollars or more each year.[20]

Olmsted was primarily an artist. It was the aesthetic appeal of nature which captured him, and in the long run provided the basis of his greatest contribution to the American culture.

Religious Background

To deal with Olmsted in any one of his roles or vocations—whether farmer, litterateur, city planner, or conservationist—one must constantly understand him as a reformer, intent upon perfecting society. In this motivation the religious factor was strong. It was only four years before Olmsted was born, in 1818, that Connecticut had adopted a new constitution which severed the union between the state and the Congregational church.[21] Faced with the encroachments of Episcopalianism and the victories of the Unitarians in Massachusetts, orthodox Congregationalists in Connecticut turned increasingly towards revivalism to bolster their position.[22]

The religious orientation and training of young Olmsted were intense and pervading. His parents were typically Puritan, and Olmsted's inculcation into the Protestant ethic both at home and at school was complete. Olmsted's father, while kind and indulgent, was also "a man with a strict sense of justice and of duty, exacting toward himself rather than toward others." His stepmother, who had raised him, "was a Puritan, a model of order and system, most efficient as an organizer and full of interest in Nature and Man."[23] In early childhood, Olmsted's education was put in the hands of Congregational ministers. Olmsted explained that his father was "brought up in a superstitious faith in preaching and didactic instruction, and knowing how little he could by deliberate purpose do for me in that way, my father's affection and desire to 'do right by the boy' made him always eager to devolve as much as practicable of the responsibility of my education upon ministers." This attitude on the part of Olmsted's father may perhaps have been inspired by the early death of Olmsted's mother. As a result, young Olmsted was "successively in charge of six ministers" whose educational qualifications were for the most part of little account, and who did not neglect to teach the harsher aspects of Calvinism preached in rural Connecticut.[24] Thus the problems of predestination and salvation, of duty and obligation, of self-doubt and social responsibility, of human depravity, and public conversion through revivalism, were an abiding influence upon Olmsted all his life.

How deeply he felt in this regard can be gathered from a series of letters written by the father to his son, Frederick Law Olmsted, Jr., who became one of America's leading landscape architects. As a man of seventy-two, the elder Olmsted admonished his son,

> Keep it all the time well in mind that you are now in a school of which you are yourself the headmaster. Your most important business is now that of school-master to yourself—Professor to yourself. What will you do with him? How best train him for his future responsibilities; to do his duty; to fairly, honestly and squarely *earn* the living for his wife and children, as well as fill a responsible place in the machinery of civilization? Do not neglect to think of *your* duty to others as well as to yourself in determining how this ward of yours is to be educated. . . . How is your health—physically, mentally, morally? Do not be backward in telling me. I also am a sinner and after a long and hard discipline am still awfully neglectful of my duty to myself and to you and others. Do I hate myself for it and keep stirring myself to do better? I hope so.[25]

Religion, as a motivating factor, had become deep-seated for Olmsted by the time he was twenty-four years old. In 1846 Olmsted was informally attending lectures at Yale College in the company of his brother John and a number of devoted friends who were students at the College. Nathaniel Taylor still ruled the Yale Divinity School. Attacked by the tenets of Taylor's New Divinity and succumbing to the doctrinal liberalism of Unitarianism, the power of orthodox Calvinism was declining in New England.[26] Efforts were made to liberalize Calvinist theology to make it palatable to a sophisticated audience. The doctrine of original sin was set aside. Predestination and human depravity were softened and obfuscated. Taylor and his liberal co-workers attempted to make God an enlightened, lawful Governor who ruled the universe under a rational law understandable to an enlightened people. "Such Calvinism was really not very objectionable, but it also was not Calvinism. It was the faith of the fathers ruined by the faith of their children."[27]

With revivalism and Taylor's New Divinity, Congregationalism was endeavoring to hold adherents who had become increasingly self-assured through business and political successes and who felt that they were neither as sinful nor eternally damned as orthodox Calvinism would lead them to believe. It seemed evident that a good, just, and loving God had blessed the American people with all manner of good, rewarded virtue with success, and forgiven sin.[28] Furthermore, the urban sophisticates were escaping the embarrassments of self-denunciation and public conversion involved in Congregational revivalism by turning to Unitarian and Episcopal churches.

In the Great Retreat of Calvinism "it became increasingly necessary to defend dialectically doctrines which were actually losing credibility."[29] By the middle of the nineteenth century Puritan theology had been so softened by Taylor and others that it had wholly lost its power.[30]

Resting his New Divinity upon the Scottish common-sense philosophy, Taylor's theological dialectics were radical enough to make the Divinity School at Yale the center of religious controversy.[31] It was while Taylor was expounding and defending his theology as head of Yale's Divinity School that Olmsted, his brother, John, and their intimate friends, Charles Brace, a divinity student, and Frederick Kingsbury, were attending classes and becoming deeply enmeshed in theological discussions. The door of religious controversy, once opened, led them immediately to the awareness of an even more radical figure in the development of Congregational doctrine—the Reverend Horace Bushnell of Hartford.

Bushnell was a product of Yale's Divinity School, but a rebellious one. He rejected both the hard orthodox faith of his rural upbringing and Taylor's New Divinity as inappropriate and sterile.[32] In his search for a new approach to religious experience more acceptable to a sophisticated urban society, Bushnell turned to Samuel Taylor Coleridge and the romantic philosophy. From this springboard Bushnell made the transition from "classic to romantic" within the context of Congregational theology. His accomplishment was considerable. He turned away from the rationalism and individualism which characterized traditional Calvinism and followed the lead of the German theologians, Friederich Schleiermacher and Johann Neander, whose works he had read in translation. Thus influenced by romanticism, Bushnell held that the essence of religious feeling lay in the spiritual idea of a direct revelation. In his rejection of rational theology he claimed that man could apprehend God and achieve salvation only through the emotions, and that religious feelings are based upon intuitions that transcend language and form. He held that regeneration requires the "goodness of 'perfect feeling'."[33] "The life of man," Bushnell said, "is in his heart, and, if he does not live there, I care not what other successes may befall him, he does not live. The roots that nourish a man's life are in his love, local love, family love, love of old friends and familiar scenes."[34] In his book, *Views of Christian Nurture,* first published in 1846, Bushnell revealed his rejection of the atomistic psychology of Paley (Bushnell's first "model") by turning to the organic notion of society. In place of isolated, technical, individual conversion to transform the individual, Bushnell substituted the inculcation of the love of Christ in children through continuous parental love and piety. It is the parental feeling of love which reveals the love of Christ. A church composed of such Christian families became for Bushnell an organic church which expresses the universal unity of the spirit and is also opposed to and transcends sectarianism. Bushnell's notion envisioned a world-embracing church of the spirit with a millenial purpose. An important influence upon Bushnell's theology was Coleridge's *Aids to Reflection.* It is through this medium that Bushnell imported German romantic philosophy to leaven the theology of Congregationalism. Bushnell himself stated that he "was more indebted to Coleridge than to any extra-Scriptural author."[35] It was also through his reading of Coleridge that Bushnell was lifted from the "pedestrian" thinking of Paley to the imagery and symbolism of "a range of realities in higher tier, that I must climb after, and, if possible, apprehend."[36] From Coleridge and German idealism Bushnell acquired the conception of the universe as a spiritually organic unity, and he infused this idea into his religious doctrine. "All society," he said, "is organic— the church, the state, the school, the family," permeated throughout by a spiritual unity. In applying this conception Bushnell knowingly undermined the extreme individualism of existing Congregationalist doctrine.[37]

In his *Christian Nurture,* Bushnell adopted the metaphors characteristic of the romanticists who stressed the organic unity and interdependence of the parts of the universe. There is an "organic connection of character subsisting between parent and child." There cannot be and never has been a "pure, separate, individual man, living *wholly* within, and from himself." Thus, the child is dependent nutritionally and mentally upon the parent, "as when the sap of the trunk flows into a limb" or as the growing plant is dependent upon its germ and the sun for its characteristics and its growth.[38] Bushnell carried over into his reinterpretation of Congregational theology those very analogies from the plant and vegetable world so profusely used by the German idealists and by Coleridge and Thomas Carlyle to characterize the relationship of the artist to nature, the individual to the universe, the hero to his milieu.

To the doctrine that society is spiritually united in an organic whole,

Bushnell related the notion, also developed by the German idealists, that there exists among the members of society an involuntary communication and sympathy—an "unconscious influence." In his sermon, "Unconscious Influence," Bushnell started from the organic principle that each individual is a "fractional element of a larger and more comprehensive being." In the final analysis, "all adhere together, as parts of a larger nature, in which there is a common circulation of want, impulse, and law. Being thus made common to each other voluntarily, you become one mass, one consolidated social body, animated by one life." Within this mass there is an involuntary (i.e., unconscious) communication and sympathy among the members which determine character. Bushnell believed that this

> always results in what men call the national or family spirit; for there is a spirit peculiar to every state and family in the world. Far down in the secret foundations of life and society there lie concealed great laws and channels of influence, which make the race common to each other in all the main departments or divisions of the social mass— laws which often escape our notice altogether, but which are to society as gravity to the general system of God's works.[39]

Bushnell's influence in revising American Protestantism through the uses of romantic idealism and the repudiation of the Lockeian associational psychology was the culmination of a task originally entertained by another Congregational minister, James Marsh.[40]

The Olmsteds, Frederick and John, and their friend, Charles Brace, had already come under the influence of Bushnell in Hartford before arriving at Yale. (Bushnell was the pastor of Hartford's North Church.) Frequently Bushnell preached in New Haven pulpits and lectured to the Yale students. In 1842, in a letter to his father from Yale, Charles Brace reported, "Bushnell gave the good people of New Haven quite a curious and certainly a splendid lecture. It has set the *big-wigs* in tremendous excitement. . . . The young men like it to distraction—they praise his originality, his liberality, and his independence."[41] It was the juxtaposition of the two opposing theological conceptions (Taylor's individualistic rationale of "legal" divinity versus Bushnell's organic religion of "feeling") which instigated controversial religious discussion among the students. For Olmsted, his brother, and their friends, religious problems of atonement, original sin, sectarianism, human depravity, conversion, the hereafter, election, and the millenium, became of paramount importance. The letters between friends and family and the reports of informal discussions show a preoccupation with religion. The issues of religious ferment at Yale led Olmsted to the study of the contemporary theological literature of the New England ministers.[42] His letters also mention such religious figures as Irenaeus, Luther, Milton, and Jonathan Edwards.[43]

Although described by his friend Brace as having a "regular Dr. Taylor mind in its analytic power!" and "another Taylorite in his virtue theory," Olmsted was developing a strong commitment to the idealism derived from German philosophy. His letters indicate a continuing interest in the exponents of theological romanticism. In a letter to his father he wrote, "We are reading now Morrel's [*sic*] Philosophy of Religion which is very fine."[44] Later, Olmsted wrote that he "bought and tasted Neander's Life of Christ; . . . it is the only readable commentary I ever opened."[45] At another time Olmsted recommended James Martineau's *Endeavors after a Christian Life* to his family and friends as "the most readable book of *sermons* I ever saw."[46]

In recalling the college years and those immediately following, Frederick Kingsbury remarked that the Olmsted brothers and their circle of friends were constantly engaged in discussion. "There were very few subjects that did not come up, at one time or another, in our discussions," Kingsbury remembered, and, "of course, religion, theoretical and practical, general and personal, entered largely into these discussions."[47] How true this is can be seen in the intensity of Olmsted's religiosity as displayed at this time in his letters to his friends and his father. His correspondence indicates a scepticism of orthodox theological ideas. The discussions in his letters between 1846 and 1850 show a probing, provocative mind searching out and testing religious ideas raised in the Bushnell-Taylor controversy at Yale. The attempt by Olmsted to thrash out religious doctrine was grounded upon his own need to establish a value position for himself. Or at least so he seemed to think.

Olmsted's religious interest was reflected in this letter written to Brace in 1847:

> My deepest religious feelings suggested by the writings perhaps of others, have evidently been common to others. Indeed, so much has been written by so many different sorts of men, particularly of reflective and exhortative character, that little is left at the present day but to translate from the *fathers* into the language of the day or to the form most likely to interest. But we have work to do, as well as to think and feel. Let us help each other then to give our thoughts a practical turn. We must learn to labor and to wait. Throw your light on the path in Politics and Social Improvement and encourage me to put my foot *down* and *forwards*. There's a great *work* wants doing in this our generation, Charley, let us off jacket and go about it. Our great Example distributed bread to the thousands as well as preached to them and created wine to make his neighbors merry in this world as well as prayed for them and exhorted them that they might prepare for the next. Oh! how we do need God's light and strength. Faith without works—How dangerous it is. What shall we do? How shall we do it? Dear Charles I very much want your especial prayers for God's guidance and strengthening Grace.[48]

And in a mood of depression and contrition, revealing his religious feeling, Olmsted wrote to Brace,

> This is my truest and most solid and sustainable standpoint. I am quite as much what every body, even you and I, calls an infidel as I am a Christian in belief and perhaps in practice, but not I hope in Faith. I never expect to be a real good man and I always expect to be in this world a downright sinner—I believe circumstances make it morally impossible for me to come up to even the ordinary standard of Christian life. I expect it less than ever—if there's a Hell, besides I am bound to suffer it—there's no use whining about it now—very much the contrary. The fear of it will do me no good—I'll have to take my chance of it, but meantime I'll enjoy the pleasure of doing all the good that chains will let me *reach* to.[49]

At this stage of Olmsted's life the impact of Bushnell's influence was substantial. Olmsted's letters manifest a personal as well as a pastoral and intellectual relationship. From his farm in Guilford, Connecticut, Olmsted wrote to his brother John of Bushnell's visit with him.[50] In still another letter to his brother Olmsted described a visit with Dr. Bushnell in Hartford in which they discussed landscape beauty and the beauty of all nature, the "Theory, Economy, and Moral Philosophy of Love and Courtship," as well as the idea of atonement. The letter continues: "I have found the doctrine he advocates very important to me. It has influenced me to the good. I have grown better for believing it. I have never assented with understanding or cordiality to any other."[51]

Later in his life Olmsted derogated the role of theological doctrine and the unwholesome effect of "hard" points of Calvinism. Writing to his old friend Kingsbury, he intimated that doctrinaire religion imposed a "restricting influence upon the free action of the mind and conscience, the compounding of undefinable social duties by the performance of certain codified duties, and the cultivation of a special disguised form of self-conceit and contempt—pitiful contempt." He questioned "whether the evil effects of those most powerful mutual admiration clubs called churches . . . does [sic] not more than compensate their good influence on Society."[52] He rejected the notion of theological sin as a "terrible and cruel burden" upon himself which happily no longer burdened his children. Without having to bear the onus of the doctrine of election or damnation he would have lived, Olmsted claimed, a happier life.[53]

Though his religious belief declined, the psychological sanctions which gave direction to practical conduct in the form of an ethic remained with him. The influence of romantic idealism, particularly as it affected his artistic activities, loomed increasingly significant.

Olmsted's "Prophets"

Olmsted's congenial introduction to romantic idealism through Bushnell's guidance was reinforced through his reading of other transcendentalists. The study of Thomas Carlyle, John Ruskin, and Ralph Waldo Emerson had a particularly significant impact upon Olmsted's thinking. Each of these writers influenced Olmsted to evolve a world view which, in turn, contributed to the development of his aesthetic doctrine.

With their introduction in the 1820s Carlyle's writings enjoyed a growing distinction in the United States. Carlyle was the first to transmit to Americans the philosophic idealism of Germany.[54] Octavius Brooks Frothingham states that the enthusiasm for Carlyle's papers was widespread. His interpretations of German philosophy and literature "had great weight with people to whom German was an unknown tongue."[55]

Olmsted found Carlyle's writings interesting because at the time he read Carlyle's *Sartor Resartus* he was seeking answers to the same religious and moral questions to which Carlyle addressed himself. While Carlyle's treatment of human problems and of man's ethical role was not based upon dogmatic theology, the issues he raised provoked religious thought. Throughout his writings Carlyle's Calvinism, but without its dogmatics, permeates German idealism.

In explaining his attraction to *Sartor Resartus* Olmsted wrote, "I suppose it was because perhaps a little, I had this vagabond feeling that I fancied Sartor Resartus. . . . [W]hen I got along about the 'Everlasting No!'—I was enchanted with it and some parts I have laid on my bed and read and thought over by hours—again and again."[56]

Olmsted was sensitive to Carlyle's doctrine that man's whole duty consisted in working to the utmost in that specific work to which each is called by his special, innate capacities. In striving towards his vocation, Carlyle held, each individual must combine his inner talent with the outward environment to achieve his maximum capability. It is only through a harmonious self-development in work that man can know himself, realize his potentialities, and hope to find happiness.[57] Carlyle asserted that man himself is "a Symbol of God."[58] Insofar as he follows his moral duty to work unstintingly, he follows a "God-given mandate" which brings him into harmony with the divine law of the world.[59] In this respect, Carlyle stated, man evidenced divinity and was bound into an organic unity of humanity and of the universe.

Carlyle vehemently opposed the rationalist-empirical explanations of the material world exemplified by Jeremy Bentham and the Utilitarians. In his "Clothes-Philosophy" Carlyle presented all matter and material things as spirit.[60] He viewed the visible, physical world of matter as a world of appearances or symbols; the universe itself is one vast symbol or "Garment of God."[61] For Carlyle the artist or the seer discovers reality in the deep, mysterious, invisible forces—the "Divine Essence"—when he pierces and transcends the world of appearances.[62] But even the lives of the run of men, whose conscious, daily experiences are seemingly circumscribed by their small, visible existence, extend into the invisible deep of the unconscious.[63]

The reading of Carlyle's *Sartor Resartus* was an illuminating and enthusiastic experience for Olmsted. He wrote to his father:

> I have been reading Sartor Resartus. It took me about three weeks, but I was intensely interested before I finished. And now if anybody wants to set me down for an insane cloud dwelling Transcendentalist, because I like Carlyle, I hope they'll gratify themselves. I do think Carlyle is the greatest genius in the world, with a greater intellect than Scott, Bulwer, Dickens, Hemans and all the lady writers of the age together. I perfectly wonder and stand awe-struck as I would at a Hurricane. Have you read his Cromwell?[64]

Reminiscing on her early days with young Frederick Olmsted, his brother John, and their circle of friends, Frederick Olmsted's wife recalled that "*Sartor Resartus* and *Modern Painters* were our text books."[65]

With the publication in the United States in 1847 of his book, *Modern Painters,* John Ruskin achieved a position of great influence and importance in America, first as the arbiter of aesthetic taste and art criticism and later as a social critic and reformer. As James Flexner states, "The critic who had by far the most readers in mid-century America was the Englishman John Ruskin."[66] Ruskin exerted an enormous influence upon the intellectuals and artists of the United States.[67]

In reading John Ruskin's early volumes of *Modern Painters* and *The Seven Lamps of Architecture,* Olmsted and his group were immediately captured by the didactic and moral aspects of Ruskin's writing. Olmsted found in Ruskin a rigidly-trained Calvinist who was as much devoted to the improvement of the morals of society as he was. Ruskin offered in his early volumes the aesthetic impulse as the means by which man is to be the "witness of the glory of God, and to advance that glory by his reasonable obedience and resultant happiness."[68] For him aesthetics was to act as the mediator between nature and man to reveal the divinity and the spirituality within the physical manifestations of nature. He believed that moral and social reform could be achieved through the contemplation and appreciation of natural beauty. Ruskin offered a mode for moral regeneration which was more attractive to an educated, urban middle class than a crude revival theology.

Ruskin's lifelong appeal for Olmsted appears in his early correspondence. Writing to his father from his farm on Staten Island, Olmsted reported that he, his brother John, and their friend Charles Brace were reading and discussing Ruskin's *Modern Painters* and *The Seven Lamps of Architecture*. They felt that the first volume of *Modern Painters* contained such a strong religious feeling that Brace, an ordained preacher, considered it appropriate to "read some extracts from it" in his Sunday services preceding his sermon. "From what I saw," Olmsted wrote, "I am sure it will do us all good to read it—great—immeasurable good."[69] The correspondence of Olmsted with his parents and friends between September 1848 and August 1849 shows that *Modern Painters* and *Seven Lamps* were read and discussed again and again.[70]

Olmsted was not only attracted to Ruskin from the religious side. Ruskin is one of Olmsted's links to romantic aesthetics. Ruskin's views were transcendental, deriving and holding in common many of the concepts held by Carlyle, Coleridge, and Wordsworth. In Ruskin's writings Olmsted found principles in landscape painting that were to guide him in his own artistic work. When Olmsted turned to planning urban parks and cities he invariably found the opportunity to invoke Ruskin to support his thesis that beauty, and particularly the beauty of natural landscape scenery, must be the means to improve the quality of life.

But long before Olmsted had any thought that he would find his vocation in planning parks and cities, he had turned to Ruskin's writings with enthusiasm. Ruskin's colorful descriptions of the natural beauty of Europe's landscapes reminded Olmsted of his own childhood travels with his parents through New York, New England, and Canada, and also of the travel books by Silliman, Dwight, and Martineau that his father had read to him. Both Ruskin and Olmsted possessed what Francis Townsend describes as "the landscape feeling."[71]

Just as pleasure in landscape "was a ruling passion" in Ruskin's life,[72] so it was with Olmsted. "I love beautiful landscape and rural recreations, and people in rural recreations, better than any body else I know," Olmsted wrote to Calvert Vaux, his partner and collaborator in designing Central Park.[73] His regard for nature approached reverence. Olmsted tried to explain his feelings: "Nature treats me so strangely; it's past my speaking sensibly of, and yet, as a part of my traveling experience, I would speak of it. At times I seem myself to be her favorite, and she brings me to my knees in deep feeling, such as she blesses no other with."[74]

When Olmsted purchased his farm on Staten Island, New York, in 1848, he found that one of his neighbors on the Island was Judge William Emerson, the older brother of Ralph Waldo Emerson. William Emerson was an able lawyer with a Wall Street office, who was known for his literary tastes and thorough scholarship.[75]

Olmsted's correspondence manifests a cordial entente between the two neighbors. "I have been to Mr. Emerson's again and taken a lot more books," Olmsted wrote to his father.[76] A few months later Olmsted described a visit to Emerson's home:

> Returning from there [New York City to Staten Island] in company with Judge Emerson, I accepted an invitation to dine with him, and then on account of the storm, to spend the night. An exceedingly agreeable visit. Excellent family, Mrs. Emerson, lovely character. . . . He had the Knickerbocker with Charley's [Charles Loring Brace] Critique on Emerson [Ralph Waldo Emerson] with which he was much pleased, and is anxious to know the author. You had better read it.[77]

William Emerson was uniquely capable of giving Olmsted a critical appreciation of the literature of German philosophy and its English interpreters. After graduation from Harvard he was persuaded by George Ticknor and Edward Everett to continue his theological studies at the University of Göttingen in Germany. While in Germany he developed a thorough enthusiasm for Herder, Wieland, Eichhorn, Schleiermacher, Schiller, and Goethe, and for the German university system. Upon his return to the United States William Emerson abandoned the ministry for the law. But he maintained a continuing interest in German literature. During the period of his legal apprenticeship in a New York law firm he gained some recognition for his lectures and writings on German literature.[78]

The older Emerson's direct experience with the great German romantic scholars, his critical knowledge of Carlyle and the English idealists, as well as his lifelong, close relationship with his brother Ralph, made him an authoritative intellectual guide for Olmsted and his circle of friends.[79]

The Concord, Massachusetts Emersons were frequent visitors to Staten Island. If the Olmsted brothers and their friends did not come under the personal influence of Ralph Waldo Emerson during his visits, they certainly came under his intellectual influence. It would seem inevitable that a "cloud-dwelling Transcendentalist," as Olmsted described himself, should be drawn to the conceptions of the American Transcendentalists and to Emerson in particular. His letters show this. Olmsted wrote to his father in Hartford: "Get . . . 'Nature, Addresses,' etc. by R. W. Emerson. Scip [*sic*] the first [part] at first and you will say the addresses are the best things you ever read—almost. St. Paul would have enjoyed it."[80]

The influence of Emerson took deep root in Olmsted and his friends. Olmsted's brother, John Hull Olmsted, who lived with him on the Staten

Island farm, wrote to a mutual friend: "What on the whole do you think of Emerson and his influence on us. We continue to get inspiration from him."[81]

In his analysis of New England Transcendentalism, Frothingham asserted that "The Transcendentalist was by nature a reformer." He described Emerson as a "recreator from the inside, rather than as a reformer of the outside world."[82] Olmsted and his circle on Staten Island seemed to look upon Emerson not only as a purveyor of provocative ideas but as the leader in a reform movement that affected practical life. Both aspects of Emerson's influence appear in the correspondence of the Olmsteds and their friends. Olmsted's brother John expressed the enthusiasm Emerson engendered in the following letter: "We want you to come and work, and work against the material tendency that is swamping us. That will be your next task . . . to direct the fierce energies here, to lead towards divine things, to join Emerson in his work, in a different way, to speak a word, and never cease speaking a word for ideas."[83]

However, Emerson's significance lay as well in implementation as in intellection. Writing to Theodore Parker on behalf of the Olmsted group, Charles Brace said, "I wish, if you meet Emerson, you would express the exceeding gratitude of myself and my friends here for what he had done for them. I can scarcely think of a teacher who has done more. Next to Dr. Arnold, Emerson has given many of us here the strongest impulse we ever received. . . . [H]is thoughts come up continually anew in practical life."[84]

New England Transcendentalism was not only carried into Olmsted's farmhouse on Staten Island in books, it also was personified in the visits of Theodore Parker. Parker was "The Preacher" of New England Transcendentalism. His reputation and influence as a scholar, reformer, and preacher was enormous.[85] His association with the Olmsted group must have been felicitous and provocative. Brace wrote: "Your visit left a delightful impression on us all, and was of real good, I think, to our friends on Staten Island."[86]

Many years later, in looking back, Olmsted showed how significantly these men had influenced his intellectual and artistic development. "I was led up at that time to Emerson, Lowell, and Ruskin, and other real prophets who have been familiar friends ever since," he wrote. "And these gave me the needed respect for my own constitutional tastes and an inclination to poetical refinement in the cultivation of them that afterwards determined my profession."[87]

If Olmsted had not yet by 1850 found his vocation, he had undoubtedly found his ideological milieu. His Calvinist training and his indoctrination in romantic idealism gave him the best possible orientation to follow his "prophets."

It is within the context of transcendental idealism that Olmsted finally found his way towards the reform of society that his youthful letters express as important to him. With Bushnell, Carlyle, Emerson, and Zimmermann as his intellectual heroes, it must be obvious that Olmsted derived his social and aesthetic ideals mainly from the English and American interpreters of German romantic philosophy and not from Bentham and Bentham's Utilitarian disciples as Albert Fein claims.[88] It was with such an orientation that Olmsted embarked between 1852 and 1856 upon a literary career. His report on slavery in the pre-Civil War South was a result. From 1857 onward he entered into the vocation of planning parks and towns.

In his essay of 1844, "The Young American," Emerson deplored the absence of public gardens in the United States. He complained that the beautiful, large-scale gardens which he found so pleasant in Europe were unknown in his own country. It is, said Emerson,

> the fine art which is left for us, now that sculpture, painting, and religious and civil architecture have become effete, and have passed into second childhood. We have twenty degrees of latitude wherein to choose a seat, and the new modes of travelling enlarge the opportunity to selection, by making it easy to cultivate very distant tracts and yet remain in strict intercourse with the centres of trades and population.[89]

It was Frederick Law Olmsted's significant achievement to formulate in the United States the aesthetic theory for the fine art of landscape architecture.

By incorporating the notions of romantic philosophy, Olmsted created great works of public art. He was convinced that in using the aesthetic impulse he could effect a psychological transformation in the viewer that would reform society.

3

The Organic Principle

Though the organic principle became an integral part of Olmsted's aesthetic theory, he was impressed by the conception in its social context long before he had entertained any notion of creating parks.[1] In his three-volume analysis of Southern slavery Olmsted attempted to show that slavery had an adverse effect upon the entire culture of Southern society. In Olmsted's view the subjection of the black man had stifled the economic development of the small-scale farmer and favored the large landholder. The result was the development of an aristocratic class whose habits and attitudes were inimical to the progress of a democratic society. It demeaned the dignity and morality not only of the black man but of the slave owners as well. The slave society, Olmsted held, is a patriarchal society. It is characteristic of such a culture to be in a retrogressive transitional stage—"abusive of intelligence, comfort, and morality." The institution of slavery retarded education and brought into effect habits of viciousness and cruelty.[2] Olmsted believed that a democratic civilization could unfold only in a society of free, educated individuals. Mental, moral, and material prosperity could emerge only in a democratic social milieu.[3]

Congruity: The Art to Conceal Art

In 1858, Olmsted and Vaux were commissioned to landscape a municipal public park—The Central Park in New York City. In one respect their *Greensward* plan was similar to the work of the great English landscape gardeners such as William Gilpin, Uvedale Price, Humphrey Repton, John Claudius Loudon, and their American disciple, Andrew Jackson Downing. Their landscaping followed the so-called natural style of the English garden. But in a most signficant way the underlying aesthetic basis of Central Park differed radically from any previous ventures in the landscaping art. Primarily, in Olmsted's mind, the conceptualization of the park manifested the metaphysics of the idealist school of philosophy united with Olmsted's functional refinements.

The English and the American landscape gardeners who preceded Olmsted implicitly or explicitly belonged to the classical school of aesthetics with its dependence upon associational psychology and empirical rationalism.[4] Their work was technical and very often dilettantish and gardenesque. In the hands of the English practitioners it served the pleasures of rich landlords. One of this school, Humphrey Repton, explained: "I hope never to lose sight of the great and essential object of my profession, the elegance, the magnificence, and the convenience of rural scenes, appropriated to the uses of a gentleman's habitation."[5]

In the first half of the nineteenth century Andrew Jackson Downing was America's best known horticulturist and writer on rural architecture and landscape gardening. He was also the editor of the *Horticulturist*, one of the most influential publications of its kind, from its beginning in 1846 until his death in 1852. The journal published some of the most important American contributions to the periodical literature of horticulture. It was through the *Horticulturist* as well as his books that Downing exerted considerable influence on rural tastes and landscape gardening.[6] But he was also instrumental in influencing the configuration of New York City. With William Cullen Bryant and other prominent New Yorkers he exerted great efforts to realize the introduction of a city park in Manhattan.

Downing and Olmsted possessed in common not only an interest in scientific agriculture, but a desire to refine and cultivate the public appreciation of rural tastes. With Downing's untimely death in 1852 and Olmsted's appointment to the position of Architect-in-Chief of Central Park in 1858, Olmsted in effect assumed Downing's mantle. But, while Olmsted may have become Downing's successor, he was not his disciple. Downing was at best a landscape gardener, who stressed the horticultural style more appropriate for small-scale grounds. He had nothing in his theory of landscape gardening to offer Olmsted which Olmsted had not already himself learned through his own early reading in Gilpin, Price, Loudon, and Repton.[7] Like Repton, Downing preferred the natural style over the formal, classical geometric landscape. However, he offered, like Repton, no significant aesthetic basis for it. These landscape gardeners had adopted a new informal style of landscaping, while still adhering to the older, formal, mechanistic theory of aesthetics. Downing, for example, said, "The true artist breathes a life and soul, which is beauty, into the dead utilitarian materials . . . and they speak a language that is understood as readily as that of animate nature."[8] This is precisely the nature of artistic genius which the German, English, and American idealists rejected. A. W. Schlegel stated the contrast:

> Form is mechanical when it is imparted to any material through an external force, merely as an accidental addition, without reference to its character. . . . Organic form, on the contrary, is innate; it unfolds itself from within, and reaches its determination simultaneously with the fullest development of the seed. . . . In the fine arts, just as in the province of nature—the supreme artist—all genuine forms are organic.[9]

Olmsted, as a landscape architect, differentiated himself from the landscape gardeners. His aesthetic theory for the design of large-scale, natural landscape was based upon the aesthetics of romantic idealism. Olmsted attempted to explain the difference between Downing and himself in this sense. "Although he had a philosophic turn of mind, . . . the plans and instructions which he gave to the public were far less excellent with reference to their ostensible ends, than they were with reference to the purpose of stimulating the exercise of judgment and taste in the audience addressed."[10]

Olmsted gave to the natural school of landscape design an aesthetic theory based upon the organic concept of art. He consciously set out to raise his calling "from the rank of a trade, even of a handicraft, to that of a liberal profession—an Art, an Art of Design."[11] He adopted the designation of landscape architecture at the suggestion of his partner, Calvert Vaux, to distinguish his work, "because it helps to establish the important idea of the distinction of my profession from that of gardening, as that of architecture from building—the distinction of an art of *design*."[12] Olmsted placed his art "side by side with the fair sisters, Poetry, Architecture, Music, Acting, Painting, and Sculpture."[13] Indeed, he looked upon his work as combining the artistry of the architect, the painter, the poet, as well as the gardener. Defining the principles of his art, Olmsted noted:

> Landscape Architecture is the application or picturesque relation of various objects within a certain space, so that each may increase the effect of the whole as a landscape composition. It thus covers more than landscape gardening. It includes gardening and architecture and extends both arts, carrying them into the province of the landscape painter. In all landscape architecture there must not only be art, but art must be apparent. The art to conceal art is applicable to the manipulation of the materials, the method by which the grand result is obtained, but not to the result which should not be merely fictitious nature, but obviously a work of art—cultivated beauty.[14]

In his plan for the Mount Royal park in Montreal he described the completed, matured park as a "sustained landscape poem."[15] He compared each separate section of the park to a stanza of a poem, which when completed makes an integrated whole.

In describing his role as a landscape architect Olmsted asserted:

> I shall venture to assume to myself the title of artist and to add that no sculptor, painter or architect can have anything like the difficulty in sketching and conveying a knowledge of his design to those who employ him which must attend upon an artist employed for such a kind of designing as is required of me. The design must be almost exclusively in my imagination. No one but myself can feel, and without feeling no one can understand . . . the true value or purport of much that is done in the park. . . . My picture is all alive—its very essence is life, human and vegetable.[16]

Because of the nature of the materials with which he worked, Olmsted was able to embody the organic conception in the most direct manner and in a way most characteristic of the romantic philosophers and aestheticians. A cardinal theme of these nineteenth-century theorists was the organic process of the spontaneous outward unfolding from an inner vital seed or root. The analogy characteristically used was the growth of a vegetable or a plant. M. H. Abrams says that it is J. G. Herder's use of the life process of a plant and his generalization of this process into a world view that "must be accounted a turning point in the history of ideas." The Herder thesis is that "nature is an organism, and man, inextricably a part of that living whole, is in himself an organic indissoluble unity of thought, feeling, and will, exhibiting in his own life the same powers and functions as the nature without." Herder used the paradigm of the growth process of a plant to overthrow the mechanical view of nature and man and artistic creativity.[17]

The vegetable world, the unfolding world of live nature, was indeed Olmsted's realm. He made this clear when he said,

> In gardening in the natural school our efforts should be to prepare a field for the operations of nature. We should depend on nature, not simply as some teach, [or] appear to do so, but actually trust nature only offering certain encouragements by means of ground work. *The details must be left to shape itself* [sic]. All that is not to be thus treated should be clearly artificial. There should be no doubt about it. No compromise.[18]

In stressing the organic unity of Central Park, indeed in each of the parks which he created, Olmsted subordinated the artificial and manmade objects to the vegetation. To the extent that roads, bridges, walks, seats, and buildings must be constructed for the convenience of a mass of people, they detract from the aesthetic element of the park. But where they are required, they must be subordinate and harmonious with the natural features. They must not conspicuously obtrude.[19] Whatever necessary construction must be introduced must be "fitted to nature" so that it will blend naturally with the pastoral or picturesque vegetative environment. In advising the architect preparing a public house to be located in the Mount Royal park for the convenience of visitors, Olmsted directs that "the conspicuous parts are of ax-finished timber, not to be painted; it is fitted to sit on a saddle of rock, so surrounded by natural low wood, growing on ground declining from it, that while commanding from its upper parts a magnificent outlook the building will scarcely be seen except by those who have occasion to use it."[20] To maintain the integrity of this principle, Olmsted vehemently fought with every means available to him against the Tweed Ring, park commissioners, recreational groups, unknowing do-gooders, patriotic groups, businessmen, real estate speculators, newspaper editors, and others who attempted, and in some cases succeeded, in destroying the wholeness of his artistic work. Central Park, particularly, was continually subjected to pressures for revision. Were Olmsted to have had his way there would have been no zoos, no statues, no buildings, no flower gardens, no swimming pools, no theatres, no cafes to destroy the organic unity of the design he and Vaux conceived and executed. Any recisions of the vegetation or gifts for the park, no matter how well-intentioned, would be analogous to "improving" Rembrandt's *Aristotle* by painting in a necktie.[21]

So imperative to Olmsted was the organic principle that it led him to consider the fitness of the artistic design in relation to the region and locality. The result in a design had to be locally congruous and appropriate to the "original conditions of the locality."

In planning the urban parks of Boston's Back Bay area Olmsted undertook to solve three problems: to control flooding, to correct the unhealthy conditions caused by brackish water, and to beautify an uninteresting area. The first two problems were matters of engineering which posed no difficulty of solution for Olmsted. It was the landscaping problem which gave Olmsted, the artist, momentary pause. The organic principle of art required him to conceive of an artistic composition which would utilize the "several broader constituents," the vegetation, the meandering water, the blooming islets, indigenous to the Back Bay. Olmsted planned to create an effect in "labored urban grounds" which would represent "no affectation or caprice of taste." He intended his design to be a

> direct development of the original conditions of the locality in adaptation to the needs of a dense community. So regarded, it will be found to be, in the artistic sense of the word, natural, and possible to suggest a modest poetic sentiment more grateful to town-weary minds than an elaborate and elegant gardenlike work would have yielded.[22]

One aspect of the Back Bay project in Boston was the construction of the Fenway—a city-suburb parkway in which Olmsted creatively attempted to incorporate the assets of natural beauty while providing the utility of a broad highway for the efficient flow of vehicular traffic. To aid him in the construction of parkway bridges Olmsted called upon his neighbor and long-intimate friend, H. H. Richardson, the outstanding American architectural pioneer, with whom he had maintained over the years a professional association. The compatibility of Richardson's architectural principles with Olmsted's can be seen in their joint endeavors. In the Fenway bridge there is plainly visible the organic beauty-function aesthetic. Richardson had early established the practice of using local materials so that his buildings would be congruent with their surroundings.[23] Henry-Russell Hitchcock describes the Fenway bridge as really two bridges—one of Roxbury (Massachusetts) puddingstone across the water and the other of metal over railroad tracks and street. The bridges are simple and without embellishment; the result, says Hitchcock, is inconspicuous. The puddingstone bridge "is harmonious with the curves of the landscape, quite as the metal bridge is appropriate to the straight lines of the railroad." Hitchcock describes Olmsted's Back Bay planning as a "remarkable example of a new and more intelligent attitude toward the problem of large-scale urban planning and landscape design."[24]

In presenting proposals for his various projects Olmsted was wont to be didactic. He was not satisfied merely to formulate a plan; he frequently included an elaborate rationale to educate his clients and the public to his aesthetic principles and to convince them of the judiciousness of adopting his proposals. Often the material which he presented was tangential, but it was not without purpose. For example, in response to the request of the Commissioners of the Park Department of Boston, Olmsted prepared a statement to the public explaining and detailing the plans for Franklin Park. To explicate the organic principle as the paramount one in fashioning the park, he used an illustration which might have been meaningful to the new suburbanites of Boston in 1886—the building and landscaping of a dwelling.[25] In his illustration Olmsted used the principle of "congruity." He said,

> In a region of undulating surface with a meandering stream and winding valleys, with much naturally disposed wood, there is a house with outbuildings and enclosures, roads, walks, trees, bushes, and flowering plants. If the constructions are of the natural materials of the locality and not fashioned expressly to manifest the texture and the grain and the hues that such materials will naturally become if no effort to hide or disguise them is made, if the lines of the roads and the walks are adapted to curves of the natural surface, and if the trees and plants are of a natural character naturally disposed, the result will be congruous with the general natural rural scenery of the locality, its rural quality being, perhaps, enhanced by these unobtrusive artificial elements.[26]

He went on to reject as "cheap and fragmentary" efforts to fashion wooden houses with decorations copied from houses of masonry or to paint them white. Wooden houses, Olmsted affirmed, should be left in their natural color or tinted to harmonize with natural objects.[27]

The consistency with which Olmsted applied his aesthetic conceptions is further manifested in his original plan for the layout of Stanford University in California (see fig. 2). The design of the buildings and grounds of the University, Olmsted asserted, must be "a matter of art. It must have scholarly dignity. It must not be ostentatiously costly, and it must be unobtrusively incidental to a means of a manifestly useful purpose."[28] What is unique in the planning, yet wholly consistent with his aesthetic theory, is the fact, as Diane McGuire points out, that Olmsted was the first to realize completely how architectural forms and landscape materials suitable to West Coast conditions could be properly used in a functional and aesthetic manner in order to meet the needs of large numbers of people.[29] As part of the organic notion he considered the characteristics of the California topography and climate and the use to which the grounds would be put. From these considerations Olmsted rejected the customary traditional approach of building and landscaping in imitation of the East Coast. He employed instead Richardson's Romanesque style of architecture—similar to the California Mission style, which in turn, as McGuire indicates, "was derived from the Mediterranean Romanesque."[30] In the landscaping aspect, too, Olmsted abjured the plants, trees, and turf of the East Coast for a vegetation common and natural to the climate of southern Spain and the Mediterranean lands as being adaptable to the natural circumstances of the California climate and the site of the University.[31]

As Olmsted turned his attention to the planning and the development of suburban towns, the organic principle acquired multiple applications. First, the plan of the town must be consonant with the topography; it must be a self-contained artistic whole. If, therefore, the site of the development were to be artistically "true" then the plan must unfold in relation to the natural environment. There would be no arbitrary graphlike rectangularity, no forcing of straight streets where a glen or a rock promontory would more naturally call for a curve. The regular and monotonous grid pattern would have no place where irregularity and picturesqueness were the more natural.

But in the suburban towns Olmsted was faced with a problem which did not concern him in the park—the towns were places of permanent residence. The organic principle still must apply. Not only did the plan of the town need to reflect Olmsted's aesthetic principles, but it also had

Figure 1. Plan for Proposed Improvement of Back Bay, Boston, 1879
Olmsted combined a brackish tidal estuary (right) with a fresh water
stream (left).

(Courtesy National Park Service
Frederick Law Olmsted National Historic Site)

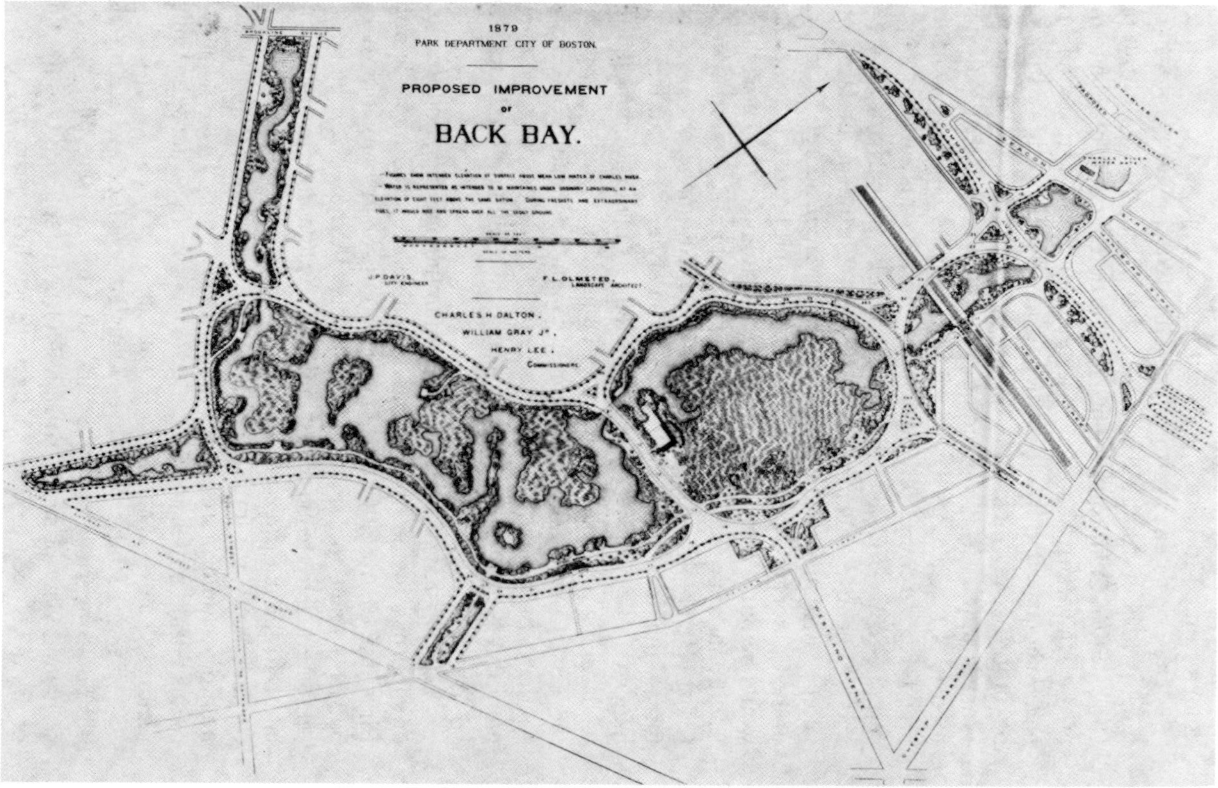

Figure 2.   Plan for Campus, Leland Stanford University, Palo Alto, California, 1888
*(Courtesy National Park Service
Frederick Law Olmsted National Historic Site)*

to functionally provide for both the individuation and the "harmonious" integration of the resident families. The plans for the suburban communities of Riverside, Illinois and Riverdale in New York City are examples of Olmsted's use of the organic, beauty-function aesthetic. The organic conception of humanity is combined with an organic aesthetic, fusing into a unified whole by which Olmsted hoped to overcome the "unnatural" conditions of alienation fostered by antagonisms engendered by trade and commerce and the friendless, impersonal relations characteristic of large cities.

These principles led Olmsted to advocate the need for a comprehensive city plan for great and rapidly growing cities such as New York, Boston, and London which would preclude the "immeasurable waste of life, strength, and property." As early as 1870, in a speech before the American Social Science Association, he advocated the need for a "comprehensive and impartial study" of cities. He held that these surveys should result in a complete city plan to insure a beautiful, spacious, healthful city, which would not neglect the interests of commerce but would provide for the moral, social, and psychological happiness of the urban community.[32]

In consonance with the world view that the universe is an organic whole, Olmsted similarly conceived of the city as an interrelated, dynamic subsystem. The city for him was the seat of civilization undergoing a continuing process of growth. He accurately predicted the continuing urbanization of western society. To forestall the random internal and external sprawl of the city he brought his aesthetic theory to bear upon the problem.

To provide beauty and efficiency and a sense of community to its inhabitants Olmsted believed that the great city must have a rational, comprehensive plan for its growth.

The Influence of Schelling's Philosophy

The significant elements of romantic idealism to which the Americans were attracted were the concept of an interrelated, organic universe in which the world of matter or objective nature (i.e., the world of appearances) is subsumed into the subjective realm of spirit. This organic whole is animated by an immanent God (i.e., the Absolute or Reason) in whom all opposites are united. To go beyond an understanding of the material world of experience into the realm of spirit (of which the material world of nature is but a symbol) requires the intellectual intuition or imagination of the creative genius possessing the capability of reason to pierce the world of matter and transcend it by realizing its corresponding and coincident realm of spirit. In order for the mind to apprehend this relationship it requires an individualism based upon a freedom which may disregard all man-made rules, yet is bound by the natural laws governing a God-suffused universe and the laws which reason dictates in creative activity. Therefore, as a part of nature, man is divine, and is an analogue of God, the Artist, in creative activity wherein reason (the Absolute or God) is manifested as the unification of the material and the spiritual. As formulated by the German idealists, this philosophy rejected the sensationalism based upon the Hobbes-Locke philosophy, the associational psychology of Hartley, a mechanical universe, the limitations of social customs, and the formalism of inherited rules.

The idealist philosophers urged a spontaneity that came with the freedom of the individual's capability to use his imaginative powers to apprehend the reason which controls the material universe.

The impetus in the development of idealism in philosophy came from Schiller[33] and was directly related to the German literary artistry of the Weimar and Jena groups. The emphasis of German idealism supported in the artistic field the aesthetic reason and in the religious sphere the "aestheticism of individuality" in the writings of Schleiermacher.[34]

The romantic idea of individuality was therefore different from the Hobbesian atomic idea of individualism. In its emphasis upon the unique worth of each man, the romantics focused upon the genius in whom individuality is more fully developed than in others. To the artistic genius the romantics ascribed the greatest insight into the processes of the universe; his creative abilities are a consummation of spiritual insight, individuality, and harmony—a reflection of nature itself.

The idealists rejected the empiricist-utilitarian psychology because, they claimed, it reduced man to an isolated, self-contained atom in a universe of similar atoms. Coleridge criticized this psychology because it considered man to be nothing more than a "hydraulic machine."[35] It did not take into account his unique potentialities, his individuality, his vitality, his spirituality, or the miracle of his divinity. Instead of considering man as an integrated and interdependent part of an organic universe both material and spiritual in nature, it portrayed him as a malleable form operating principally from a simple, egoistic pain-pleasure motivation. For this type of human mechanism, who learns and knows only what exists in his experience, the institutional patterns—the mechanisms of society—make the personality; to alter the personality, alter the mechanisms. The romantics turned away from "the absurdity of the corpuscularian or mechanic system," as Coleridge called it.[36] They centered their attention upon the individual rather than upon social mechanisms. And in so doing they emphasized the diversity existing in mankind and the unique qualities possessed by each individual. For the romantics it is the individual through his genius who molds the society and creates the symbols which inspire action.

While the impetus for philosophical idealism may have stemmed from Schiller, it was the work of F. W. J. von Schelling, "the father of German *Naturphilosophie*," whose formulations consistently issued forth in the writings of the British and American romanticists. Implementing the notion of the organic universe and its derivative vital force—the unconscious—Schelling developed his theory or philosophy of identity.

In originating the philosophy of identity Schelling asserted that subject and object coincide in the Absolute. The essence of the Absolute is Reason or God in whom all opposites are united. For Schelling, while nature rejuvenates and recreates itself by an opposition of forces, these natural forces are actually an organic unity in terms of the world-soul or God who is present everywhere as "the One in this totality."[37] Schelling was intent upon showing that "the power which flows forth in the mass of nature is essentially the same as that represented in the mental world."[38] In Schelling's system of idealism the natural or objective world is invested with spirit—thus that which exists in the human mind and in external nature is essentially one. Schelling resolved the dialectic in the subject (ego)/object (nature) opposition by unifying the two poles in his theory of identity. According to Schelling it is in intellectual intuition that the absolute is realized. In his philosophy Schelling began with the subjective-ego and derived from it the laws of objective nature. Then, to arrive at the unity of knowledge, he started from the objective—nature—and deduced from it ego—the subjective. His intention was to show the identity of the soul and nature—the ideal and the real. In his system of transcendental idealism, Schelling explained how intellectual intuition identifies the real and ideal, being and thought, object and subject. In sum,

> The complete theory of Nature would be that whereby the whole of Nature should be resolved into an intelligence. The dead and unconscious products of nature are only unsuccessful attempts of Nature to reflect itself, and dead Nature, so called, is merely an unripe Intelligence; hence in its phenomena the intelligent character peers through, though yet unconsciously. Its highest aim, namely, that of becoming completely self-objective, Nature reaches only in its highest and last reflection, which is nothing else than man, or, more generally, what we call reason, by means of which Nature turns completely back upon itself, and by which is manifested that Nature is originally identical with what in us is known as intelligent conscious.[39]

With Schelling's identity of real and ideal as a living bond, nature becomes a divine vitality in which all "sanatory power is only in nature."[40] The reconciliation of knowledge through intellectual intuition overcomes the various dualities. In this process there is expressed a relative form of the absolute. Since God alone is the Absolute, man can know the ultimate unity or absolute identity of all things only in a relative sense. It is therefore in the intellectual intuition or the imaginative impulse of the artist in his creative activity that he reveals an aspect of the absolute reason and partakes of the creative activity of God. Reason is achieved as the genius gives concrete embodiment to the ideal in sensible forms. It is in the coalescence of the ideal and the real, Spirit and Nature, unconscious and conscious, that antithesis is abolished and the spectator learns what reason is and identifies with God, the Absolute, whose Intelligence is manifested and embodied in the universe—both the most perfect organism and most perfect work of art. For Schelling the purest expression of philosophy is embodied in the identity achieved in the work of art. Art is the "universal organon of philosophy"; it is the keystone of Schelling's system of transcendental idealism.[41]

In the course of the diffusion of German romantic philosophy to Britain and then to the United States the importance of Schelling's philosophy for Coleridge and Carlyle and the Americans who were attracted to idealism becomes apparent. In his *Biographia Literaria,* Coleridge wrote, "Let whatever shall be found in this or any future work of mine, that resembles, or coincides with, the doctrines of my German predecessor [Schelling], though contemporary, be wholly attributed to him."[42] Coleridge's aesthetic theory, his development of the theory of identity, and his conception of the role of intellectual intuition or the philosophical imagination are based upon Schelling's philosophy of idealism. J. Shawcross, the editor of *Biographia Literaria,* points out that "the large verbal borrowings from Schelling" in the *Biographia* as well as Coleridge's essay "On Poesy or Art" are "largely the language of Schelling."[43]

Thomas Carlyle, as well, found support for his romanticism in Schelling's philosophy of identity. Charles Harrold explains that "It is possible that much of the element of symbolism in Carlyle came from Schelling, in whose 'philosophy of identity' it naturally had a major position."[44]

Unlike Coleridge and Carlyle, Ruskin had little direct experience with the philosophical works of the German romantics, yet his "first principles represent a continuation of the romantic tradition."[45]

Though Ruskin rejected what little he knew of the philosophy of the German romantics, his aesthetic theory shows that through the back door he introduced as much as he could understand of it into his formulations.[46] Ruskin's lack of German metaphysics hampered the development of his aesthetic theory, yet his reliance upon the poetry of William Wordsworth and the writings of Coleridge impelled Ruskin (at least in the first two volumes of *Modern Painters*) into an acceptance of elements of the philosophy of idealism.[47]

Ruskin's reliance upon Wordsworth was profound. In the first two volumes of *Modern Painters* (the two which influenced Olmsted so strongly) Wordsworth's poetry is copiously quoted. In what regard Ruskin held the poet the following explains: "Wordsworth may be trusted as a guide in everything, he feels nothing but what we ought all to feel—what every mind in pure moral health must feel, he says nothing but what we all ought to believe—what all strong intellects must believe."[48]

Ruskin's defense of the landscape painter Joseph Turner (the basis for writing *Modern Painters*) was occasioned by Ruskin's view that Turner's landscape painting was a counterpart to Wordsworth's poetry. Throughout volumes 1 and 2 of *Modern Painters* Ruskin points out the aesthetic parallelism of Turner's painting and Wordsworth's poetry.[49] Ruskin's absorption of many of his aesthetic notions from Wordsworth's romantic poetry is interesting in the light of recent research. E. D. Hirsch points out that Wordsworth and Schelling, writing contemporaneously, independently developed and expressed a metaphysics so similar as to be astonishing. Though Wordsworth and Schelling "did not influence one another," Hirsch settles upon the thesis that each developed independently an identical *Weltanschauung* as the "most probable explanation of the remarkable congruence" between the two.[50]

In the development of Emerson's aesthetic theory the importance of Schelling's philosophy of identity cannot be overestimated. Henry Pochmann claims that Emerson resolved the metaphysical problem of a dualistic universe in finding and accepting Schelling's philosophy of identity. With this idea, which he pre-empted and called the "universal law of Identity and Centrality," Emerson was, says Pochmann, able to repudiate the dualism he sought to transcend by arriving at the union of the ideal and the real in an absolute. Emerson's frequent copyings and references to Schelling in his *Daybooks, Journals*, and other writings indicate that he "regarded Schelling's idea of Identity as all important."[51]

From the Ascetic to the Aesthetic

Educated Americans were piqued by the criticism levelled against them in 1820. American writers and artists were reproached for having produced up to that time nothing that was worthy of serious consideration. During the next thirty years this criticism provoked the ambition among American intellectuals to express indigenous American culture through the arts.[52] The movement was somewhat similar to the desire of German intellectuals. In Germany the league between literature and philosophy marked an efflorescence of German national culture. This was in no way narrowly nationalistic in a political sense. Though the new German literature and philosophy aroused a national pride and self-confidence it stressed the freedom of reason through the development and the realization of the individual within a universal humanity.[53]

In shaking off the bonds of neoclassical aesthetics, Americans turned to German romantic philosophy to find the elements of an aesthetic theory which would provide the artistic freedom for a new expression. Hans Kohn notes that the American intellectuals influenced by the German idealists were similar in their outlook to many of the German idealists. Both groups were urging the expression of cultural nationalism in their arts, but in both cases the substance of art was not intended to be merely a narrow assertion of nationalism, but must represent the highest universal ideals and standards.[54]

The decisive significance of the interrelationship of philosophy and art lay in the emergence of a new aesthetic theory. It is precisely in its aesthetic principles that the German romantic philosophy most strikingly influenced the religious and artistic thought of the New England transcendentalists.

However, serious impediments to artistic expression existed among Americans. Frontier conditions allowed few activities other than those contributing to survival. Also, the Puritan tradition of New England acted as a restraint upon the production of anything that had no utility. Max Weber asserted that Puritan asceticism "descended like a frost" upon the fine arts. He explained that the Puritans rejected any attitudes "without objective purpose, thus not ascetic, and especially not serving the glory of God." They favored a "sober utility as against any artistic tendencies."[55]

Calvin had warned his followers that man must not use his creative abilities which God had granted to paint or carve anything that would diminish and insult God's majesty.[56] The Puritan may not have been insensible to the beauty of nature and man, but the ascetic principle channeled his glorification of God into enthusiasm for mundane work rather than the aesthetic. Calvin's warning against "images" and the restraint and utilitarianism of the Puritans tended to limit the development of the aesthetic sense. "Human effort, social institutions, the world of culture, are (to the Calvinist) at best irrelevant to salvation, and at worst mischievous. They distract man from the true aim of his existence and encourage reliance upon broken reeds."[57]

"It is unfortunate," writes Thomas Wertenbaker, "that the spirit of American Puritanism found few media for its expression." The Puritans of New England produced neither painting, music, architecture, stained glass nor sculpture which reveal their religious feelings.[58]

Olmsted was astringent in his criticism.

The Puritans, whatever their moral elevation, were very low in civilization, and they possessed and bequeathed to their descendents one element of public opinion strongly antagonistic to civilization. Their requirements were meagre. They considered the fine arts for instance as devices of the devil. They strangled or turned into savage directions the natural demands for festive recreations.[59]

The decline of the importance of the legalism of the Calvinist theology and the joining together of the Calvinist notion of mission with romantic aesthetic idealism marked a departure point in the development of American aesthetic theory (and theology).

The New England idealists rejected the Calvinist notions of salvation for a predestined elite and the damnation of the rest of depraved humanity, the utter religious loneliness of the self-examining individual, and the pessimism that goes with these notions. In their place they substituted the idealist's view of the divinity of all nature, of which man is an integral part, and the conception of an interrelated organic humanity and universe. But far more important, the New England Transcendentalists undertook to achieve a holy community by softening with an aesthetic sense the severe aspects of Puritan asceticism with its hard requirements of duty, utility, work, and self-denial. The introduction of the aesthetic sense inspired the expression of feeling, the sense of personal enjoyment in one's labor, pleasure in recreational activity, the tempering of duty by a feeling for humanity, and an acceptance of the ordered universe as an object of beauty created by God, the Artist, for man's pleasure and moral improvement.[60]

In the sphere of creative art this nucleus of romantic philosophy provided Emerson with the material to formulate an aesthetic theory which rejected the prevailing restrictive neoclassical aesthetic theories. It represented a new departure in the development of American aesthetics.[61]

The Puritan ascetic element plays a role in combination with the romantic aesthetic in a unique way. It emerged as a unification in art of the organic form with a practical purpose or function. In the romantic aesthetic the growth and development of a work of art is analogous to the natural growth of a plant. It is an organic form in that it possesses its own vital or germinal power by which it shapes and develops itself from within outward. It is the inner vital organizing power which unites the diverse component parts into an interrelated unity and determines the outward form. The romantics held that a work of art exhibits the organic properties of a work of nature. The beauty of a work of art, like that of nature, consists in the variety of component parts which are drawn into a unified whole. Coleridge called it "Multëity in Unity."[62] Impelled, however, by their Puritan background, the American romantics combined organic form with purpose or function into a complete aesthetic theory that would give moral or social purpose to a work of art. In their version of unfolding, both in nature and in art, there is the notion of the economy of utilization—the fitness and interrelation of parts which make up the whole. The organic conception contains within it a functional aspect. Emerson discussed this in terms of "Fitness."[63] Using the organic form Emerson developed an aesthetic theory in which art is the creation of beauty and beauty cannot exist without the useful.[64]

Horatio Greenough, an American sculptor, adhered to the same aesthetic convictions as his friend Emerson. While Emerson applied the organic principle in working out his aesthetic doctrine, Greenough used the principle to develop an aesthetic theory for art and architecture that incorporated the notion of functional beauty.[65]

Carrying the organic analogy from nature to art, they saw in organic natural forms a utility which for them comprised beauty. In their conception of beauty art is so stripped to its very essentials—free of all embellishment and decoration—that it may be called an ascetic beauty. In his essay "Beauty" Emerson wrote, "The very definition of art is, the inspiration of a just design working through all the details. But the forsaking the design to produce effect by showy details is the ruin of any work. Then begins shallowness of effect—intellectual bankruptcy of the artist."[66] In this respect Greenough was even more rigorous:

> The normal development of beauty is through action to completeness. The invariable development of embellishment and decoration is more embellishment and more decoration. The *reductio ad absurdum* is palpable enough at last; but where was the first downward step? . . . [It] was *the introduction of the first inorganic, non-functional element, whether of shape or color.* If I be told that such a system as mine would produce *nakedness,* I accept the omen. In nakedness I behold the majesty of the essential instead of the trappings of pretension.[67]

Notwithstanding the great influence that Ruskin's aesthetic criticism wielded over Americans, the conception of functional beauty held by Emerson and Greenough (and subsequently Olmsted) was more rigorous than Ruskin's view. At the same time the Americans were more forward-looking in their application of organic functionalism. This is particularly true in relation to architecture and technology. Ruskin turned back to the medieval Gothic form in architecture as an ideal; he feared and abhorred the machine. Greenough (perhaps more than Emerson), on the other hand, rejected the older architectural forms as inapplicable to the evolving culture of America. He was firm in his conviction that the best application of his aesthetic theory would be in developing new forms of architecture and in such practical arts as new machines and tools where the functional aspect is uppermost.[68]

An essential component in Emerson's conception of beauty is the aspect of economy. He observed that "there is not a particle to spare in natural structures."[69] Like natural structures, artistic structures must be free of superfluous embellishment. In Emerson's view "beauty rests on necessities. The line of beauty is the result of perfect economy."[70]

In Greenough's aesthetic theory the artist's first aim for beauty should be to seek the essential, because it is in finding and expressing the essential that completeness or unity can be achieved in art.[71] Nonfunctional embellishment exhibits the inadequacy of the artist's aesthetic conception and attempts to compensate for the incompleteness of the artist's effort.[72] The organic-functionalism of nature is the paradigm of beauty, economy, organization, and completeness for both Emerson and Greenough. In their view nature manifests the highest principles of aesthetic truth. It is in nature that the best examples of art and beauty are to be found. And, according to Greenough, in nature the dominant element that the Creator inculcates in his works is the principle of "unflinching adaptation of forms to functions."[73]

It is in the transfer to his art of the principles of the divine organization and completeness that the artist expresses his genius. Romantic writers considered the artist to be a second creator and his work a part of nature, since artistic creation was viewed as a process of nature.[74] Goethe viewed a perfect work of art as the product of the human soul "and in this sense, also, a work of nature."[75]

With Emerson's view that beauty rested on necessities and embodied perfect economy, and Greenough's view that beauty is promised in function, there is the further equation which they project: a work of art simulates nature in functional economy and completeness and at the same time becomes part of nature and the "absolute utterance of the Godhead."[76]

By combining beauty in art with utility, or function with nature, and describing the whole as an emanation of God, the aesthetic theorists of New England Transcendentalism joined the ascetic aspect of Calvinism with an aesthetic appreciation of God as the Artist. In their view God could be glorified through beauty and artistic creativity rather than by self-denial. In this modification there is found an emphasis upon the optimistic enjoyment of this world as opposed to the dour preparation for other-worldly existence.[77]

Among the New England Transcendentalists there was no conception of art for art's sake. Beauty in art must serve a moral or social purpose.[78]

Only in this way can the aesthetic sense displace the ascetic. The social implications of the beauty-function aesthetic are apparent in architecture and the useful arts. In the fine arts, even in his special field of literature, Emerson found it necessary to impose a function or use. This he provided by requiring the fine arts to provide to an audience, or an observer, a moral or social improvement.[79]

Like Emerson and other American Transcendentalists Olmsted united the Calvinist ethic with the romantic aesthetic imported from England and Germany. With this new concept the Americans continued the journey to Christ's Kingdom—the Holy Community—but now the aesthetic reason was enlisted to accomplish the mission.

Form and Function

From the first, when Frederick Law Olmsted took up his career as a landscape architect and later as a city planner, he found it necessary to make a public justification for each of his creative efforts. The creation of a great public park involved the outlay of thousands and even millions of dollars in the purchase of hundreds of acres of land and equipment, the hiring of thousands of laborers, and continuous maintenance. For any municipality to undertake such a project, as many did after 1858, implied public support. But it also involved Olmsted in the continuous oversight of municipal boards, councils, and state legislatures as well as newspaper editors. Further, the effort of a municipal administration to engage itself in such a project was a pioneering one. For Olmsted, the great city public park and later the planned suburban subdivision became the investment and vehicle by which he meant to pursue the reform of a society rapidly becoming urban.

Aggressively and zealously he used every legitimate means available to him to publicize and gain acceptance for the aesthetic rationale which supported his creative work. As an artist he was uncompromising in his commitment to embody his aesthetic theory in whatever work he undertook. Because his city parks were particularly vulnerable to spoliation or neglect by changing political administrations, he constantly fought both "good" or reform municipal office-holders, such as the New York reformer, Andrew H. Green, as well as the corrupt ones, such as the members of the Tweed Ring.[80] They would not or could not understand that the external functionalism of the park (its social purpose) would be diminished or destroyed if the internal unity (its "fitness" or organic relationship) fashioned by the artist were undermined. Olmsted's aesthetic theory embodied both aspects—art must be socially useful, beauty and utility are components in a work of art.[81]

Though Olmsted derived the elements of his aesthetic theory from the writings of the European and American Transcendentalists, he was intellectually capable of independently educing and refining his own theory relating to landscape architecture and city planning. Yet his organic beauty-function theory is similar to Greenough's "form and function" theory.

There are strong possibilities that Olmsted was familiar with Greenough's writings. In 1855 there was a notice in *Putnam's Monthly Magazine* of the publication of a new weekly magazine devoted to art. The magazine, *The Crayon*, was edited by two followers of Ruskin, William Stillman and John Durand. (The latter was the son of the famous American landscape painter Asher Durand.) In the early issues of *The Crayon* the editors published a number of articles from Greenough's book, *The Travels, Observations, and Experience of a Yankee Stonecutter*, originally published in 1843. As one of the editors of *Putnam's* it might very well have been Olmsted's task to review the new magazine which included Greenough's articles.[82] He must have known *The Crayon* well. He quoted from it in a few instances in his volumes on the South.

Whether Olmsted arrived at the "form and function" concept independently or from Greenough is of little concern here. The following quotations from Olmsted and Greenough indicate two points: first, the salience of the concept as a controlling one in Olmsted's landscape architecture and city planning; and second, the striking similarity to Greenough's formulation.

In *City Planning* Frederick Law Olmsted, Jr. recalls a discussion relative to town planning in which his father said,

> Let a thing be supposed, of greater bulk than the largest of our fine Fifth Avenue private habitations, to have been made for a mere common purpose of trade by the work of many men,—not one of them ranking among artists, not one of liberal education, men not at all delicate, not nice-fingered, not often even clean-handed; muscular, sweaty, and horny-handed; no small part of them rude and clumsy in their ways, tobacco-chewing, given to liquor, slang and profane swearing. Suppose the thing so produced to have no beauty of carving or color, to be mainly smeared black and white, and any touch of decoration upon it to be more than barbarously childish and clumsy.
>
> It can hardly be easy for those who represent what we have been more particularly gaining of late in esthetic culture to believe that such can have given the world a thing of supreme beauty. It will be still harder to realize that the coarse, rude, sensual men producing it had, in general, a deep artistic sense of its characteristic beauty, so that they would protest, in stronger terms than Mr. Ruskin ever used, against the putting upon it of anything by which the rare refinement of it might be marred.
>
> Alas! that I must speak of this as of a lost art; for it is of the "Baltimore Clipper" of fifty years ago, the like of which will never again be seen, that I speak. What is admirableness, dependent on no single thing done for admiration, no decoration, no ornament, no color of splendor, of a sailing ship?
>
> Whatever else it may be in the last analysis, it cannot be separated from this fact,

that a fine clipper ship, such as we had in America just come to build and rightly sail when the age of such things passed away, was as ideally perfect for its essential purpose as a Phidian statue for the essential purpose of its sculptor. And it so happened, in much greater degree than it can happen in a steamship, or in the grandest architecture, that the ideal means to this purpose were of exceeding grace, not of color, but of form and outline, light and shade, and of the play of light in shadow and of shadow in light. Because of this coincidence it was possible to express the purpose of the ship and the relation and contribution to that purpose of every part and article of her, from cleaving stem to fluttering pennant, with exquisite refinement.

No writer, poet, or painter can ever have told in what degree it lay in a thousand matters of choice—choice made in view of ideal refinements of detail, in adaptation to particular services, studied as thoughtfully and as feelingly as ever a modification of tints on painter's palette. One needed but a little understanding of the motives of seamanship to feel how in the hull every shaving had been counted, and how in the complicated work aloft every spar and cloth, block and bull's eye, line and seam, had been shaped and fined and fitted to do the duty required of it in the most sinewy way. These qualities, with the natural stateliness of the ship's motion set off by the tuneful accompaniment of the dancing waves, made the sailing ship in its last form the most admirably beautiful thing in the world,—not a work of nature nor a work of fine art.[83]

If Olmsted's statement is compared with the following from Green-ough, the parallelism becomes apparent. F. O. Matthiessen describes the following excerpt as Greenough's "most eloquent expression of the pos-sibilities of American art":[84]

Let us now turn to a structure of our own, one which, from its nature and uses, commands us to reject authority, and we shall find the result of the manly use of plain good sense, so like that of taste, and genius too, as scarce to require a distinctive title. Observe a ship at sea! Mark the majestic form of her hull as she rushes through the water, observe the graceful bend of her body, the gentle transition from round to flat, the grasp of her keel, the leap of her bows, the symmetry and rich tracery of her spars and rigging, and those grand wind muscles, her sails. Behold an organization second only to that of an animal, obedient as the horse, swift as the stag, and bearing the burden of a thousand camels from pole to pole! What academy of design, what re-search of connoisseurship, what imitation of the Greeks produced this marvel of con-struction? Here is the result of the study of man upon the great deep, where Nature spake of the laws of building, not in the feather and the flower, but in the winds and waves, and he bent all his mind to hear and to obey. Could we carry into our civil architecture the responsibilities that weigh upon our shipbuilding, we should ere long have edifices superior to the Parthenon, for the purposes that we require, as the *Constitution* or the *Pennsylvania* is to the galley of the Argonauts. Could our blunders on terra firma be put to the same dread test that those of shipbuilders are, little would be now left to say on this subject.[85]

It is commonly agreed that Greenough's original work in developing his theory of organic-functionalism for architecture was never applied by his contemporaries. He and his writings were forgotten. His theory seems to have made no impact upon the "Chicago school" of architects (spe-cifically Dankmar Adler, Louis H. Sullivan, and Frank Lloyd Wright) whose revolutionary work in the 1880s embodied the essence of Greenough's aesthetic.[86]

However, Greenough's principle was sustained in Olmsted's landscape architecture and city planning. Olmsted's organic-functionalism, which shows so marked an affinity to Greenough's theory, projected forward to the "form follows function" thesis of the American architect, Louis Sullivan.

From 1858, when Olmsted and Calvert Vaux began their work on Central Park, the organic-functional aesthetic was a controlling feature of the municipal parks and the cities planned by Olmsted. Olmsted's work was highly visible to Sullivan. South and Jackson Parks (see fig. 3) and the grounds of the 1893 Columbian Exposition, in Chicago, were Olmsted's. In the last chapter of his *Autobiography* Sullivan criticized the architecture of the Chicago World's Fair of 1893 as a betrayal of "American prowess, particularly in its architectural aspects." Only one facet of the Fair, "the landscape work, in its genial distribution of lagoons, wooded island, lawns, shrubbery and plantings, did much to soften an otherwise mechanical display" of the Classical and Renaissance architectural representations of the eastern architects who had been imported by the Fair's administrator, Daniel Burnham. Sullivan praised only Olmsted, the Fair's landscape architect.[87] The whole of the last chapter of Sullivan's *Autobiography* is an indictment of popular or eclectic American architecture. Olmsted was, in like manner, antagonistic to the architects who favored the Classical and Renaissance style of the Beaux Arts school of architecture. However, it is not so much their dislikes which unite Olmsted and Sullivan as their agreements. Both men used an aesthetic theory which derived from the German romantic philosophy. Like Olmsted, Sullivan saw himself as a social reformer through the aesthetic impulse. Just as Olmsted considered his public park a "sustained landscape poem," Sullivan considered the finest expression of architecture to be "poetic."[88]

To implement his appreciation of Olmsted's organic-functionalism Sullivan had, in addition to the Chicago parks, the nearby suburban community of Riverside, a town completely planned by Olmsted and Vaux. In conception and execution Riverside is a landmark in suburban planning. Sullivan's occasional visits to the Riverside home of his early employer, William LeBaron Jenney, gave him every opportunity to see the application of the form follows function principle. The aesthetic principle which Olmsted used horizontally in his landscape architecture, Sullivan, exploiting a new technology and new materials, applied vertically to architecture.[89]

Writing in 1905, Oscar Lovell Triggs stated his belief that a fundamental change was occurring in American art. He claimed that American

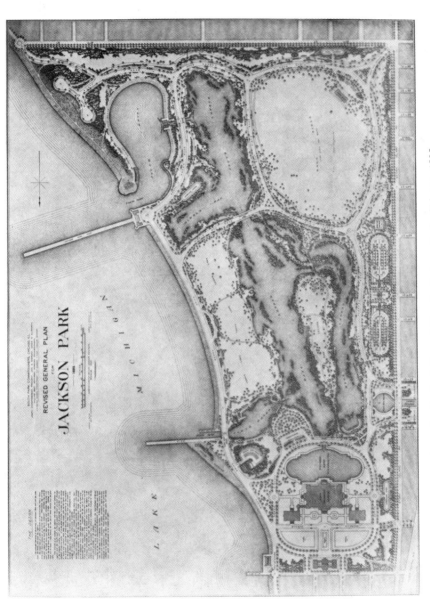

Figure 3.   Revised General Plan for Jackson Park, Chicago, 1895
(Courtesy National Park Service
Frederick Law Olmsted National Historic Site)

art was casting off its traditional and aristocratic characteristics and identifying with contemporary social forces. " 'Art for art's sake is giving way,' " he said, to " 'art for life's sake.' " Triggs found it noteworthy that

> the creative impulse in America finds other channels than the conventional ones. The fine arts are not quite native to us; they are with us derivative, the result of conscious and willful seeking and adaptation. But in certain popular and industrial forms our art has been original and creative. We originated the public park, for instance, and have carried its aesthetic forms to a perfection not equalled elsewhere in the world. America's greatest artist is a landscape architect. We created also commercial architecture, and today the American steel-frame business temple represents the one new and original departure made in the art of architecture since the period of the Gothic. *After Olmsted our most distinctive artist is Sullivan, an architect.*[90]

Triggs was an early and ardent advocate of Sullivan's architecture. He saw in it the same elements of creativity, functionalism, and "social consciousness in respect to art forms" that evoked his unqualified praise for Olmsted's genius. The significant fact as far as this study is concerned is that Triggs perceptively recognized the genius of Olmsted in creating a uniquely American art form based upon the organic beauty-function aesthetic. He looked upon Olmsted as one of America's greatest artists.

4

The Development of an Aesthetic Theory

Olmsted's creative works were accomplished in the romantic mode, but he provided no comprehensive statement regarding his aesthetic theory. We can only attempt to construct his theory from fragments that appear in his reports and letters. There is no doubt that he carried in his mind an operational theory that controlled his creative efforts. The evidence shows that his notions regarding the creative process and his conception of the aesthetic experience contain nuclear elements derived from the philosophy of German idealism.

The Unconscious in Art

Along with the organic view of the world, the romantics developed and adapted to their aesthetics the conception of the unconscious. In their hands the role of the unconscious in epistemology and in the psychology of artistic creativity was to achieve increasing importance. For Olmsted the conception of the unconscious and its use were of foremost importance.

"Hurrah for 'unconscious influence' all the world over!" writes the exuberant young Olmsted to his friend Brace in Europe.[1] Olmsted acquired the idea of the unconscious as an aspect of the organic principle from Horace Bushnell. Although it was published in 1847, Bushnell had delivered his sermon on "Unconscious Influence" in 1841.[2]

The idea of the unconscious has become a commonplace since Sigmund Freud. But in the 1850s in the United States, when Olmsted began to use the notion of the unconscious in his literary work and to relate it to his own art as a creator of parks and towns, it was a remarkable intellectual advance.[3] L. L. Whyte describes the period in which Olmsted was working with the concept as still one of discovery. It was not until about 1870 that it entered common usage.

In the manner in which Olmsted received the idea of the unconscious from Bushnell it has a synthesizing and socializing function. There is, Bushnell tried to show, an involuntary communication and sympathy which he called an "unconscious influence." It is this unconscious influence "between the members of a state or family" which is sovereign over character.[4] Olmsted accepted the unconscious as an active element in the human learning process. However, he extended the function of the unconscious into his aesthetic theory when, first, he considered it as necessary in the creative process of the artist and, second, when the unconscious becomes the link by which the artist reaches the spectator. It is, ultimately, the means by which art achieves the reform of society.

Like many of the romantics, Olmsted did not consider the unconscious mind as a memory file in the manner of the associational psychologists. The unconscious absorbs and synthesizes individual human experience and is a reservoir of potentialities which can affect man's thoughts and behavior. In advising his half-sister how to educate herself in her European travels, Olmsted wrote:

> The best thoughts come to us unawares; not by study; that is, not directly by study. But if entirely without study, you will not have knowledge enough or strength enough to pick up the gold you stumble upon. But don't let study or what you have arrived at or hope to arrive at by study be the end, only the means. . . . What you want is unconsciously and incidentally to cultivate your eye and the eye of your mind and heart.
> It will come when you don't know it—this appreciation of excellency, never fear.[5]

To the sophisticated reader, accustomed to the use of the concept of the unconscious, Olmsted's meager reference to the idea in an obscure letter in 1855 may have little significance. It was not a meager idea for Olmsted. The unconscious was integral to his epistemology. In 1892, while on a trip for professional study in Europe, accompanied by two young students, Philip Codman and Olmsted's son, Frederick Law Olmsted, Jr., Olmsted described the learning process of his two charges in a letter to his stepson.

> Both are learning more incidentally and unconsciously, without effort, than otherwise. Much more so than they think, I believe, consequently they value less than I do for them constant opportunities to be used without intention or effort. . . . I don't think that either Phil or Rick realizes the value which close observation of all sorts of things that may come under observation (but observation which is not recordable, or even to be given form verbally) may come to have in future practice, in aiding inventive design.[6]

Describing his own experience, Olmsted continued:

> I am, perhaps, because of a more nervous and undisciplined constitution, but largely, I think also, because of a sense, coming thro' experience of the value of what may be caught and stored in this way; which may become confused and lost to distinct re-

membrance, and yet, by some subtle process, consciously, affect [*sic*], long after-wards, essentially original inventive action of the intellect, and important convictions. I don't think the seeds of thought, their germination and conditions of growth, are sufficiently regarded in our current theories of education and metaphysics. Nor are all the injuries that result from cramming and didactic processes.[7]

Olmsted revealed his reliance upon the unconscious as the vehicle by which he influenced the development of landscape architecture. Writing retrospectively to an old friend, Olmsted stated his conviction that through his works of art he had exerted a primary educative influence upon the profession which he created. He made the claim that in the new works of the artists who were following in his footsteps his planned parks "are having an educative effect perfectly manifest to me—a manifestly civilizing effect. I see much indirect and unconscious following of them."[8]

His enthusiasm for *Sartor Resartus* and Carlyle's other writings strengthened Olmsted's reliance upon the notion of an unconsciously organized organic universe already planted in his mind by Bushnell's influence. Olmsted found in *Sartor* a view of an organic universe subject to and motivated by unconscious influences.[9] According to Carlyle, the universe consists of a multiplicity of invisible, interrelated factors and forces which surround, invade, and influence the individual. The material world of nature and the conditioned realm of society, directly and indirectly, through time and space, have ineluctable effects upon the whole.

Carlyle gave to the unconscious a paramount position in creative activity. Since he believed the unconscious to be a mysterious inner arena, the creative act was for him an inexplicable process, even a divine one. For some men who possess the facility of understanding, some aspects of the unconscious can be united with the conscious into organized knowledge. But for those elect who possess the highest intelligence—the seer or artist—the unconscious is the source of creative thought and achievement. Possessing the genius of deepest insight into the "Divine Idea" of the universe with the capability of Reason, Imagination, or Fantasy (Carlyle seems to use these conceptions interchangeably), the self-conscious ego or mind of the seer or the artist, man becomes the nexus of his own unconscious and the material world of sensation.[10] The "Archimedes lever" which initiates this process is the imagination.[11]

To develop his special individual talents each man must work. *"The end of Man is an Action,"* wrote Carlyle, *"and not a Thought, though it were the noblest."*[12] Work or activity is self-conscious action in which man manipulates or conquers the material world of nature according to a preconceived and guiding idea. But the totality of the complete work is not known to the conscious—only as the work progresses according to the preconceived idea, a conscious outline, is the work completed by elements of the unconscious which rise up from the inexhaustible "deep" through an intuitive process.[13] According to Carlyle, below the visible and conscious is the invisible, mysterious realm of the dynamic and vital unconscious.[14]

The study of the role of the unconscious received its impetus from Johann Gottfried Herder. Herder insisted upon regarding the life of a people as the common life of an organism in terms of a national spirit and a national character. The attempt to seek out the underlying sociopsychological tone of a society, or the spirit of the folk derives from Herder's formulation that every society contains within it an underlying spirit or unconscious elements residing within the race which are indigenous to it and are continually unfolding.[15]

Succeeding German philosophers proceeded to modify Herder by making particular applications of his generalizations in the development of the imaginative aspects of human thinking—specifically to the nature of genius in art in the field of aesthetics. The working out of this problem finds its expression in the scheme of the dialectic: the subject-object antagonism. Among a complex of related anitheses Fichte, Schiller, Goethe, and Schelling gave systematic expression to the questions of the relationship of the mind to the outside world (i.e., the Ego and the Non-Ego) and the conscious-unconscious conflict as they relate to the pyschology of the creative process. These German philosophers and writers were dominant in this development, and it is largely their influence which Coleridge and Carlyle reflect.[16]

Olmsted also reflected their influence. His analysis of the process of his own artistic creation shows that he embodied the salient elements of romantic thought as they related to artistic invention. Olmsted deliberately attempted to focus directly upon the psychological process by which he created the design that would determine his artistic product. Forced by public and private clients to justify his park plans, he provided in a few instances the process that he believed controlled his own creative efforts. He gave us, however, no systematic essay. The information comes from a few letters which Olmsted wrote to a number of his private clients or to public officials.[17]

For Olmsted there were two general areas of operation in creative activity. First, there was the inductive process. This involved the rational, conscious element of his effort in which he became empirically familiar with the topography of the ground with which he worked. This required a comprehensive study involving the relations of the parts to one another and to the whole, the character of the construction, and the emergence of a general plan or design incorporating some idea of the principles to be undertaken. Once the awareness of the design was secured, then the

Figure 4. Frederick Law Olmsted, ca. 1860
*(Courtesy National Park Service
Frederick Law Olmsted National Historic Site)*

planning could "go in a deductive way, from comprehensive to incomprehensive,[18] larger to smaller, from the more controlling to the less controlling features."[19] What Olmsted meant by the "deductive" in the creative process is the welling up of unconscious elements into consciousness to provide the detailed substance in which the general empirical design is filled in to complete the grand design. It is in this latter process that the genius of the artist emerges and manifests itself. Unlike "inductive reasoning" the "deductive" operation is "a natural, spontaneous, individual action of imagination—of *creative fancy*," Olmsted said.[20] "It is a matter of *growth*; involuntary and unconscious growth. I cannot come to a designing conclusion just when I want to. I must muse upon the conditions to be dealt with, have them upon my mind, and, after a time, I find a conclusion. I do not make it. It has come to be in my mind without my knowing it."[21] "A well-considered plan," Olmsted wrote, "cannot be had by any forced mental process. It must be reached by a natural and fluent, deliberately contemplative action of the imagination."[22] In specifically referring to his artistic work in Central Park he asserted that

> the best conceptions of scenery, the best plans, details of plans—intentions—the best, are not contrived by effort, but are spontaneous and instinctive and no man would be worthy of my office, who did not know that he must depend for his best success less upon any strong effort, than upon a good instinct. . . . The work of design necessarily supposes a gallery of mental pictures, and in all parts of the park I constantly have before me, more or less distinctly, more or less vaguely, a picture, which as Superintendent, I am constantly laboring to realize.
> . . . The design must be almost exclusively in my imagination. No one but myself can feel, and without feeling no one can understand . . . the true value or purport of much that is done in the park, of much that needs to be done.[23]

What Olmsted described here is a dialectic method in which the artist resolves the antagonisms in the unconscious-conscious conflict within himself on the one hand and the ego/non-ego or spiritual-materialistic conflict on the other hand. The synthesis by the creative artist results in a product which is a rational and harmonious organic unit.

Olmsted's analysis of the psychology of creative activity reflected a similar activity which preoccupied the philosophers of German idealism. However, it is in the philosophy of Schelling that the aesthetic act becomes all encompassing as the highest act of reason.

Schelling maintained that the concrete forms of matter in nature are symbolic—analogous with the processes of consciousness. For him matter is potential mind or spirit and spirit is potential in matter. In the fusion of the subject (self) and the object (nature) identity is achieved. In this identity the individual discovers himself by finding in nature his own external expression. It is the perception of the self which makes it possible to create a unity of the multiplicity to be found in nature. The self can organize the universe in terms of its own experiences and infuse individual personality into the realm of nature. The aesthetic act embodies such a process. In Schelling's view reason reaches its complete development in a work of art and art stands as the purest expression of philosophy. Schelling combined two elements of nature into a unity which is itself a manifestation of nature. In his identity concept Schelling offered a positive approach to the problem of alienation. He asserted that the individual's identification with nature allows the revelation of various forms of universal life. The separation of the individual from nature leaves the self a "dead object" unable "to comprehend how life is possible outside" a being's existence.[24]

To explain the syntheses of the parallel but mutually opposing "Ego or Intelligence" and "Nature," "conscious" and "unconscious," "freedom" and "necessity," "subject" and "object," Schelling turned to the creative activity of the artist. In the unconscious-conscious activity of the artistic genius, Schelling explained, the antitheses are abolished and the aesthetic reason is realized. Feeling within himself an opposition, the inability to fuse the unconscious and the conscious, the artist is driven to expression. In this activity the artist achieves satisfaction as well as an "infinite harmony" in his product. "The work of art," Schelling said, "reflects in us the identity of the conscious and the unconscious."[25]

"More than anyone" it is Schelling who is responsible for making the concept of the unconscious "an ineluctable part of the psychology of art."[26] Schelling asserted,

> It has long been perceived that, in art, all things are not performed with a full consciousness; that with the conscious activity an unconscious energy must unite itself; that the perfect union and reciprocal interpretation of the two is that which accomplishes the highest in art; works wanting this seal of unconscious power are recognized by the evident want of a self-sufficing life, independent of the producing life; while on the contrary, where this operates, art gives to its productions, together with the highest clearness of the understanding, that inscrutable reality by which they resemble works of nature.[27]

Schelling and Coleridge viewed artistic creation as a rational process. The romantic idealists held that the genius is autonomous. As artist the genius may overthrow the merely mechanical rules of art that bind him. But they believed that in the course of artistic invention the artist subjects himself to his own law—a law that emerges in the creative process.[28] Coleridge insisted that "no work of true genius dare want its appropriate form; neither indeed is there any danger of this. As it must not be so neither can it, be lawless! For it is even this that constitutes its genius— the power of acting creatively under laws of its own origination."[29]

However, the "extremists" among the romantic writers, emphasizing the unconscious, considered the creative act to be impulsive and lawless. For them the unconscious assumed superiority over the conscious.[30] The extremists rejected the idea of the organic unity of content and form and the reciprocity of conscious and unconscious in the aesthetic act.

In his all too brief accounts of the psychology of his own creative activity Olmsted showed that he belonged to the rationalists rather than the anarchists of the romantic school. In his description of the process by which the artist arrives at synthesis it is apparent that Olmsted was careful to explain that a necessary awareness of empirical factors of area, topography, climate, and function consciously gave form to his creative effort. For Olmsted the artistic invention was a reciprocating activity between the conscious and the unconscious. A work of art achieves completion in this intimate union, and not outside the limits of consciousness.

The Artist as a Moral Agent

The religious and social responsibilities which motivated Olmsted were enduring elements in his activities as an artist and planner. His Calvinist training infused him with a sense of guilt from which he hoped he might purge himself in some sense by a continuing activity to reform society. In his correspondence with his friend Brace he confessed,

> But this much—I feel just so as you do only—I have cause to feel ten times "more so." Our consolation must be that we in preparation must [labor] in the hope of *yet* doing something for the good and help and salvation of our fellow sinners and the honor and glory of Christ through whose *all powerful atonement and mediation—as we believe,* we can hope to be saved from *Justice.*[31]

At the same time Olmsted assumed that he enjoyed the grace by which he would accomplish his mission. This is precisely the sense of Calvinism which Troeltsch describes when he points out that the "Calvinist is filled with a deep consciousness of his own value as a person, with the high sense of a Divine mission to the world, of being mercifully privileged among thousands, and in possession of an immeasurable responsibility."[32]

The two elements of guilt and divine agency flow together into a single aspect with Olmsted's aesthetic theory and artistic vocation. Not only must moral purpose possess the artist's activities, but also the artist reveals his character in his work. The artist is the link between God and man in whom the essential nature of reason comes to its full realization in the work of art. Acting as a conductor, a moral agent, he reveals to lesser men the reason, the beauty, the divinity that reside unconscious in nature.

Olmsted must have been convinced that he possessed the requisite qualities of moral leadership. In performing his duty in his role and call-ing, he must have viewed himself as one of Carlyle's elect—the seer, the artist—the "inspired Maker" whose spiritual vision rendered the "God-like" visible.[33] Writing to his friend Brace in 1863, five years after he and Calvert Vaux had planned and created New York's Central Park, Olmsted asserted: "None the less is there work to do always by every man,—chiefly for you and me to keep up the faith of people and make them look far ahead, as is not their custom in everyday affairs."[34]

Among the romantics there was the widely shared view that, since the artist is the vehicle by which the divine is revealed and moral instruc-tion imparted, there must be a correlation between artistic excellence and moral excellence. Schelling made this point when he declared that the "soul of the artist" becomes visible in the essential "goodness" of the artist's creative performance.[35]

Coleridge regarded genius as a "divine effluence." He used Shake-speare and Milton as examples to demonstrate that morality is one of the attributes of the genius. Coleridge asserted that in disclosing the character of a "divine mind," Shakespeare's dramatic works show a sense of mo-rality superior to his contemporaries and "calculated to make his readers better as well as wiser."[36] He stated that the sublimest parts of Milton's *Paradise Lost* are revelations of the grandeur and purity of the author's mind.[37] Carlyle equated the poet with the prophet since the poet, like the prophet, can "penetrate into the sacred mystery of the Universe" and reveal the "Divine Idea of the World" in his writing. According to Carlyle the poet discloses his moral nature in his creative effort.[38]

In his essay on "Art" Emerson also held to the view that the work of art is a revelation of the artist's personality. "In proportion to his force," he said, "the artist will find in his work an outlet for his proper character."[39] Emerson implied that the greater the manifestation of gen-ius, the more moral the artist must be. Emerson perceived the artist as a prophet or an angel.[40]

The strongest position of the moral purpose of art and the artist was stated by John Ruskin. For Ruskin, the "impressions of beauty . . . are neither sensual nor intellectual, but moral."[41] The whole purpose and labor of the artist must be to prove "that no supreme power of art can be attained by impious men."[42]

The Artist as Analogon of God

Among those of the romantic orientation the moral excellence of the personality of the artistic genius is revealed in his work. Matched with this is the view of the unconscious activity and growth of the man of creative genius—an internal process similar to the organic processes of external nature. The internal activity of the human mind in producing great art and the nonhuman involuntary processes of natural growth are linked in conception—both are processes of nature and each activity results in a natural product. Creative activity, then, is the result of the same powers which are integral to nature and is a manifestation of nature. In his dialogue, "On the Truth and Probability in Works of Art," Goethe stated this: "A perfect work of art is a work of the human soul, and in this sense, also, a work of nature." Since the perfect work of art displays the achievement of a comprehensive mind, the creation of the artist is "above nature, but not unnatural."[43]

Schelling, Coleridge, and Emerson conceived of the aesthetic reason as the vehicle by which the identity of subject and object is finally achieved. A work of art completes the synthesis. With this aesthetic motif the universe itself becomes a manifestation of the most perfect organism and the most perfect work of art. "The universe is in God as an absolute work of art and fashioned in eternal beauty," said Schelling. It is in the artist whose imaginative genius intuits the harmony of the universe and expresses it through himself that the divine universe is represented and realized. The fundamental principle which the true artist must express is "the holy, eternal, creative original force of the world which produces all things out of itself."[44] According to Schelling, the process by which the artist finds expression and harmony in a work of art is through the necessity of the artistic genius to realize a synthesis of the contradiction in the unconscious-conscious activity. "Within the artist is felt an 'infinite opposition,' the '*pati Deum*,' the inability to bring together the two activities, the unconscious and the conscious. This opposition drives him to expression. Then follows an 'infinite satisfaction' in the artist, and his product is an infinite harmony."[45]

The same conception appears in Coleridge's essay, "On Poesy or Art." For Coleridge art mediates and reconciles nature and man. It stamps the diversity of nature into "unity in the mould of a moral idea."[46] The artist manifests his genius inasmuch as his product realizes the identity of thought and nature.[47] Coleridge believed that were it possible to discern the thought in the whole and in every part of nature, nature itself would be seen by the religious observer as a work of art—"the art of God."[48] He maintained that the human mind is not merely a passive recipient of sensory phenomena but an active, creative agent "made in God's image." For Coleridge the creative process of the poet or artist is "a dim Analogue of Creation."[49]

The view that "a work of art is an abstract or epitome of the world" and "the expression of nature in miniature," as Emerson phrased it, was easily equated with the notion that the creative act is a divine one, similar to God's creation of the universe.[50] The parallel to this is the creative genius, conceived as an aspect of the divine mind, emulating the creative power of God. In the heterocosmic analogue—the parallel between the inventive activity of the artistic genius and God's creation of the universe—art must imitate the organized productive power of nature. The God-possessed artist creates autonomously through an integral, indigenous, natural power, like a second maker. As God modeled the universe so the artist patterns his product.[51]

The exaltation of genius by the romantic idealists is an aspect of their rejection of the philosophy of mechanism of the eighteenth century derived from Hobbes and Locke and Bentham. The romantics could not accept Hobbes's assertion that the physical and mental abilities of all men are so equal that "when all is reckoned together, the difference between man, and man, is not so considerable, as that one man can thereupon claim to himself any benefit, to which another may not pretend, as well as he."[52] They believed that since nature conforms to no regular and uniform model, but manifests diversity, society likewise cannot be made up of similar, equally-endowed individuals. Within organic society there exist unusual men who far surpass others in their insight and creative genius. With the romantic idealist the artist becomes a creator, an analogon of God, who creates a work of art representative of nature following the patterns upon which God modeled the universe.

These conceptions were conjoined in Olmsted's landscape architecture and planning and were implemented in his artistic activity. Olmsted's concern throughout his work was to develop an aesthetic theory by which to effect social reform. His underlying motivation was moral. Olmsted labeled his own artistic creation, such as Central Park in New York, "a specimen of God's handiwork," that will have an effect upon the physical and mental health of the observer equal to a visit "in the White Mountains or the Adirondacks."[53] He considered his urban park "the work of nature, invulnerable to criticism, accepted by all, as well the cultivated as the ignorant, and affords a limitless field for interesting observation and instruction."[54] In formulating his design for Mount Royal, Olmsted offered to the people of Montreal an urban park which would remind them of the Garden of Eden. In his report Olmsted declared that like the "original Gardener of Eden," he would create sacred places "of indescribable loveliness."[55]

Writing to Mariana Griswold Van Rensselaer in 1893, Olmsted defined the nature of his art, distinguishing it on the one hand from architecture and on the other from gardening. Architecture, he pointed out, ought to be limited to works of buildings but gardening must be limited to garden work. His own art of landscape architecture, he asserted, included both activities and transcends them. It involves "exposing great ledges, damming streams, making lakes, tunnels, bridges, terraces, and canals." This is a conception of architecture on the grandest scale, analogous to God's work. He asked, "Did not Milton use the word architecture for the working out of the divine design for the heavens?"[56]

Certainly Olmsted was aware in his first project—New York's Central Park—that he had embarked upon an enormous artistic venture. Olmsted took complete responsibility for implementing his design formulated with Calvert Vaux. From an unsuitable, barren tract of land of more than 800 acres of granite ledge and swamp, occupied by a few squatters, scavengers, and goats, Olmsted evoked one of the finest examples of art of the nineteenth century. Writing in 1890, Olmsted explained that the nature of his administration was such that he had completely controlled the employment and instruction of four thousand men and the disbursement of monies.

> It was to be an intimate combination of such work as is commonly directed apart, respectively, by engineers, architects and horticulturists. Thus, there was to be grading, quarrying, dam-building, sewering; there were to be many costly bridges on all sorts of foundations; there were to be numerous small buildings: there were to be many miles of heavy retaining walls, many miles of roads. Three hundred thousand trees were to be planted on ground, the greater part of which was a bare ledge of granite and another considerable part of swamp. . . .
>
> The experts swore that the work was the best of its kind in every respect of which they had any knowledge . . . and at length reported that the force was well directed and under rarely good discipline.[57]

Olmsted was so successful in carrying out his design that to the unknowing spectator Central Park, like most of Olmsted's parks, seems but a preservation of an original, natural state with the addition of a few man-made appurtenances. The artistic deception is a deliberate part of Olmsted's plan to fashion such an ideal "natural" environment. To create the effect, Olmsted required thousands of tons of soil to be brought to the park site. The fact is, Olmsted explained, Central Park "has nearly everywhere a shallow made soil laid upon a solid flooring of rock. Almost anywhere for example on the green and between the elm trees of the mall, when the ground is saturated with moisture a walking stick may be thrust down to the rock."[58]

Olmsted's genius lay not only in the manner in which he used a vast space, but time as well. It was necessary for him to fashion his immediate work with vegetation in such a way that the total design that he envisioned would be realized forty or fifty years after the original plantings.[59] The results of his creativity are works of art in a two-fold sense in his uses of land, water, and vegetation to form the park and in the park as a creation of the human mind.

In the romantic proportion, just as the universe is God's perfect work of art, fashioned in eternal beauty, the parks which Olmsted created through the natural force of his imaginative genius, are microcosms of the universe—representations of nature. They are not mere mirror imitations of nature; nature, unassisted, often presents a landscape that is unappealing, composed of weak, deformed, barren elements, Olmsted pointed out. The work must be encouraged and idealized by the imaginative activity of the artist applying rational principles. By cooperating with nature the artist produces a poetic charm no less natural than the original scenery.[60]

Olmsted looked upon his parks as symbols of nature in which the essence of nature is expressed in art. In the Transcendentalism of Carlyle, Coleridge, and Emerson the reconciliation of thought and matter, of spirit and nature is activated in the symbol. Olmsted found the doctrine in Carlyle's *Sartor Resartus*. In the symbol, Carlyle declared, "the Infinite is made to blend itself with the Finite, to stand visible, and as it were, attainable there."[61]

In artistic creation the ideal for the neoclassicist was a precise reproduction of nature according to universally accepted rules that reflected the order of the universe. The work of art was a mirror image of nature. The romantic idealists sought the absolute by turning their efforts to idealizing and remaking nature. But no matter how great the natural potency of the greatest artist, his potentialities are ultimately derived from an absolute or God. Reluctantly, perhaps, the romantic idealists realized that there existed an insuperable barrier which their efforts could not overcome. They could at best speak in terms of participating in a minute way in the infinite powers of God. By the infusion of man's natural powers as thought or spirit into matter they claimed that their great works of art are part of nature in that the processes of their creation are similar in kind to God's artistry which is exhibited in nature. The great work of art is a symbol of the God-like.

The Ideal Landscape

Olmsted gave to romantic aesthetic theory the ultimate service. If the ideal of the artist is to create a work of art that reflects the generative vitality of an organic world, if the work of art is a microcosmic recreation of the organic world, then Olmsted achieved the romantic ideal in the artistry of his landscape designs. He had consciously developed the art of landscape architecture, equating it with the other fine arts. Olmsted's landscape designs were composed as natural scenes that impart a pictorial effect. His parks are composites of "naturalistic pictures."[62] They have a likeness to the kind of landscape paintings Ruskin favored in his *Modern Painters*. However, there is a significant difference between landscape painting and Olmsted's natural scenes. In contrast to an inanimate landscape painting Olmsted's natural scenes are vitally and generatively alive with vegetation and people. His parks were manifestations of physical nature yet ideal expressions of nature; they were analogous to nature yet homologous with it. "My picture is all alive—," Olmsted asserted, "its very essence is life, human and vegetable."[63] The natural scenes that Olmsted created were in a continuous process of growth and change from season to season and year to year. He even considered the human observers who peopled his parks as part of his picture. As the people and animals moved about, the scenery constantly changed, giving his natural pictures a kaleidoscopic effect. In a description of Central Park Olmsted wrote:

> The Park has attractions to those who visit it, merely as a picture; people walk, and drive, and ride there, not only because the walks, and ride, and drive are superior, but because the eye is gratified at the picture that constantly changes with the movement of the observer. . . .
>
> The lawn, the flowers, the trees, the water, all combine to form this picture, and each adds to its attractiveness.[64]

Olmsted did not intend the visitors to his parks merely to view nature but to become participants with other spectators in a constantly changing picture of natural scenery.

The Artist-Spectator Relationship

In Olmsted's aesthetic it is only in the mind of the spectator that the creative idea can achieve the purpose which the artist intended. It is not enough that the artist attain the highest synthesis in a work of art. The fact that in the creative process the artist discovers himself and his own idea in the materials with which he works is only part of the total aesthetic experience.[65] The identity principle must also include the spectator. The artist cultivates and predisposes the mind of the observer to see the world as the artist has organized it. Art and nature and art as nature attain significance through the aesthetic reason. The circle of aesthetic experience achieves closure when the spectator realizes the intent of the artist.

Olmsted's public was the heterogeneous mass of population which flooded into the cities of the United States during the latter half of the nineteenth century. His municipal parks presuppose a confidence in the ability of all men to enjoy creative intuition. He wrote,

> It is unquestionably true that excessive and persistent devotion to sordid interests cramps and distorts the power of appreciating natural beauty and destroys the love of it which the Almighty has implanted in every human being, and which is so intimately and mysteriously associated with the moral perceptions and intuitions, but it is not true that exemption from toil, much leisure, much study, much wealth, are necessary to the exercise of the esthetic and contemplative faculties. It is the folly of laws which have permitted and favored the monopoly by privileged classes of many of the means supplied in nature for the gratification, exercise and education of the esthetic faculties that has caused the appearance of dullness and weakness and disease of these faculties in the mass of the subjects of kings.[66]

Olmsted rejected the elitist notion that the common man neither appreciates nor deserves the highest art. "There is," he declared, "a sensibility to poetic inspiration in every man of us, and its utter suppression means a sadly morbid condition."[67] In his plan for Mount Royal he directed the following remarks to the people of Montreal: "Please reflect . . . whether it may not be a teaching of snobbishness and vulgarity against which every true man should rebel, that good art is above the heads of the common people. Those whom all accept as the highest authority regard the highest art to be that which was made for public places and for the use of all."[68]

Olmsted's optimistic premise that every man possesses an intuitive sensitivity to beauty in art and nature subjected him to the criticism of his friend, Charles Eliot Norton. Upon reading the plan for the Mount Royal park, Norton commented,

> And here it seems to me is your only error, you expect too much from men who have not culture enough to enable them even intellectually to conceive of such a state of mind as yours, much less to appreciate beauty when they see it. They positively prefer ugliness, they think it beautiful. You are preaching truths above the comprehension of our generation. A few may, through their rare humility and docility, take on trust your doctrine, without loving it; but the most will according to their nature, reject and scoff at it. Your native optimism comes out in your hope for anything but this.[69]

Olmsted's optimism about every man's ability to realize the creative idea of the artist was no less pronounced than Ralph Waldo Emerson's. For Emerson, too, the aesthetic process was consummated with the observer's reaction to the artist's product. In his essay "The Poet," for example, Emerson granted to all men the aesthetic sensibility by which they may identify with the creative intuition of the artist. He asserted, "If imagination intoxicates the poet, it is not inactive in other men."[70]

Emerson believed that every man who was susceptible to the "enchantments of nature" was a poet.[71]

Both Olmsted and Emerson held that the aesthetic experience must lead to a socially useful end, that social impact must give art and literature that worth. Both men agreed with Greenough's thesis that function and beauty are essentially bound together. In order to provide the aesthetic impulse with a function, they imputed a social value to it. This is particularly true of Olmsted. It gave him a rationale for the huge metropolitan parks he designed for the enjoyment of a mass of urban dwellers.[72] He intended that his parks be enjoyed for something more than green oases in teeming, fetid cities. They must be enjoyed through the aesthetic reason. In this way the parks would have social value to the spectators who came to them. Olmsted "was firmly convinced that the prime function of his own art, as of all the Fine Arts, was to bring inspiration and delight to *others* than [the] artists."[73] Inherent in his idea of the public park was Olmsted's presumption that every man is capable of the aesthetic impulse.

The relationship of the creative artist to the observer, especially in moral or ennobling effects, was also a question of some importance to both German and English writers of the romantic school.[74] As an example, Schiller offered the aesthetic experience as an impulse to play, the play-drive, as an effective vehicle for the moral education of man.[75]

For Carlyle there are two classes of men—the heroes and the average men. The first are the few "Prometheus-like," imaginative, creative, inspired makers. They are moral agents with divinely endowed intellects who fashion the souls of men by limning new paths for humanity. They pierce the world of appearances and reconstruct the world of nature through new symbols. The second class, the average men, are "blinded, dwarfed, stupefied, almost annihilated." Carlyle respected both classes, but he pitied the average men who are defaced by labor and deprived in body and soul from knowing freedom. Only the reason or right judgment of the hero as artist or "inspired Thinker" can reveal to the average men the "Divine Idea" that pervades the universe.[76] Carlyle allowed to the average man little possibility of imaginative thought that would lead to the kind of freedom in which the individual can psychologically free himself of his social constraints and assess his relations with the world.

In contrast to Carlyle, Olmsted, like Emerson, displayed a confidence in the average or common man for self-development. If men are not alike in their capacities for the highest creative achievement, most have some degree of creative ability. Olmsted firmly believed that the artist and his product must educate, civilize, and refine the spectator.[77] He said, "It must be observed, also, that a really fine, large and convenient park exercises an immediate and very striking educational influence, which soon manifests itself in certain changes to taste and of habits, consequently in the requirements of the people."[78] The enjoyment of the park scenery inspires the spectator to participate in the chain of aesthetic experience that is vaguely similar to the artist's path of creation. In this process the observer identifies with the creator in an apprehension of the divinity of nature.[79] If the artist is a dim analogue of God, the observer is a dim analogue of the artist.

Olmsted was optimistic concerning man's potentialities for creative development. Examination of his view of the slaves of the pre-Civil War South reveals his conception of human nature. He rejected the notion that blacks as a race are inferior and have little or no capacity for improvement. The slave system reduced their natural capacities and demoralized and debased them. To prove that social development and character are results of environment and conditioning, Olmsted compared the various conditions of slaves (domestic or house and field slaves).

> The character and intellectual condition of the more privileged [domestic] negroes is so superior, that I deem it in itself the strongest evidence against the first hypothesis—which affirms that the negro race has but little capacity for self improvement. . . . At present I take the hypothesis more generally accepted by the world . . . that the race is capable of indefinite elevation; that the same general laws of progress apply to it that are admitted for our own race; that all are descended from one parent stock, and that the difference of physique is due to outward circumstances, and has followed rather than caused the difference of mental character which has distinguished the races.[80]

Olmsted joined the Calvinist doctrine of the individual's duty for self-development to his conception of human nature. "Our first duty," Olmsted urged, "is that which is the first duty of every man for himself—improvement, restoration, regeneration."[81] This rationale supported Olmsted's view that his public parks would provide the vehicle by which an urban society would be transformed by the aesthetic reason.

In planning his parks Olmsted desired to communicate an immediate sense of pleasure to the spectator. Like Coleridge, Olmsted held that a work of art must evoke as its immediate object an emotional or an aesthetic response of pleasure.[82] He considered the visual delight elicited by the perception of beautiful scenes of nature to be a primary step in aesthetic education. Describing the composition of his parks, Olmsted wrote, "The landscape is arranged to please the eye: it presents a picture more exquisitely pleasing to the mind through the sense of vision than the most distinguished work of any master."[83]

But Olmsted did not consider sensuous pleasure in itself as the object of his artistic work. In addition to pleasure he urged that the contemplation of scenes of natural beauty would invigorate physical and mental health, the intellect, and moral perceptions and intuitions.

He believed that the continued subjection to the artificial patterns of the city was harmful to man's mental and nervous system and, ultimately, to the whole human constitutional organization of the urban dweller.[84] By creating parks composed of pleasing rural scenery he offered the city dweller what he assumed to be a desirable antidote to the rigidity and confinement of the city. In contrast to the city's environment, he said: "Hill and dale, wood and water, grass and green leaves, are the natural food and refreshment of the human eye—an organ of sense so delicately adjusted as to require something more than dull colors and uninteresting forms, and is but little ministered to, in a pleasant way, in the portion of the city devoted to plain, straightforward business, or even domestic routine."[85]

Given the nature of his art, Olmsted's concentration on vision is understandable. It is no less notable than the similar reliance upon the sight which characterized two men whose writings he greatly admired— Ralph Waldo Emerson and John Ruskin. In the first chapter of Emerson's "Nature," a work which enchanted Olmsted, Emerson described himself as "a transparent eyeball" who sees all.[86] In her critique of Emerson's aesthetic doctrine Vivian Hopkins notes Emerson's emphasis on sight as the basis upon which the aesthetic experience begins for both artist and spectator. It is mainly through the eye that the artist must capture the attention, if he would educate the perceptive faculties of the beholder.[87]

Like Emerson, John Ruskin was one of Olmsted's "prophets." Young Olmsted eagerly absorbed the pronouncements he read in Ruskin's *Modern Painters*. He acquired the same devotion to vitalizing the visual sense that permeated Ruskin's descriptions of landscape scenery and critiques of landscape paintings. During his literary period Olmsted was displaying the disciplined exercise of the visual sensibilities which Ruskin was trying to teach in *Modern Painters*. Graham Hough makes the point that "Most of *Modern Painters*, indeed, is not about painters at all, but about what the natural world really looks like." Ruskin's purpose, Hough claims, was to educate the uncultivated sense of sight in order that the beauty of God, the artist, might be revealed in the truth of nature. Hence it is that "visual sensations are heavily charged with moral and reflective overtones."[88] At the same time Olmsted was himself attempting the education of his readers by providing visual commentaries on his experiences. This is illustrated by his first book, *A Walking Tour of an American Farmer in England*. But it is especially true of his three volumes on the antebellum South. They were meant to educate his readers to perceive the social and economic conditions of the slave culture, the details of husbandry, and the landscape of the South and Southwest. His expert picturization of the territory he traveled and the conditions he reported gives reliability to his study.

When Olmsted turned to the designing of public parks he continued his campaign to educate the eye. The arranged landscape beauty of his city parks was meant to stir into conscious activity the faded and dormant perceptive faculties of the urban population who visited the parks.

Through art in nature he undertook the education of the observers of his parks. "The idea of education, it must be confessed by all," Olmsted insisted, "unquestionably culminates in the development of the reflective faculties, but the reflective faculties—which are secondary—can never, it is obvious, be healthily exercised if the perceptive faculties—which are primary—are neglected and starved."[89] The area in which he believed there must be universal appeal, where the educational process would be fruitful, is nature, since nature "affords a limitless field for interesting observation and instruction."[90]

Assuming that there is a sense of appreciation for the beauty of nature in everyone, Olmsted employed his art to provide natural environments which are visually pleasurable. This sense Olmsted called taste. Though taste is instinctive, it is found in individuals in varying degrees. "The power of scenery to affect men," he elaborated, "is, in a large way, proportionate to the degree of their civilization and the degree in which their taste has been cultivated."[91]

In its elementary sense taste is passive. The artist must make an appeal to the sensory apparatus of the beholder (i.e., "to delight the eye"). But taste has an active side. Taste can be refined and cultivated. One of the purposes of the park is to do precisely that. In various reports Olmsted explained that one of the virtues of the park is its influence "as an educator of the popular taste."[92] He confidently asserted that Central Park was "doing much towards elevating the general public taste of the country, not only in the more extended and spacious public and private dwellings and gardens, but in the adornment of the more numerous and less pretentious habitations of our rural population."[93] When art and nature are creatively fused in the park those who resort to it will experience sensations which are latent. With the exercise of the perceptions which the continuing use of the park will alert, the dormant tastes will come to life superseding old habits "less favorable," Olmsted maintained, "to health, to morality and to happiness." He stated that the tastes encouraged by his parks would be more natural and desirable than the wasteful and even degrading habits to which the inhabitants of cities are accustomed.[94]

Olmsted was close to Schiller's view that the simple pleasure in beauty—the aesthetic taste—frees the soul from "all those material inclinations and brutal appetites, which oppose with so much obstinacy and vehemence the practice of the good." Schiller held that taste "implants in us, nobler and gentler inclinations, which draw [us] nearer to order, to harmony, and to perfection."[95]

The casual park stroller, exposed to the beauty and grandeur of nature, is invited to participate in the creative reason of the artist. The visible world of the park provides the mnemonic to the unconscious and activates dormant potentialities. In his assessment of the value of his parks Olmsted insistently relied upon the unconscious. In a letter written in 1877 to the president of the Department of Public Parks, Olmsted asserted that if the millions of dollars poured into the construction of Central Park had any relevance,

> in the last analysis it will be found to be to produce certain influences on the imagination of those who visit it, influences which are received and which act, for the most part, unconsciously to those who benefit by them. These influences come exclusively from the natural objects of the park as they fall in passing them into relations and sequences adapted to the end in view.[96]

For Olmsted the unconscious was as significant in the artist-spectator relationship as in the creative activity of the artist.

Some romantic critics analogized the unconscious in man to the system of all phenomena in nature. Just as the unconscious is a realm of experience, processes, laws, and powers in man, the physical universe is the unconscious of the Creator. The organic unity of both realms is concealed and their elements are known to most only involuntarily as blind necessities and unrelated, discrete phenomena. Both realms become intelligible as the seeming multiplicity of variegated phenomena achieves organization or unity in the consciousness of man. It requires the reflective power of the human mind to bring its disparate elements to consciousness. According to Coleridge, "in the objects of nature are presented, as in a mirror, all the possible elements, steps, and processes of intellect antecedent to consciousness, and therefore to the full development of the intelligential act."[97]

Through his art Olmsted offered the spectator a new awareness of nature by which latent senses and feelings are reactivated and brought to consciousness. When the reason which lies in nature—the art of God— is made visible through the creative product of the artist, the beholder can identify himself with the processes of nature. The identification implies the recall of a period in the history of man when he was one with nature, rather than the alienated, depersonalized creature civilization has made him. The philosophic position was stated by Schelling:

> If *all* nature rises to a higher power up to consciousness, or if it leaves nothing—no monument—of the different steps through which it passes, then it would be impossible for it to reproduce itself with reason, whose transcendental memory, as it is well-known, must be refreshed by visible things. The Platonic idea, that all philosophy is recollection, is true in this sense; all philosophy consists in a recollecting of the situation in which we were one with nature. . . . Then we can go in different directions—from nature to ourselves, or from ourselves to nature, but the *true* direction, for him to whom *knowing* is of supreme value, is that which nature itself has taken.[98]

Olmsted considered his parks to have the same kind of effect upon the mind as does the nature poetry of Wordsworth and Emerson. He believed that the natural landscape exerts a charm that transforms the beholder.[99] The aesthetic of the park leads the spectator's mind into a musing or poetic mood. It induces contemplation.[100] Olmsted explained that the creation of Central Park

> is not simply to make a place of amusement or for the gratification of curiosity or for gaining knowledge. The main object and justification is simply to produce a certain influence in the minds of people. . . . The character of this influence is a poetic one and it is to be produced by means of scenes, through observation of which the mind may be more or less lifted out of moods and habits into which it is, under the ordinary conditions of life in the city, likely to fall.[101]

The faculties are freed from the rigidity and confinement into which they have been repressed by the routine convention, the daily grind of specialization, and the city environment. The spectator can now realize himself to be with other men, unified into a total organic whole, living within the universal laws that determine all natural processes. The aesthetic experience offers the spectator the opportunity to contemplate the world as an interrelated whole. The contemplation of natural scenery gives man the opportunity, as Emerson said, to apprehend "the unity of Nature,—the unity in variety,—which meets us everywhere."[102]

The artist-spectator relationship reaches full circle when contemplation results in inspiring the imagination of the spectator. Olmsted believed that the common people for whom he created his parks are not only able to appreciate good art, but that they are also capable of creative thought. "There is," he said, "a sensibility to poetic inspiration in every man of us." Olmsted maintained that though Wordsworth may have had greater poetic sensibility than others, he was neither differently constituted nor more affected than other men by the beauty of nature.[103]

Olmsted designed his parks so that the pictorial effects of the beauty of natural scenery would produce the free play of the imagination. "A great object," Olmsted emphasized, "of all that is done in a park, of *all* the art of a park, is to influence the mind of men through their imagination."[104] The keystone to the understanding of Olmsted's creative efforts was his intent to free the imagination of the observer through aesthetic experience. He construed the monotonous grid patterns of paved streets, the blank walls of high-rise buildings, fences, and the artificial constructions of the city to have the psychological effect of enforcing the sense of rigidity and confinement.[105]

To overcome the condition of visual limitation in the city Olmsted required large expanses of greensward interwoven with varieties of vegetation, rocks, ledges, water, and even the horizon to provoke the sense of limitless space in the spectator. His purpose here was to inculcate in the spectator the feeling of freedom. He said, "*A sense of enlarged* freedom is to all, at all times, the most certain and the most valuable gratification afforded by a park."[106] The atmosphere of the park should be open, free and inviting. Olmsted's belief that the natural scenery of his parks must induce the sense of freedom was so strong that he opposed the use of any barriers that obtruded upon them. He was particularly adamant against the use of the spiked, iron fence; artistically he considered it to be offensive. "We should undertake nothing in a park," he asserted, "which involves the treating of the public as prisoners or wild beasts."[107] Olmsted believed that the aesthetic experience in the rapprochement achieved by the beholder of all great art as well as natural beauty has the effect of freeing the flow of the imagination. Music and, especially for Olmsted, the poetry of Robert Burns and Wordsworth have such an effect.[108]

The aesthetic factor was the controlling one for Olmsted in the choice between planning a large public park for a city or a number of small ones. He admitted to the city's need for a large number of small urban grounds. They act as "Breathing-Places," he said. They are "lungs" for the city. They serve such purposes as exercise, protecting public buildings from noise and the spread of fires, allowing light and view to public buildings, honoring an historical or natural feature, playgrounds for children, and neighborhood conveniences. They are conveniences, even necessary ones, but limited in visual impact by special purpose. However, it is in the aesthetics of the great public park that Olmsted meant to bring about the education of his audience. It is in the environment of ideal rural scenery that Olmsted hoped to effect the psychological transformation and moral ennoblement of the park's spectators.[109]

Despite his frequent references to the development of the imagination in the observers of his art Olmsted did not set out a theory of imagination.

He did not define it nor did he adequately describe its activity in the artist-spectator relationship. This is not to say that he did not have his own aesthetic theory, derivative though it might be, in which the imagination played a significant part. This much can be gathered from his plans and his correspondence. There are no instances in Olmsted's writings in which he dissected and examined with any intensity the nature of the imagination. Nevertheless, from his letters and his reports it is possible to discern from his uses of the imagination the significant role it held in his own creative activity as well as its importance in the development of the aesthetic reason in the artist-spectator relationship.

5

Olmsted, Ruskin, and the
Roots of Beauty

Ruskin viewed the perception of beauty in nature and in art not only as a moral but also as a religious activity. In landscape painting particularly, he held that the artist revealed the beauty of God's universe by the genuine portrayal of the truths of nature. In the perception of beauty man is witness to the Glory of God. Olmsted and his circle were intrigued by Ruskin's identification of beauty in art and nature with morality and religion. When Olmsted turned to designing landscapes he found a use for Ruskin which he had not at first anticipated in his early study of Ruskin's writings. Ruskin's critical analyses of landscape paintings gave Olmsted guidelines for the development of his own art of landscape architecture. Along with his study of Sir Uvedale Price's *The Picturesque,* William Gilpin's *Forest Scenery,* and the works of the English landscape gardeners such as Repton and Paxton, Ruskin's writings became part of the intellectual corpus with which Olmsted approached landscape design. He averred that "as to general principles and spirit of design, all of Ruskin's art works are helpful."[1]

Olmsted was aesthetically more progressive than was Ruskin. He was closer to the aesthetic theory of his countryman, Horatio Greenough— that form is related to function. Unlike Ruskin, Olmsted did not accept the Gothic as the ultimate form in architecture, although, like Ruskin and the Americans, Greenough, Sullivan, and Wright, he hated the neo-Renaissance architecture of Hunt and Mead, McKim, and White. Olmsted turned readily to new forms of architecture. In his *Description of Design for the Central Park* he suggested that an exhibition hall in the style of Paxton's Crystal Palace be constructed in the park. He stated, "We believe no architecture is so well fitted for the purpose as the glass and iron style, in which New York has already had a success unsurpassed in its way. The Crystal Palace itself might be placed here."[2] In contrast to Olmsted Ruskin rejected the form, technique, and materials of the Crystal

Palace, looking upon it as an admirable piece of mechanical ingenuity but not art.[3]

Olmsted always conceived his planning work as containing elements of the picturesque—those elements of roughness and ruggedness which Price distinguished from the beautiful—the smooth and undulating. For Olmsted the characteristic features of the picturesque (i.e., mountains, forests, rocks, woodland) served as contrast and variety to the pastoral of the meadow and field. The picturesque provided for him the essential naturalism which he sought to obtain in his artistic achievements. As Olmsted considered the picturesque, it was an essential part of natural beauty. He therefore included the picturesque in his artistic recreations of nature. Ruskin, on the other hand, rejected the picturesque. He considered it to be a degraded form of artistic expression, except in the very special character given to it by the British landscape painter Turner.[4]

Admirer of Ruskin though he was, Olmsted's planned public and private parks, as reconstructions of nature, would seem to run counter to Ruskin's aesthetic principles. Ruskin advised landscape artists to choose their models directly from nature as the "highest examples of the ideal forms." He warned that only thus can the artist achieve truth and impress upon the spectator "some elevated emotion" and exhibit to him an exalted beauty.[5] But the ideal expressed in nature can only be realized for a plant or animal existing in that environment with which it is compatible. A specific form of nature was ideal for Ruskin insofar as it displays that "moral ideal which is dependent on its right fulfilment of its appointed functions."[6]. Any interference by the agriculturalist or the landscape gardener destroys the true and artistic ideal. Ruskin maintained that

> man never touches nature but to spoil; he operates on her as a barber would on the Apollo; and if he sometimes increases some particular power or excellence, strength or agility in the animal, tallness, or fruitfulness, or solidity in the tree, he invariably loses that *balance* of good qualities which is the chief sign of perfect specific form; above all, he destroys the appearance of the free *volition* and *felicity*, which . . . is one of the essential characters of organic beauty.[7]

It would follow that it is not in the man-made park that essential beauty can be found, only in the natural or the wild state, untouched by man.

If Olmsted had unreservedly followed Ruskin, he could never have claimed that Central Park in Manhattan, Prospect Park in Brooklyn, Franklin Park in Boston, and all the other great public grounds designed by him, were recreations of nature. Olmsted said that man can rationally give to nature a better aspect than nature itself could produce unaided.[8] In his plan for Mount Royal in Montreal, he asked, "Why is it more irrational to . . . sympathetically cooperate with nature for the end which you have in view in your use of this property, than for that of raising apples, corn, or buckwheat, where nature, left to herself, would not provide them?"[9] The artistic function of the landscape architect is "to so select the material of planting, or the native material to be left growing, that, within reasonable limits, the principle upon which Nature, unassisted, proceeds in her selections (though often very imperfectly) shall be emphasized, idealized, or made more apparent in landscape quality."[10] In contrast to Ruskin's view, Olmsted claimed that the landscape architect creates beauty in nature by epitomizing and idealizing it through his genius. He reformulates it as a landscape painter would by selecting, leaving out, and including. This way the artist removes the blots of ugliness, decay, and enfeebled forms and progresses towards a harmonized conception of natural beauty.[11]

Olmsted, as a creative artist, differed from Ruskin, the aesthetic critic, at various points. Nonetheless, he respected him and turned to his writings for support.

> Mr. Ruskin may be thought not only unpractical but fanatical, and many of his sayings may be regarded as wild, but that he is inspired by a great good motive, few will doubt. What is the ruling conviction of his zeal? In his own bitter words, it is that "This is an age in which we grow more and more artificial day by day, and see less and less worthiness in those pleasures which bring with them no marked excitement; in knowledge which affords no opportunity of display."[12]

It is likely that the reason for Olmsted's copious use of Ruskin lay not only in his affinity for Ruskin's moral and aesthetic position, but also in his tactical purposes. Much of Olmsted's writing, including his reports, surveys, and planning projects, was, like Ruskin's, didactic. To implement his position he was wont to use Ruskin's popularity as an arbiter of aesthetic taste.

Typical and Vital Beauty

In the second volume of *Modern Painters*, Ruskin offered the elements which he conceived to be the roots of beauty: typical beauty and vital beauty. The first consists of that "external quality of bodies . . . which, whether it occur in a stone, flower, beast, or in man, is absolutely identical, [and] which . . . may be shown to be in some sort typical of the Divine attributes." The second consists of "the appearance of felicitous fulfilment of function in living things, more especially of the joyful and right exertion of perfect life in man."[13]

In the discussion of vital beauty he viewed the universe as an organic whole in which every plant and creature exists and functions in a necessary, God-given, relationship. The thesis that Ruskin developed is that while the inner vitality of all beautiful things is physical, its significance to man and to art is moral—moral in the sense that it pertains to character and conduct. Ruskin invested the physical world of nature with divine or spiritual qualities.[14] He idealized nature in its sensual and functioning aspects and sanctified landscape. "In landscape it is nearly impossible to introduce definite expression of evil," he said.[15]

Olmsted's use of the characteristics of typical beauty followed Ruskin's aesthetic doctrine. The six moral qualities comprising typical beauty which may be reflected in natural objects are infinity, unity, repose, symmetry, purity, and moderation. By pleasing the eye these objective qualities of beauty make an immediate appeal to the senses without any direct and definite exertion of the intellect. The spontaneous experience arouses the spectator to progress, through the activity of the mind, to a higher level of contemplation. In this mental process the spectator is brought to the realization that the objective qualities of beauty that inhere in nature (or in art) represent spiritual qualities—"typical of the Divine attributes."[16]

The six qualities of beauty were for Olmsted at once principles of artistic composition, moral qualities, as well as the means to achieve a functional realization of social purpose through art. The qualities which Olmsted emphasized in his plans are those of repose, unity, and infinity.

Repose

Olmsted defended the city for the conveniences, comforts, and the economic, educational, and cultural opportunities it offered. But he observed that these advantages were accompanied by inconveniences, sickness, poverty, and social and psychological disorganization. For Olmsted there was no necessary relationship between the advantages and the dysfunctional conditions of urban living. However, he considered city life to be artificial. Divorced from a meaningful relationship to nature, people in cities are physically confined by overwhelming buildings and monotonous, linear, geometric street patterns. Large compacted populations live in an impersonal, commercial society under social conditions of tension; the natural agencies of social control such as family and neighborhood are weak or non-existent.

To provide a relief from the anxieties provoked by the discrepant conditions of the city Olmsted urged the creation of large municipal parks. The natural scenery offers a "suggestion of freedom and repose which must in itself be refreshing and tranquilizing to the visitor coming from the confinement and bustle of crowded streets."[17] In contrast to the artificiality of the city the park would "secure an antithesis of objects of vision to those of the streets and houses which should act remedially, by impressions on the mind and suggestions to the imagination."[18] Olmsted attempted to achieve this by creating scenes of landscape beauty that would soothe and refresh; he recreated in the heart of the city a composition of open, pastoral landscapes and sylvan scenes that emulated the rural quiet and tranquillity of his native Connecticut countryside.

Aiming for the sense of repose, Olmsted rejected the wild, rugged, mountainous landscape scenery for the urban park. Olmsted maintained that "mountains suggest effort."[19] His view is like that of Ruskin, who wrote:

> Mountains are to the rest of the body of the earth what violent muscular action is to the body of man. The muscles and tendons of its anatomy are, in the mountain, brought out with force and convulsive energy, full of expression, passion, and strength, the plains and the lower hills are the repose and the effortless motion of the frame. . . . This, then, is the first grand principle of the truth of the earth. The spirit of the hills is action, that of the lowlands repose.[20]

However, long before he had read Ruskin's *Modern Painters* Olmsted had come to the conclusion that the quality of repose is an essential feature of great art. He found the notion in his early study of Price's essays *On the Picturesque,* a work which Olmsted considered "the Bible" for the landscape architect. Price set forth the notion that a gently sloping bank of soft and smooth turf, the flowing lines and breadth of a grassy meadow, the gently swelling hillocks of soft and undulating form, and the tranquil surfaces of a lake give the soft, pleasing effect of repose and characterize the beautiful. In his discussion Price distinguished between that which is characteristically beautiful and that which is picturesque in painting and landscape scenery. The beautiful, he said, consists of "the quality of smoothness, and consequently of ease and repose to a person while he is viewing it. . . . His heart seems to dilate with happiness, he is disposed to every act of kindness and benevolence, to love and cherish all around him. These are the sensations which beauty, considered generally, . . . does, and ought to excite."[21] In contrast, Price said the picturesque consists of rough, rugged, and abrupt surfaces such as forests, tangled thickets, rocky projections, and fragments of rock and large stones lying in irregular masses.[22] He associated the ideas which these elements convey with ideas of irritation, animation, variety, and curiosity.[23] Though the ideas of repose contained in beauty and those of roughness in the picturesque contrast, Price felt that the qualities of both are found blended in nature and in great works of art.[24] He asserted that in one sense beauty is a "collective idea" which blends and "includes the sublime as well as the picturesque."[25] In designing his parks Olmsted viewed beauty in the collective or blended sense suggested by Price.

Olmsted's concern to establish a haven of repose within the city came also from his study of *Solitude,* a work by the Swiss physician, Johann Georg von Zimmermann (1728–1795). Olmsted regarded this book to be "one of the best books ever written."[26] Zimmermann's book was widely read. It made a strong impact upon Emerson and the members of his group, and especially upon Thoreau.[27]

Zimmermann's purpose was "to exhibit the necessity of combining the uses of Solitude with those of Society."[28] He carefully pointed out that there are disadvantages, even vices, in living life in extremes. There are, he said, mutual advantages to be derived from a prudent blending of social life with occasional solitude.[29] The civilization of man can be attained only in society. Society unites men with a community of pursuits and interests which "may greatly assist the cause of Truth and Virtue, by advancing the means of human knowledge."[30] Yet, said Zimmermann, metropolitan society is an arena of vice, avarice, antagonisms, tensions, and anxieties. These weaken or destroy virtuous conduct and dignity of character, or they distract and confuse the mind.

To surmount the disadvantages of society Zimmermann advised occasional solitude, primarily in an environment of unembellished nature. Solitude prompts self-communion which "fosters and confirms our virtuous inclinations" and banishes latent vices. Amid the repose and tranquillity of rural scenery or natural landscape, solitude

> induces a habit of contemplation which invigorates the faculties of the soul, raises them to the highest energies, and directs them to purposes more elevated and noble than it was possible for them amidst the business and pleasures of public life to attain. It tends, indeed, to unfold the powers of the mind to so great an extent, that we are ashamed of having thought that our talents were confined within the limits we have prescribed.[31]

The repose and serenity of green pastures and still waters free the imagination so that it may turn the mind to the development of worthy and virtuous sentiments. Even a walk through an "English garden," an art form which, as Zimmermann noted, reunites art and nature, affords the possibility for the mind to know truth and nobility by the contemplation of nature.[32] In the solitude of rural repose man may re-create himself and return to society to carry out the inevitable duties which everyone—whatever his station in society—must perform "to promote the welfare and happiness of his fellow creatures."[33]

The idea of repose was never far from the idea of duty in Zimmermann, Ruskin, or Olmsted. They did not consider repose to be a state of indolence or intellectual torpidity. Zimmermann explained repose as an "interval of relaxation which divides a painful duty from an agreeable recreation."[34] It is a stage of freedom in which the mind, unconsciously, sharpens its faculties and perceptions. Repose fosters reflection and re-creation; it encourages the mind to find inspiration and to become aware that "human life is but a loan to be repaid with use."[35]

For Ruskin, too, repose was not a state of "inanition, nor of luxury, nor of irresolution, but the repose of magnificent energy and being; in action, the calmness of trust and determination; in rest, the consciousness of duty accomplished and of victory won."[36] Implicit in the state of re-pose, said Ruskin, is an earthly vitality to which he attributes the quality of divinity. Hence repose in nature, as in art, has moral extensions. Fol-lowing Wordsworth, Ruskin believed that the longing for repose is uni-versally instinctive in man, and "no work of art can be great without it, and that all art is great in proportion to the appearance of it. It is the most unfailing test of beauty."[37]

For Olmsted the quality of repose is of utmost importance for the fulfillment of the social function for which the park is created. He said, "the most essential element of park scenery is turf in broad, unbroken fields, because in this the antithesis of the confined spaces of the town is most marked."[38] The conception of re-creation of the mind and body from urban oppressions through repose or tranquillity is a dominant fea-ture in the planning of each of his large city parks. To retain the atmo-sphere of repose Olmsted frequently rejected the demands of various recreational groups to allow the park to be used for sports such as ball playing or a drill-ground or any special purpose appealing to a particular group.[39] To Olmsted the park, in its artistic and social aspects, was com-patible with the idea of re-creation in the sense of the establishment of a poetic mood leading to contemplation, rather than with the contemporary idea of recreation in the sense of exercise through sports activities. In the enjoyment of the "beauty of the fields, the meadow, the prairie, of the green pastures, and the still waters" Olmsted intended the park to be restorative primarily (but not solely) to the mind.[40]

The quality of repose, then, is necessary to the park as a work of art. In its social sense repose inspires a tendency, according to Olmsted, to contemplation and the free use of imagination.

Unity

In interpreting the features of his first venture in park planning, Central Park in New York (see figs. 5, 6, and 7), Olmsted asserted: "The Park throughout is a single work of art, and as such subject to the primary law

Figure 5. View of Original Site for Central Park, New York City
This photograph illustrates the condition of the land before construction of the park.
(Courtesy National Park Service
Frederick Law Olmsted National Historic Site)

Figure 6. View of Landscaped Site in Central Park, New York City
(*Courtesy National Park Service*
Frederick Law Olmsted National Historic Site)

Figure 7. General Plan for Central Park, New York City
(Courtesy National Park Service
Frederick Law Olmsted National Historic Site)

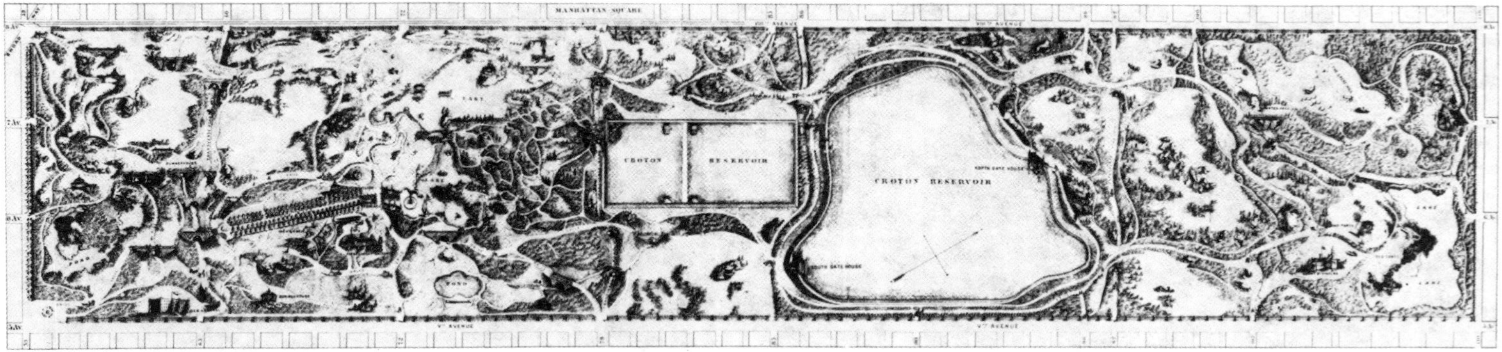

of every work of art, namely, that it shall be framed upon a single, noble motive, to which the design of all its parts, in some more or less subtle way, shall be confluent and helpful."[41] Olmsted went on to explain that

> the 700 acres allowed to the new park must, in the first instance, be subdivided definitely, although it is to be hoped to some extent invisibly, into five separate and distinct sections, only connected here and there by roads crossing them. . . . The problem to be solved is . . . making some plan that shall have unity of effect as a whole, and yet avoid collision in its detailed features with the intersecting . . . sunken transverse roads.[42]

As Olmsted progressed from one project to another he attempted to refine his theory. He was self-consciously endeavoring to establish and define an area of art which incorporated the techniques of the painter, the gardener, the botanist, the engineer, and the architect. He denominated the result as the art of landscape architecture. In the process of refinement and definition Olmsted purified his conceptions of what his art should be. In the projected development of Prospect Park in 1866 he pointed out that in the formation of park scenery in the natural style it was not his intention merely to imitate nature. This, he said, is not art, no matter how successful he might be in providing a mirror of nature. The concern of the artist in recreating scenes of nature's beauty is to realize that a

> scene in nature is made up of various parts; each part has its individual character and its possible ideal. It is unlikely that accident should bring together the best possible ideals of each separate part, merely considering them as isolated facts, and it is still more unlikely that accident should group a number of these possible ideals in such a way that not only one or two but that all should be harmoniously related one to the other.[43]

Only the genius of the artist can discover the law of harmonious relation between multitudinous discrete details and bring them together into an organic whole. In asserting this Olmsted reflected aesthetic doctrines similar to those held by Coleridge and Emerson. Coleridge defined the beautiful as "That in which the many, still seen as many, becomes one . . . 'Multëity in Unity.' "[44] The greatness and richness of a work of art are determined for Coleridge by the unity of a varied quantity of interdependent segments into an organic whole.[45] Olmsted restated Coleridge in his plan for Mount Royal:

> In works of art which the experience of the world has stamped of a high grade of value, there is found a strong single purpose, with a variety of subordinate purposes so worked out and working together that the main purpose is the better served because of the diversity of these subordinate purposes. The first secures the quality of unity and harmony; the others, that of a controlled variety.[46]

In the raw state, nature often exhibits characteristics of ugliness in decay, barren and uninteresting surfaces, forlorn and spindly and injured trees, arid or water-soaked pockets of poor soil. It is an error in art, Olmsted said, in creating a park to imitate nature in this sense and to preserve this scenery. The landscape architect, as an artist, must idealize nature. He begins with nature, but transforms it in the creative process. To realize a park as a work of art meant for Olmsted a semblance to nature, a process of selection of details which are skillfully and economically interwoven into a controlled design, and the production of a work which gives to the beholder an impression similar to that which nature itself gives.[47] The achievement of this comes from the shaping power— the sense perceptions, the memory, the imagination—of the creating artist.[48]

Olmsted illustrated these principles in describing the process by which he developed the plan for Mount Royal (see fig. 8). "It is so to select the material of planting, or the native material to be left growing, that, within reasonable limits, the principle upon which Nature, unassisted, proceeds in her selections (though often very imperfectly) shall be emphasized, idealized, or made more apparent in landscape quality."[49] By this method the artist rationally and sympathetically cooperates with nature to produce a new perception of nature "which will in truth be equally natural in aspect . . . and far more charming than the best that nature, *unencouraged*, would much more slowly give you."[50] In the Mount Royal plan he promised that the new aspect which he would create through his art would be even more natural than its current appearance.[51]

Olmsted's aesthetic conception of his parks as organically united works of art carried over into his town planning and led him to the advocacy of comprehensive city planning. It is a world view of an organically united universe, applied aesthetically and functionally to landscape architecture and to town and city planning. He applied the same aesthetic principles which obtained in planning parks to suburban communities. When Olmsted and his partner, Calvert Vaux, were commissioned to plan the layout for a suburban community near Chicago at Riverside, Illinois, the objective was to create a united community of families who would combine the enjoyment of the conveniences and services of the city with the tranquillity and beauty of the country. The physical plan was drawn to provide individual, secluded house sites, yet there were facilities specifically providing for communal integration.[52]

In his projected plan for the new wards in Riverdale in Manhattan, Olmsted, collaborating with J. James R. Croes, the civil engineer of the Department of Public Parks, developed a design for a suburban community within the city limits of New York. The design integrated the street

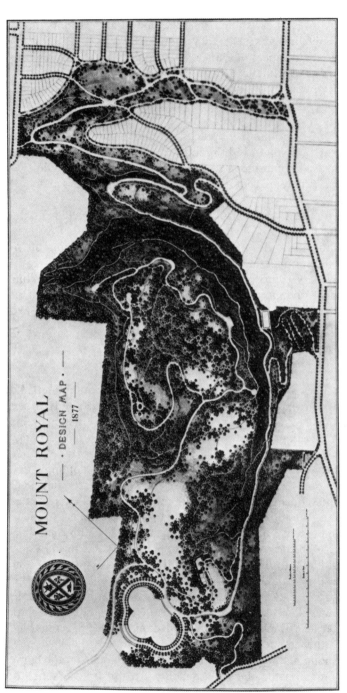

Figure 8. Plan for Mount Royal, Montreal, 1877
Mount Royal is a distinctive landmark overlooking the city, offering to
Olmsted an ideal opportunity for a park. Olmsted first visited Montreal
in 1873.

(Courtesy National Park Service
Frederick Law Olmsted National Historic Site)

system, rapid transit facilities, shops, schools, and public gardens into a pattern that followed Olmsted's aesthetic principles.[53]

Since the functional aspect of Olmsted's aesthetic theory was as controlling for him as the aesthetic aspect, he was prompted to advocate comprehensive city planning as a necessary means to prevent epidemics, plagues, and conflagrations; all of these conditions were attendant upon old city street patterns and congested city neighborhoods. Since the development pattern of cities had been piecemeal and desultory, their rapid and unplanned growth resulted in burgeoning problems of slums, inconveniences, and disease for enormous concentrations of population. Olmsted asserted that these problems required the exercise of human judgment, which must result in comprehensive planning.[54]

In his plans for New York City and Boston Olmsted called for the integration and the protection of the various functional parts of the city into a rational whole. The designs for both cities reveal systems of intracity parkways interconnecting a greenbelt of parks and open "breathing spaces." Interspersed are protected, in-city, residential subdivisions within easy reach of commercial, manufacturing, and shipping areas of the city. Olmsted envisaged cities whose parts are functionally separated into localities of specialization but organically united.[55]

Infinity

To the urban dweller, confined by the blank walls of city buildings and restricted by the grid pattern of streets, Olmsted offered in his urban parks the suggestion of great, open spaces—a sense of vast distance. His object in creating this impression was not mere contrast, a mere change of view for the sake of change. Convinced that the all-important avenue to the mind is "through the eye," he considered the city as confining and inhibiting. The buildings and street patterns of the city, Olmsted believed, must have a psychological effect upon the mind which limits or truncates man's conception of the universe and his role in it. The impulse to imaginative thought and a sense of freedom are curtailed by the physical barriers characteristic of the city. Olmsted undertook to overcome this physical and psychological block to the spirit of the city dweller. As a controlling element in his aesthetic theory he instilled the quality of infinity in his landscape scenery as a necessary antithesis to the city pattern. The sense of infinite space which he sought to provoke in the mind of the park spectator is deliberately implanted in his landscaping art.[56] He regarded spaciousness as "the essence of a park."[57] He created the illusion of infinite space by inducing the vision of the spectator to focus on the curve of the horizon. For Olmsted the artist's ability to impart the sense of infinity was central because "this character is the highest ideal that can be aimed at for a park under any circumstances, and . . . it is in most decided contrast to the confined and formal lines of the city."[58] Olmsted illustrated this motive in explaining an aspect of his design of Central Park.

Vista Rock, at the southwest corner of the reservoir in Central Park, New York, is the most distant natural eminence which can be seen from any point in the southern part of the park. If the observer enters the park from the southernmost entrance (at Columbus Circle) the visitor's eye falls upon an unbroken meadow which extends nearly a thousand feet. The artistic purpose of the meadow is meant to give the suggestion of freedom and repose, a refreshing and tranquilizing effect in contrast to the confinement and bustle of crowded streets. But, Olmsted explained, there is more to the scene:

> The observer, resting for a moment to enjoy the scene, which he is induced to do by the arrangement of the planting, cannot but hope for still greater space than is obvious before him, and this hope is encouraged, first, by the fact that, though bodies of rock and foliage to the right and left obstruct his direct vision, no limit is seen to the extension of the meadow in a lateral direction; while beyond the low shrubs, which form an undefined border to it in front, there are no trees or other impediments to vision for a distance of half a mile or more, and the only distinct object is the wooded knoll of Vista Rock, nearly a mile away, upon the summit of which it is an important point in the design . . . to erect a slight artificial structure, for the purpose of catching the eye and the better to hold it in this direction. The imagination of the visitor is thus led instinctively to form the idea that a broad expanse is opening before him.[59]

Inducing the eye to a distant point where the verdure of the field meets the light of the horizon was one of three artistic techniques which Olmsted employed to implant a sense of infinity in the observer. Another is the use of gradation through chiaroscuro, as explained by Olmsted:

> The pleasing uncertainty and delicate, mysterious tone which *chiaro-scuro* lends to the distance of an open pastoral landscape certainly cannot be paralleled in rugged ground, where the scope of vision is limited; but a similar influence on the mind, less only in degree, is experienced as we pass near the edge of a long stretch of natural woods, the outer trees disposed in irregular clusters, the lower branches sweeping the turf or bending over rocks, and underwood mingling at intervals with their foliage. Under such curcumstances, although the eye nowhere penetrates far, an agreeable suggestion is conveyed to the imagination of freedom, and of interest beyond the objects which at any moment meet the eye. While, therefore, elements of scenery of this class (which may, for the present purpose, be distinguished as picturesque sylvan scenery) would both acquire and impart value from their contrast with the simpler elements of open pastoral landscapes, their effect, by tending to withdraw the mind to an indefinite distance from all objects associated with the streets and walls of the city, would be of the same character.[60]

By the imaginative clustering of trees, shrubbery, mosses, and rocks Olmsted contrived intricate scenes of nature in which the dispersion of lights and shadows "would create a degree of obscurity not absolutely impenetrable, but sufficient to affect the imagination with a sense of mystery."[61] Just as a painter uses the colors of his palette he used the natural colors of vegetation and the sunlight to show gradations of light and color. The subtle combination and interplay of the "soft commingling lights and shadows and fading tints of color" in the varicolored context of undergrowth encourage the possibility of infinite space.[62]

The third device which Olmsted used to obtain the sense of infinity is the curve, since, he thought, by its changes of direction the curve divides itself infinitely. He believed, with Ruskin, that "there are no lines nor surfaces of nature without curvature" and that all curves are more beautiful than right lines.[63] Olmsted utilized these conceptions in every aspect of his planning of parks and cities. He planned the roads of his parks in such a fashion that the effects of the physical characteristics of the park would not be overwhelming in a "torrent-like way." They would lead the spectator through the park unobtrusively so that the impressions produced would be like "the gentle, persuasive dew, falling so softly as to be imperceptible, and yet delightfully reinvigorating in its results."[64] Though conceived as an organic whole, the park should be enjoyed, Olmsted urged, "as successive incidents of a sustained landscape poem, to each of which the mind is gradually and sweetly led away, so that they become a part of a consistent experience."[65]

The whole panorama of the park consists of groupings of trees and shrubs, hills and outcroppings of rock, meadows and bodies of water, which he looked upon as visual stanzas in a consistent landscape poem. Each part is united with every other by means of curved roadways and walkways which permit the spectator to gain the maximum visual poetic effect—"the bracing, soothing, tranquilizing medication of poetical scenery."[66]

Olmsted's reliance upon the curvilinear pattern, as opposed to the rectilinear, was an aspect of the organic nature of his aesthetic theory. In his theory beauty and function are united, and these two qualities determined Olmsted's use of the curve. In the process of creating his parks Olmsted did not neglect to preserve, wherever possible, the existing natural beauty of the tract. This often meant that roadways and walkways were designed to make the least disturbances to the natural beauty by sympathetically cooperating with nature. For Olmsted natural beauty was preserved by planning roads to conform with the natural topographical contours of the site. For purposes of transportation, the most direct, convenient, and economical route might suffice from the engineering point of view. But this would be destructive of the natural beauty. "A road must be located not alone with reference to economy of construction in respect to convenience of passage from one point to another, but with reference to *economy in the ultimate development of resources of poetic charm of scenery;* and these resources must be considered comprehensively and interactingly with reference to the entire property."[67] The highest art and at the same time the rational approach in road building will sacrifice directness to spare the natural and picturesque qualities of the site.[68]

Moreover, the curving road may be functionally necessary. This was especially the case in Olmsted's plan for Mount Royal. In considering the roadway for a mountain park Olmsted had to take into account the road's inclination. The criterion he used for the grade of his road was "such that a good horse with a fair load" could trot up and down hill safely at a speed of ten miles an hour.[69] Combining good engineering practice with his aesthetic ideas, yet always conscious of the prime position of the aesthetic, Olmsted planned a curving roadway for Mount Royal adapted to achieve the following objectives: (1) any point in the park could be closely approached by means of the drive; (2) the characteristic variety of scenery would be seen to advantage, distant views obtained in every direction, and the curve of the horizon observed along the drive; and (3) the entire park would be drawn into a unity by bringing together the different landscape strophes and the higher and lower parts of the mountain by a "practicable directness."[70]

Occasionally Olmsted voluntarily altered the mode of his design. His park promenades were laid out along formal lines to satisfy the tendency of people to gather for social intercourse—for the enjoyment of sociability. Never, however, was the formal aspect of the promenade meant to be other than a secondary feature of the park. Olmsted always intended the promenade to be subsumed to the artistic organic unity of the whole park. The dominating characteristic was the natural aspect of the whole entity.

On those occasions in which he worked with the architects of the Beaux Arts school such as Stanford White, Charles Follen McKim, or Richard Morris Hunt, Olmsted attempted to achieve a harmony between his natural style and the formalism of the French school. Though Olmsted considered these advocates of the Renaissance architecture as his aesthetic "enemies," he explained "the apparent anomaly" of his hearty cooperation by the statement, "there is a place for everything."[71] In Chicago at the Columbian Exposition of 1893 he tried to reconcile a picturesque motif of natural scenery with the formal stateliness that his "architectural associates were determined to have in the buildings" of the Exposition. At Biltmore, the Vanderbilt estate in Asheville, North Carolina, he managed to harmonize the natural character of his landscape scenery with Hunt's Renaissance buildings.[72]

However, the aesthetics of romantic philosophy was the dominant mode through which Olmsted expressed his artistic genius. In this mode he produced natural landscape scenery which is the antithesis to the "cramped, confined and controlling circumstances of the streets of the town." And in this mode he sought to impart "to all, at all times, the most certain and the most valuable gratification afforded by a park"—a sense of enlarged freedom.[73]

6

The Uses of the Park

Olmsted's parks were at once embodiments of his theory of art and instruments for the aesthetic education of man. His aesthetic theory encompassed not only notions of beauty and taste but a social function as well. He believed that art must have social relevance. He envisioned art as a means to reform society, and he created scenes of idealized natural beauty to educate and refine the tastes and habits of those who visited his parks.

The extravagant physical enlargement and population increase of the nineteenth-century American city reflected the growth of the capitalistic, industrial economy. The failure of governments and private agencies to provide adequate services and accommodations for the inhabitants of cities had resulted in noxious conditions calling for reform. Olmsted was fully aware that the commercial-industrial society produced effects which were detrimental to the physical and mental health of the inhabitants of cities. He maintained, however, that the progressive advancement of civilization unfolded in the cities. For all their faults, cities were attractive because they offered conveniences, comforts, and opportunities not available in the small towns and rural areas. In contrast to a prevailing anti-city attitude, he considered urban life to be an expression of a higher quality of living than rural life afforded. The problem Olmsted undertook to resolve, therefore, was to provide city dwellers with an antidote to relieve them from the debilitating conditions generated by the business economy.

Olmsted was particularly concerned that the demands of modern society for specialization produced fragmented personalities—stunted, one-sided, and vexed by tensions. For Olmsted, the specialization of work resulting from the continuing refinement of the division of labor indicated a progressive advancement of civilization. He maintained that specialization had produced an increase in knowledge and technology beneficial to mankind. The dilemma which Olmsted confronted in his desire to improve and reform the condition of urban society was to retain the advantages of specialization while restoring to city dwellers the enjoyment of repressed sensibilities. To synthesize the opposing elements, Olmsted resorted to the aesthetic experience. To him the enjoyment of beauty offered relief from the compulsions "of an intensely artificial habit of life" and stimulated "simple, natural, and wholesome tastes and fancies."[1] According to Olmsted, the repose induced by the aesthetic condition provided the observer with a sense of distance from the particularisms of his life style. The aesthetic experience lifted the mind to a new level of thought and feeling and gave a sense of enlarged freedom, permitting contemplation and the flow of the imagination. Olmsted believed that the enjoyment of great art restores the fragmented psyche to organic wholeness and harmony.

Olmsted construed art as a vehicle for attaining a synthesis of mutually opposed elements. He intended the park as a work of art to act as an agency to reconcile art and nature; the rural and the urban; the expertise that comes with specialization with the harmony of the integrated psyche; the calculating, rational mind with the irrational processes of perceiving and feeling; the atomized impersonality of mass society in the city streets with the warm communality of family and neighborly gathering in the park; the rectangularity of the city streets and buildings with the free-flowing, natural lines of the park. Though Olmsted designed the park as an antithesis to the city, his purpose was to integrate the park with the city into a new organic, urban configuration.

Olmsted's conception of reform was a reform of accommodation. It was not a radical theory advocating a direct assault upon the existing social institutions. He was seeking social reform by achieving individual psychological change through the aesthetic impulse. He was attempting to change society by indirection.

In his desire to recreate society by aesthetic education Olmsted's position is strikingly similar to the position presented by Friederich Schiller in his *On the Aesthetic Education of Man*.

Civilization and Its Dysfunctions

In 1858 when Olmsted began his work with Calvert Vaux on the construction of their plan for Central Park in New York City, the city was undergoing rapid, continuing growth in population and commerce. In the nineteenth century New York was becoming a great commercial center, attracting and holding increasing numbers of foreign immigrants as well as rural Americans. Olmsted saw a continuing tendency towards the enlargement of towns. He attributed urban growth to the improved facilities for communication, transportation, and world-wide exchange. He correctly foresaw that the United States was at the threshold of an unprecedented commercial development, the effect of which must lead to an ever-growing development of cities. Olmsted observed, "We seem to be just preparing to enter upon a new chapter of commercial and social progress, in which a comprehension of the advantages that arise from combination and co-operation will be the rule among merchants, and not, as heretofore, the exception."[2] This meant for Olmsted that the rapid growth of great towns which had already occurred was but a premonition of the "vastly greater enlargement" yet to come.[3]

Olmsted clearly and decidedly recognized the serious deficiencies attendant upon rapid urbanization. The antiquated, decentralized govern-mental administration of American cities, New York particularly, could hardly handle even the caretaker aspects of servicing the needs of a bur-geoning population. New York was a "walking city" with few means of cheap, mass transportation. The consequence was a compactness of pop-ulation grouped within walking distances to work places. As the poor poured into the city from Europe and surrounding states, the housing accommodations available to them were blighted, debilitated slum and ghetto dwellings. Provisions for sanitation were haphazard, if not non-existent.

The inadequacy of housing among the poor drove them to the streets to escape the indoor crowding and the fetid air. There was little mitigation in the filthy streets. Vehicular traffic was a hazard and the city air was polluted. Olmsted declared that the concentration of population, espe-cially in slum areas, resulted in the formation of a "certain gas" in the process of respiration.[4] Debility, sickness, or in extreme cases, death re-sults, he warned, if the gas is not dissipated. The effluvium pouring from the smokestacks of the manufactories was no less a danger. The air of large, compact towns is so corrupt and irritating, he said, that "even metallic plates and statues corrode and wear away under the atmospheric influences which prevail in the midst of large towns."[5] Such conditions, Olmsted asserted, must have a detrimental effect directly upon physical health and indirectly debilitate "the mind and the moral strength."[6]

When the gridiron pattern for street layout was adopted for New York by law in 1811, the main intent was to facilitate land use in such a manner as to maximize its profitable disposition by landlords. There was little regard for the public uses of land for recreation and open space for com-munal interaction. The monotonous rectangular pattern of street platting that was to cover Manhattan made no differentiation between commercial and residential districts. Since each street became a thoroughfare, the traffic and transportation conditions were chaotic. The block structure that char-acterized the city's street pattern intensified the difficulty of communi-cation and the social isolation of the inhabitants. It hindered the development of a sense of community. The addition of high rise residential and commercial buildings cut off the sunlight and the flow of fresh air. The angularity of the city pattern, according to Olmsted, gave the aspect of living in a box—in close confinement.

Olmsted observed that physical disadvantages associated with rapid urbanization, intensification of commercial activity, and an inexpedient morphology of the city, produced a psychosocial environment inimical to the mental health of the inhabitants of great towns. There were large segments of the population, especially the poor and the newly-arrived immigrants, who were attempting to accommodate to an urban environment unprepared to receive them. They were trying to survive in a rapidly changing, unfriendly culture. Olmsted clearly recognized manifestations of anomie among them.

Olmsted argued that with the advantages that accrued to society through modern inventions, enlargement of trade and commerce, and the spread of urban habits, there emerged some serious disadvantages. He claimed that these disadvantages were still so imperfectly understood "that we but little more than veil our ignorance when we talk of what is lost and suffered under the name of vital exhaustion, nervous irritation and constitutional depression; when we speak of tendencies, through excessive materialism, to loss of faith and lowness of spirit, by which life is made, to some, questionably worth the living."[7]

Olmsted believed that modern urban life intensifies a one-sided preoccupation with manual labor, commerce, or politics. Just as the monotony of household duties has a dulling effect upon women, even the excessive preoccupation with literature and education destroys the capacity of man to enjoy his naturally endowed emotional and intellectual faculties with a semblance of balance.[8]

In the social and physical environment of the large city habits of thinking develop which Olmsted denoted as characteristic and typical. He described them as follows:

> The severe and excessive exercise of the mind which leads to the greatest fatigue and is the most wearing upon the whole constitution is almost entirely caused by application to the removal of something to be apprehended in the future, or to interests beyond those of the moment, or of the individual; to the laying up of wealth, to the preparation of something, to accomplishing something in the mind of another, and especially to small and petty details which are uninteresting in themselves and which engage the attention at all only because of the bearing they have on some general end of more importance which is seen ahead.[9]

By way of contrast Olmsted provided a description of the ambiance of the communal society. In an autobiographical fragment written when he was in his fifties, he nostalgically remembered his boyhood in the New

England villages near his birthplace, Hartford, Connecticut. The binding sentiments of kinship, friendship, and religion are evident in the warmth and sympathy of communal unity. "Every house, every room, every barn and stable, every shop, every road and highway, every field, orchard and garden, was not only open to me but I was everywhere welcome."[10] The death of a single village child evoked the sympathy of "every heart in every household" in the village.[11] From such a milieu Olmsted suggested that there emerges another kind of personality type which is characteristically communal in orientation, in contrast to the atomized, impersonal relationships of city-bred men.

In establishing the identity of the two different societies and the personality types derivative of each, Olmsted anticipated the formulations of the German sociologist Ferdinand Tönnies. In his sociological theory Tönnies described two types of societies—*Gemeinschaft* and *Gesellschaft.*

Gemeinschaft is based upon the binding sentiments of friendship, neighborliness, and kinship. People and things are not regarded as mere means but as extensions of man's sympathies and abilities. In such a society the actions of man are controlled by love, understanding, custom, and religion. It assumes a unity of human wills cooperatively related in labor. In associations characterized by *Gemeinschaft,* people reside with relative permanence in a natural, intimate, organic community such as a neighborhood or a rural village. The essence of the personality type derivative of such a society Tönnies defined as the "natural will." This type expresses a "genuine, friendly, and benevolent tendency of will, considerateness . . . , ready sympathy with other people's joy and sorrow, devotion to, and grateful memory of, friendly companions in life."[12]

As the antithesis of *Gemeinschaft* Tönnies constructed another type of social organization—*Gesellschaft.* The city and urban culture is synonymous with *Gesellschaft.*[13] Essentially a center of commerce and industry, the city is closely aligned with science and culture as well. This society is an aggregate of mobile, individualistic, socially isolated people living peacefully together under conditions of competition and tension. The predominant relationships are economic and oriented to the market place. There is a marked specialization of labor and the various individual roles are segmental. All things and relationships are reified and reduced to abstractions just as scientific concepts are abstractions in a scientific system. Although elements of *Gemeinschaft* persist, the society is controlled by formal law and contained within the state.[14]

Tönnies defined the rational will as the central phenomenon of the personality type corresponding with *Gesellschaft.* In a social milieu where every man is a trader, self-interest and purposiveness are essential. The personality which emerges from such a milieu is dry, hard, and cold.[15]

Means rather than ends become significant and sentiment and sympathetic relationships are eschewed. Among the members of the *Gesellschaft* society, relationships are impersonal and transitory and act as instruments for economic gain, political power, and knowledge.[16]

In a similar vein Olmsted observed that the city draws people together physically into an impersonal, atomized aggregate. Urban life engenders a personality type who finds himself in continued, close, physical association with men in a mass with whom there are no friendly interactions whatever. He only relates to other men to avoid collision in crowded places or to engage in the pursuits of commerce. "Much of the intercourse," Olmsted said, "between men when engaged in the pursuits of commerce has . . . a tendency to regard others in a hard if not always hardening way."[17] Such interpersonal intercourse "or contact of minds is so slight and so common in the experience of towns-people that they are seldom conscious of it."[18] Men who have been brought up in the streets of the city or, Olmsted continued, "who have been most directly and completely affected by town influences, so generally show, along with a remarkable quickness of apprehension, a peculiarly hard sort of selfishness. Every day of their lives they have seen thousands of their fellowmen, have met them face-to-face, have brushed against them, and yet have had no experience of anything in common with them."[19] This kind of impersonal transaction, he held, requires an expenditure which affects the nerves and the mind. Olmsted was attempting to describe the way in which city life has the tendency to alienate man, not only from society but from nature and from himself.

As a result of fragmentation man becomes incapable of creative activity and moral determination. Olmsted believed that the elaboration of the division of labor inevitably led to activities so exclusive and intense as to dehumanize mankind. Like Carlyle's average man, the individuals of mass society are required to exhaust their lives in almost constant, sordid labor, repressing the need and the use of their reason or feelings or both. In a seeming paradox Olmsted noted that even farmers are victims of their monotonous, oppressive labor. By implication he repudiated an essential feature of the agrarian myth: that the close communion with nature produces a contented, virtuous man. He did not hold with Emerson that farmers are invigorated metaphysically and morally because they are in the constant presence of nature or that farmers are universally virtuous. During his travels in the South and the West his experiences with the mean, avaricious, ignorant, dispirited farmers he encountered taught him otherwise.[20] Moreover, Olmsted reported, "the agricultural class is more largely represented in our insane asylums than the professional."[21]

Olmsted's appraisal of the plight of modern man shows a close resemblance to the line of thought Friederich Schiller had developed in his critical and philosophical writings. In his *On the Aesthetic Education of Man* Schiller surveyed the predicament of modern man and accused civilization itself of having sundered him. Modern society, insisting on the intense development of special skills, has destroyed psychic and social unity. As a result, Schiller wrote, mankind is fragmented so that

> one has to go the rounds from one individual to another in order to piece together a complete image of the species. With us, one might be tempted to assert, the various faculties appear as separate in practice as they are distinguished by the psychologist in theory, and we see not merely individuals, but whole classes of men, developing but one part of their potentialities, while of the rest, as in stunted growths, only vestigial traces remain.[22]

In his assessment Schiller declared that the division of labor has maimed man by divorcing enjoyment from labor, the means from the end, and the effort from the reward. Fragmented by specialization, the whole man is no longer considered as an end in himself; the community assesses his value only in terms of his special function. He becomes a cog in the monotonous wheel that he turns. His only link to a whole is in a fragmentary participation in the state which jealously controls him through an irrelevant, externally operating mechanism. Schiller asserted that "The abstract thinker very often has a cold heart . . . while the man of practical affairs often has a narrow heart, since his imagination, imprisoned within the unvarying confines of his own calling, is incapable of extending himself to appreciate the other ways of seeing and knowing."[23]

Both Schiller and Olmsted regretted the psychosocial disorganization of man as the result of the changing nature of culture. Both saw the one-sided man as a result of specialization, but saw specialization as a necessary aspect of civilization's advance. Though it has caused error and suffering, Schiller and Olmsted agreed that the intense division of labor has resulted in the attainment of knowledge and the development of techniques which have benefited the world. "The greater the division of labor at any point, the greater the perfection with which all wants may be satisfied."[24] It is, nevertheless, wrong that the cultivation of individual powers involves the sacrifice of the wholeness of the self unless there is a means by which the unity of individual nature and of society can be achieved in a new synthesis. Olmsted, following Schiller, agreed that the means of realizing this is in the aesthetic education of man.[25]

Though his appraisal of the city life was disquieting, Olmsted, unlike most contemporary critics, welcomed the city's growth. He viewed the process as a manifestation of the advance and progress of civilization. He believed that city life became an agency of human progress because of the internal forces it generated. The commercial advantages of the town make it an attractive locus for a labor force of varying, specialized skills. He declared:

> The larger a town becomes because simply of its advantages for commercial purposes, the greater will be the convenience available to those who live in and near it for cooperation, as well with reference to the accumulation of wealth in the higher forms,— as in seats of learning, of science, and of art,—as with reference to merely domestic economy and the emancipation of both men and women from petty, confining, and narrow cares.[26]

Forecasting the continuing and accelerating urbanization of the world's populations, Olmsted predicted that "the further progress of civilization is to depend mainly upon the influences by which men's minds and characters will be affected while living in large towns."[27]

Advocate for the City

It becomes apparent that at some point in Olmsted's life experience he turned away from his advocacy of the farming life and identified with the city. Indeed, he became one of the foremost nineteenth-century champions of the city.

A good part of Olmsted's early vocational training was deliberately chosen with the intent of becoming a farmer. He had hoped that training in scientific farming would give him the opportunity to become a leader among farmers, educating the old-fashioned husbandmen in the uses of new methods and tools in agricultural production. Olmsted looked upon farming as an agreeable life which offered contentment.[28] But he was not successful in his ventures in farming. Moreover, as he matured, the thrust of Olmsted's interests was intellectual and artistic—not agricultural. It was these interests—first literary, as a writer and editor, and later artistic, as the superintendent and landscape architect of Central Park—that brought him to a close identification with, of all places for a farmer, New York City.

Olmsted may also have been prompted to turn away from farming because the prospect of achieving success in agriculture seemed dim. "As to the success of the farm-laborer in gaining wealth, I cannot now speak with equal confidence as of the mechanic," Olmsted wrote in the first volume of *Our Slave States*.[29] He was reflecting here his own lack of success in his experiments at farming and the generally low condition of farming he observed in his travels in the South and the West.

Olmsted's changed view regarding the economy of agriculture can be attributed in no small measure to his study of John Stuart Mill's *Principles of Political Economy.* It is highly likely that he took seriously Mill's "fundamental law" of diminishing returns as Mill applied it to agriculture. Mill argued that "increased labor, in any given state of agricultural skill, is attended with less than proportional increase of produce."[30] Increased production in agriculture takes place at increasing cost while the contrary tendency occurs in manufacturing industry, where the larger the scale of production, the more cheaply goods may be produced. Further, Mill contended that the efficiencies that accrue to large scale industrial manufacture through the combination of labor and the refinements in the division of labor do not similarly accrue to agricultural production because it is impossible to perform its different operations simultaneously.[31] Quoting Mill, Olmsted pointed out in the third volume of *Our Slave States* that no matter how favorable the conditions for farming, production will be merely for subsistence unless there is the demand for the surplus of farm products by the population of a large town.[32] In *Political Economy* Mill states that the progress of civilization is related to the concentration of population in cities. The skills necessary to higher degrees of the division of labor and the stimulus for industrial production depend upon a large city population.[33] Olmsted concurred with Mill.[34]

But Olmsted was also critically aware of the adversities that he observed among the inhabitants of the maladministered American cities of the nineteenth century. Yet, with all its faults, some of which he recognized as pernicious, Olmsted saw in the developing city the vehicle for the advancement of civilization. He expressed this when he wrote: "Our country has entered upon a stage of progress in which its welfare is to depend on the conveniences, safety, order and economy of life in its great cities. It cannot prosper independently of them; cannot gain in virtue, wisdom, comfort, except as they also advance."[35]

Olmsted was optimistic in his belief that the development of civilization, as reflected in the city, was progressive, and that civilization is a process of progressive unfolding, stage by stage, to higher forms. With the emergence of the industrial city society had achieved a new form of civilization which surpassed that in which agriculture was the predominant style of life. It is in the industrial-commercial city with its concentration of human ingenuity and skill that the greater division of labor promotes a greater refinement of living and the increase in the wealth of the economy. The effect of this, Olmsted said, reaches agricultural production as well, since mechanization of agricultural apparatus allows increased production with a reduction in manpower.[36]

From his observations and study Olmsted came to identify the development of the industrial-commercial city with the progress of civilization.

"The Genius of Civilization"

Olmsted realized that the improvement of civilization reflected in the city was obtained at the expense of humanity working and residing in the city. The terrible task of urban man, according to Olmsted, is that of going about the business of attempting to perform his duties under physical and social conditions which are so overwhelmingly antithetical to his nature that he is overcome by physical exhaustion and psychological disorganization.

With the onset of the economic developments that brought intensive urbanization in its wake, a countervailing social force emerged. This movement, according to Olmsted, manifested itself in a widespread interest in the "soothing and reposeful influences" of the beauty of natural scenery and landscape painting.[37]

In his 1880 address before the American Social Science Association, Olmsted noted that in the previous twenty-five years there had developed in the nation a social force which "directed the investment of hundreds of millions of private capital in travelling machinery, built up many towns, replenished many treasuries . . . and swayed every commercial exchange in the world."[38] However, occurring "simultaneously with a great enlargement of towns and development of urban habits," the park movement evolved by public demand.[39] The movement became evident in 1851, the year in which legislation by the New York State Legislature made possible the Central Park in New York City.[40] Olmsted regarded this "as a self-preserving instinct of civilization"—a deep desire by man to save himself from the corruption, artificiality, materialism, and vices of commerce and cities.[41] He described it as "a common, spontaneous movement of that sort which we conveniently refer to as the Genius of Civilization."[42]

Olmsted considered the park an antidote and a therapeutic to the disabilities of city life in two main respects: physical and objective, sociopsychological and subjective. In the first case Olmsted regarded the park as an oasis from the noisome conditions of the city streets. Within the confines of the park the visitor could enjoy sunshine and pure air. The park offered a quiet and tranquillity contrasting sharply with the noise and activity of the streets. The sick, the aged, and the convalescent found refuge in the park; it was a haven from the stifling dwellings and the monotonous housewifery endured by mothers with their small children. For the poorer classes "who have no opportunity to spend their summers in the country" as do the rich, the park was a refreshment.[43]

The configuration of the park, with its free-flowing, natural lines, was the antithesis of the gridiron design of the city. Though the rural park contrasted with the rectilinear, urban pattern, Olmsted attempted to integrate the park with the city by rational planning. Where he was permitted, he provided extensions from the park in the form of parkways. These parkways radiated into the urban areas and blended with the morphology of the city. Moreover, Olmsted observed a tendency for a park to become the center of the city—the population of the city settles around the park.[44] The park and the city would remain a complementary duality, yet synthesized into an organic urban whole for the community.

Olmsted's most important objective was to use the park to restore to the alienated city inhabitants a sense of community and to the fragmented psyche a sense of wholeness. In Olmsted's view the park was an aesthetic instrument to achieve a social and psychological change in a business oriented, urban society. In explaining and supporting his design for Mount Royal, Olmsted insisted that

> It is a great mistake to suppose that the value of charming natural scenery lies wholly in the inducement which the enjoyment of it presents to change of mental occupation, exercise, and air-taking. Beside and above this, it acts in a more directly remedial way to enable men to better resist the harmful influences of ordinary town life, and recover what they lose from them. It is thus, in medical phrase, a prophylactic and therapeutic agent of vital value; there is not one in the apothecaries' shops as important to the health and strength or to the earning and tax-paying capacities of a large city. And to the mass of the people it is practically available only through such means as are provided through parks.[45]

He was convinced that the beauty he created in the park possessed an "influence of the highest curative value."[46]

Aesthetic Education

In the "Preface" to the second edition of *Lyrical Ballads* Wordsworth explained that the purpose of the writer is to make men better. Such a service is needed, he wrote, in a world where "a multitude of causes . . . are now acting with a combined force to blunt the discriminating powers of the mind, and . . . to reduce it to a state of almost savage torpor. The most effective of these causes are the great national events which are daily taking place, and the increasing accumulation of men in cities, [and] the uniformity of their occupations."[47] Here Wordsworth stated the problem and the mission to which Olmsted, as an artist, committed himself.

The key to understanding Olmsted's art is that he meant it to effect a psychosocial change; as a work of art the rural park is an educative and civilizing agency changing the tastes and habits of the people who visit it.[48]

Olmsted's conception of the use of aesthetics in the transformation of society did not come to him as an addendum to rationalize his park planning. It was a deep-seated conviction which he derived through the influence of romantic philosophy. The congenial confluence of chance and artistic genius provided Olmsted with the opportunity to use the park as his vehicle.[49] More than three years before he had any thought of a professional association with parks, Olmsted made the following observation concerning the role of government in relation to aesthetic education:

> Simple protection to capital and letting-alone to native genius and talent is not the whole duty of Government; possibly that patent laws, and the common schools, with their common teachers, and common instruction, (not education) such as our institutions as yet give to the people, are not enough. That the aesthetic faculties need to be educated—drawn out; that taste and refinement need to be encouraged as well as the useful arts. That there need to be places and time for *reunions,* which shall be so attractive to the nature of all but the most depraved men, that the rich and the poor, the cultivated and *well-bred,* and the sturdy and self-made people shall be attracted together and encouraged to assimilate.
>
> I think there is no sufficient reason why the aid of the State should not be given to assist corporations and voluntary associations for such purposes, on the same principle, and with the same restrictions, that it is in New York to schools, to colleges, and to agricultural societies. Thus, I think, with a necessity for scarcely any additional governmental offices, or increase of the friction of governmental machinery, might be encouraged and sustained, at points so frequent and convenient that they would exert an elevating influence upon all the people, public parks and gardens, galleries of art and instruction in art, music, athletic sports and healthful recreations, and other means of cultivating taste and lessening that excessive materialism of purpose in which we are, as a people, so cursedly absorbed, that even the natural capacity for domestic happiness, and, more obviously, for the enjoyment of simple and sensible social life in our community, seems likely to be entirely destroyed. The enemies of Democracy could bring no charge more severe against it, than that such is its tendency, and that it has no means of counteracting it.[50]

In his report to the California Legislature on *The Yosemite Valley and the Mariposa Big Trees* Olmsted attempted to explain the effect that the aesthetic experience has upon the psyche. He stated that there is an intimate and reciprocal relationship between the mind and the nervous and the physical systems. Assuming it to be a scientific fact, Olmsted asserted that the contemplation of scenes of natural beauty is favorable not only to physical health but also to intellectual vigor. In the contemplation of beauty both sides of the psychophysical organism are energized in the harmony of a pleasurable experience, increasing "the capacity for happiness and the means of securing happiness."[51]

In the exposition of his theory of aesthetic education, Olmsted said,

> But as with the bodily powers, if one group of muscles is developed by exercise exclusively, and all others neglected, the result is general feebleness, so it is with the mental faculties. And men who exercise those faculties or susceptibilities of the mind which are called in play by beautiful scenery so little that they seem to be inert with them, are either in a diseased condition from excessive devotion of the mind to a limited range of interests, or their whole minds are in a savage state; that is, a state of low development. The latter class need to be drawn out generally; the former need relief from their habitual matters of interest and to be drawn out in those parts of their mental nature which have been habitually left idle and inert.[52]

He explained that the enjoyment of scenes of natural beauty

> is for itself and at the moment it is enjoyed. The attention is aroused and the mind occupied without a continuation of the common process of relating the present action, thought or perception to some future end. There is little else that has this quality so purely. There are few enjoyments with which regard for something outside and beyond the enjoyment of the moment can ordinarily be so little mixed. The pleasures of the table are irresistibly associated with the care of hunger and the repair of the bodily waste. In all social pleasures and all pleasures which are usually enjoyed in association with the social pleasures, the care for the opinion of others, or the good of others largely mingles. In the pleasures of literature, the laying up of ideas and self-improvement are purposes which cannot be kept out of view.
>
> This, however, is in very slight degree, if at all, the case with the enjoyment of the emotions caused by natural scenery. It therefore results that the enjoyment of scenery employs the mind without fatigue and yet exercises it; tranquillizes it and yet enlivens it; and thus, through the influence of the mind over the body, gives the effect of refreshing rest and reinvigoration to the whole system.[53]

Inspired by beauty, the spectator reaches the aesthetic condition—a condition in which the beauty of nature or a genuine work of art releases the spectator from sensuous and intellectual constraints. In appreciation and response to the beauty of the park the mind is educated aesthetically, freeing it to unfold in disinterested contemplation. In this state the compulsions that motivate man negate each other by their mutual opposition. However, the drives of sense and reason simultaneously remain active achieving reconciliation in the perception and appreciation of beauty.[54] Olmsted's view of the conditioning influence of beauty was similar to that held by Schiller. Schiller stated that

> Beauty is the product of accord between the mind and the senses; it addresses itself at once to all the faculties of man and can, therefore, be perceived and appreciated only under the condition that he employ all his powers fully and freely. One must assemble clear senses, a full heart, a fresh and unimpaired mind; one's whole nature must be collected, which is by no means the case with those who are divided in themselves by abstract thought, hemmed in by petty business formalities, or exhausted by strenuous concentration.[55]

While the aesthetic experience may be consciously perceived, Olmsted contended, most of the effect of the experience is of an unconscious nature. He likened the condition to that which music effects: "First, the chief end of a large park is an effect on the human organism by an action of what it presents to view, which action, like that of music, is of a kind that goes back of thought, and cannot be fully given the form of words."[56] Olmsted said he could not explain the process. But in some mysterious way the charm of natural scenery effects a psychic transformation in the character. It is the grace of nature.[57] He pointed out that the capacity to enjoy sympathetically the charm of rural scenery does not need the intellectual refinement of "Wordsworth, Emerson, Ruskin, and Lowell."[58] All men, he said, have the poetic sensibility. The beauty which he created in parks acts as a charm "to make us in some way different from what we should otherwise be."[59] The conception can be applied rationally, he said, "to scenery only because of a common experience that certain scenery has a tendency to lift us out of our habitual condition into one which, were the influence upon us stronger and the moods and frames of mind toward which it carried us more distinctly defined, we should recognize as poetic."[60]

Consciously and unconsciously the contemplation of scenes of beauty results in "a sense of enlarged freedom [which] is to all, at all times, the most certain and the most valuable gratification afforded by a park."[61] It is a freedom which is to be apprehended by the energized psyche in the state of active repose. In the dynamic reciprocity of the two drives—the intelligential and the sensuous—the constraints upon the psyche are annulled and man achieves the realization of a third nature—the aesthetic or poetic. At the same moment he becomes aware of the potential powers of the self. For, as Olmsted put it, "The whole body of the susceptibilities of civilized men and with their susceptibilities their powers, are on the whole enlarged."[62]

Unlike John Ruskin, Olmsted did not claim that the elements of raw nature contain moral qualities which impart virtue by the beholder's exposure to them. With greater psychological insight Olmsted held that the contemplation of beauty in art and nature induces a condition which obtains when the drives of the body and the mind, feeling and intellect are opposed but in reciprocal concert. When man's psyche has reached this synthesis, "he is in the fullest sense of the word a human being"; he is consciously free to enjoy the "play drive."[63] With the activation of the play drive the restored individual reaches the psychological condition that makes him capable of conscious self-determination.

The Aesthetic State

"A great object of all that is done in a park, of *all* the art of a park" is to create the conditions for the enjoyment of life.[64] Olmsted contended that the people of the northern United States are so compulsively materialistic that they "probably enjoy life less than any other civilized people. Perhaps it would be equally true to add—or than any uncivilized people."[65] In the city streets conditions compel people "to walk circumspectly, watchfully, jealously, . . . [and] to look closely upon others without sympathy."[66] In contrast, Olmsted observed that under the influence of the park families and neighborly groups, the poor and the rich, freed from the conscious exertion of discipline and formalism, come together in larger numbers than anywhere else. They enjoy the beauty of the park and each other "in more complete sympathy than they enjoy anything else together."[67] He asserted, "In all my life I have never seen such joyous collections of people."[68]

In his explication of the uses of the public park Olmsted revealed a conception of play as it affects social behavior. He identified and categorized two types of recreation or play: an exertive recreation (i.e., athletics) and a receptive one (i.e., the fine arts). The latter he separated into two subgroups: the gregarious and the neighborly. Both of these are suited to the enjoyment of parks.[69]

The gregarious classification defines a condition in which a multitude of people participate in a common enjoyment. In a metropolitan community comprised of a heterogeneous population separated by lines of social class, wealth, education, and widely diverse ethnic traditions and cultural patterns Olmsted declared that the enjoyment of beauty, particularly the beauty of the natural scenery of the park, linked all in common appreciation; "There is . . . a universality in nature that affords a field of enjoyment to all observers of her works."[70] In its idealized version of nature the park essentially reflects "the work of nature, invulnerable to criticism, accepted by all, as well the cultivated as the ignorant, and affords a limitless field for interesting observation and instruction."[71]

While admitting that the fusion of differing ethnic groups into a homogeneous body would require two or three generations, Olmsted considered the metropolitan park a vehicle for the integration of the diverse social elements of the city.[72] As an effort at social unification through aesthetic education, Olmsted asserted New York's Central Park to be "a democratic development of the highest significance and on the success of which . . . much of the progress of art and aesthetic culture in this country is dependent."[73] The basis for Olmsted's assertion appeared in his description in 1870 of the ambiance of two parks he created with Calvert Vaux: Central Park and Prospect Park in Brooklyn. In these parks, he said,

> you will find a body of Christians coming together, and with an evident glee in the prospect of coming together, all classes largely represented, with a common purpose, not at all intellectual, competitive with none, disposing to jealousy and spiritual or intellectual pride toward none, each individual adding by his mere presence to the pleasure of all others, all helping to the greater happiness of each.[74]

Absorbed in the beauty of natural scenery and themselves becoming part of a living work of art, "poor and rich, young and old, Jew and Gentile are brought closely together in vast numbers in pure air and sunlight under influences which counteract the ordinary hard, hustling working hours of town life."[75]

The second of Olmsted's receptive play types is the neighborly recreation. In this type of play "the close relation of family life, the association of children, of mothers, of lovers, or those who may be lovers, stimulate and keep alive the more tender sympathies, and give play to faculties such as may be dormant in business."[76] Olmsted was concerned that the family life of immigrants and the working class degenerated in slum neighborhoods. Their children, he said, are diverted and influenced by prostitutes and strangers; street gutters, the basements of houses, and the saloons are the children's playgrounds. Olmsted assumed that the expansive, healthful, and charming properties of the park would relieve parents of the domestic routines, child-rearing, and anxieties that city life provoke: "The cares of providing in detail for all the events of the family, guidance, instruction, reproof, and the dutiful reception of guidance, instruction, and reproof are, as matters of conscious exertion, as far as possible, laid aside," and the loving sentiments of a closely integrated family are freely expressed.[77]

In these two types of recreation or play Olmsted described patterns of social interaction characteristic of the closely-knit *Gemeinschaft* society. These patterns act as the counterpoise to the hard, severe, impersonal formality of the *Gesellschaft* society.

Olmsted did not envision that a society of elite aesthetes would be generated through aesthetic education. His intention was to enhance the quality of life for all by putting his art to social use. Oscar Lovell Triggs recognized Olmsted's effort in his essay on "The Sociological Viewpoint in Art." Triggs wrote, "When art is considered as one of the processes of idealization by which all psychic forms and social institutions are shaped, its proper place appears in the circle of social agents." It is because Triggs believed that Olmsted carried this principle into effect through the creative art of his parks that he recognized Olmsted as the greatest American artist of the nineteenth century.[78]

Olmsted was convinced that aesthetic education would enliven the mind, refine sensibilities, free the imagination, and expand the understanding so that members of society would develop a better society of interrelated human beings. In this conception Olmsted expressed a doctrine of indirection. He intended that laborers, businessmen, scientists, philosophers, indeed the whole community, would be transformed by the contemplation of beauty to be freer and happier in their daily living. He expected that political and social change would ensue from this individual psychical transformation. Olmsted believed that the free, joyous behavior he observed in the park would penetrate the whole society, thereby creating within the political state his version of what Schiller called the aesthetic state.

In his essay, "Anxiety and Politics," Franz Neumann praised Schiller for his perception in recognizing the problem of alienation which modern society has inflicted upon man. Neumann asserted that aesthetic education is of foremost importance, but Schiller's ideal of the aesthetic state must not be "only a beautiful facade"; it must be implemented by practical politics.[79] Schiller himself took the position that the theoretical must be based upon the practical. However, he never implemented the aesthetic state. It remained with him a beautiful abstraction. It is to Olmsted's credit that he made a noble effort to give the abstraction concreteness. Out of living nature he created urban parks for the aesthetic education of man, and he saw them filled with throngs of people who, he was convinced, found joy and emancipation in them. But the doctrine of indirection did not solve the problems of class conflict, exploited labor, grinding poverty, and fetid slums. Olmsted's efforts to reform society through municipal parks were a noble delusion.

The Park as a Pastoral Idyll

The influence of Connecticut pastoral scenery is apparent in Olmsted's park designs. The broad fields of his parks are essentially images of the pastures of a New England farm. But Olmsted did not aim simply to reproduce nature. He was an artist working with the essential elements of nature, bringing together ideal aspects into a total picture as a landscape painter might. He did not imitate the gardenesque, English style of his predecessors the landscape gardeners. Using the aesthetics of romanticism Olmsted created a new art form. With his partner, Calvert Vaux, he named the new art landscape architecture and raised it to the level of a fine art. He considered his art to be an advancement upon previous modes of art and fit to serve the purposes of a new society and an advancing civilization.

Olmsted's conception that art should serve the needs of society, indeed, that it should lead the progress of civilization, merged with his view that civilization was continually progressing to a higher stage. As a result he viewed with misgiving manifestations of retrogression to an earlier historical and cultural stage of man's development. This can be seen in Olmsted's rejection of Renaissance architecture. He disliked the Gothic style, as well, notwithstanding Ruskin's strong support of that style of architecture.[80]

Olmsted's last great public work was the landscape design for the World's Columbian Exposition of 1893 at Chicago. Ironically, the elderly Olmsted (seventy-one years old when the Chicago Fair opened) found himself working with a group of architects whose orientation was the neoclassic of the Beaux Arts school. The architectural motif of the Fair, set by Daniel Burnham, Richard M. Hunt, Charles F. McKim and Stanford White, was the Renaissance style.[81]

Olmsted did not look upon the Fair as indigenous to or congruent with the development of American culture; he regarded it as a kind of "vacation" from it.[82]

Olmsted could only have considered the formalism of the Chicago Fair's architecture as an expression of cultural retrogression. The Renaissance architecture represented a reversion to the defensive city and the despotic militarism of an earlier epoch in the history of civilization. Indeed, Olmsted looked upon some of the Fair's architects such as Hunt, McKim, and White, advocates of the Beaux Arts architecture, as enemies of the aesthetic principles that underlay his art. He was convinced that their efforts to redesign portions of his parks would destroy the artistic unity of his work. Writing to William Augustus Stiles, editor of *Garden and Forest* and a member of the New York Park Commission, Olmsted described Stanford White and his followers of Parisian training and associations as "sincere and unquestionably strong in their convictions." He continued: "We have an organized enemy before us. . . . They are strong; they are sincere; they are confident: they are mostly cultivated gentlemen to be dealt with courteously, but they are doctrinaires and fanatics and essentially cockneys."[83]

As an artist of living landscapes Olmsted was a counterpart of Schiller's modern poet who synthesizes the ideal with the real. In his essay "On Naive and Sentimental Poetry," Schiller identified two types of poets: the naive and the sentimental. The naive poet is in unison with himself and with nature; his genius expresses simple nature and feeling and is limited solely to the imitation of actuality based upon his experience; his art is objective, displaying no reflection in his poetry. He is characterized by the absence of self-consciousness. The naive poet represents a childlike innocence, psychologically, and his product represents the stage of childhood, historically. For Schiller the naive poetry belonged mainly to ancient times and Homer is his exemplar.[84]

In contrast, the sentimental poet is a product of an age when antagonisms and pressures have torn society asunder; within the sentimental poet, sense and reason are divorced and in conflict. Aware and critical of himself, he is reflective and purposive. He is cognizant of the separation between the actual and the ideal and his poetry reflects abstract ideas distant from actuality. In his emphasis upon the intellectual, the sentimental poet is disassociated from feeling. His unity with nature destroyed, he must self-consciously seek nature in a new unity, but in an idealized representation.[85]

Among the various modes through which Schiller said the sentimental poet expresses himself (and the one which is of concern here) is the idyll, the poetic representation of innocent and contented mankind. The critical problem for Schiller was that the sentimental poet removes the location of the idyll from the tumult of everyday life into the pastoral state—prior to the beginning of civilization, when man was in the childlike age—the state of nature. This is incompatible with the conditions that the sentimental poet encounters in modern society.

The form of the pastoral idyll is appropriate for the naive poet; it is his unified world and he portrays it uncritically. When the sentimental poet, psychically divided and critically alien to society, approaches the pastoral idyll, there is the tendency to depict man in a fictional golden age. But, set before the beginnings of civilization, such poetry produces a sense of sad loss rather than joyous hope. It turns thought backward to what man was rather than what he may become. Schiller rejected the pastoral dream as an illusion. In the idyll the aim of the poet is to represent man in a condition of harmony and peace with himself and his environment. We cannot, Schiller said, return to the naive state.[86] Schiller's optimism is evident in his belief in the progressive evolution of civilization. As in the *Aesthetic Education,* Schiller instructed poets to combine the two modes and strive for "the ideal of beauty applied to actual life" by a synthesis of the naive and the sentimental.[87] It is by means of the reconciliation of sense and reason, actuality and idealism, the particular and the universal, that man progresses towards the attainment of the ideal in himself and in society. For Schiller the three modes of poetry were characteristic of historical stages in the development of man: nature, the naive, antiquity in the first stage; art (as the antithesis of nature), the sentimental, the contemporary, in the second; ideal (in which consummated art returns to nature in a new unity), synthesis, future, in the third. The highest aim is consciously and voluntarily to return to nature.[88]

In transposing Schiller's aesthetic theory from poetry to landscape architecture it seems that Olmsted accomplished what Schiller had advised modern poets to do. From the raw, barren, uninteresting grounds in New York, Brooklyn, Chicago, Montreal, and Boston he created pastoral idylls which embodied idealized versions of nature. Combining nature with ideality, Olmsted produced a beauty representing a higher nature. It is not a contradiction in terms to fashion beautiful natural scenery by art. He said, "When an artist puts a stick in the ground, and nature in time makes it a tree, art and nature are not to be seen apart in the result."[89]

Olmsted's city park was a representation of a pastoral idyll. Indeed, it was a return to the scenes of Olmsted's New England childhood. But it was a conscious, voluntary return of the contemporary artist to nature. He repudiated the nostalgic return to an earlier condition of mankind. An illustration of his position occurred in his review of *The Woods and By-Ways of New England* by Wilson Flagg. The book extolled the raw, simple beauties of farm life with its dilapidated, moss-covered house, meandering cow path, uncultivated grounds, and swamp. In an acerbic critique Olmsted declared that it was in such neighborhoods, houses, and simplicity that he had found immured, dreary inhabitants, victimized by inconvenience, insanity, and disease even more than the residents "of the densest and dirtiest of cities."[90]

Commentators who describe Olmsted as an adherent of the Arcadian myth or who maintain that his parks are representations of the myth are incorrect in their estimate.[91] For Olmsted to have conceived of his work as Arcadian would be retrogressive and a contradiction to his view of the progressive advance of civilization. It would be a return for man to the stage of barbarism or savagery.[92]

His parks were not at all meant to be an imitation of an illusory golden age of innocence set in the past. In insisting that his public parks exemplified the highest art Olmsted unified reason and nature into a new synthesis as a manifestation of what ought to be. To develop a higher quality of life for all, the urban park was meant to provide an aesthetic education. It follows that Olmsted had no intention of "educating" man to a return to the childhood stage of the psyche or to its analogous historic stage of civilization. In a guarded manner Olmsted was looking forward to Schiller's "ideal of beautiful humanity."[93] The task which Olmsted undertook was to create a condition which would emancipate man so that he might lead an active, vigorous life of expansive thought and social refinement. Olmsted's purpose was, like Schiller's, to lead man, who cannot go back to Arcady, forward to Elysium.[94]

The City in History

As a result of his continuing work in designing city parks and his new employment in planning suburbs, Olmsted was inevitably brought to the consideration of the structure of the entire city.[1] This wider arena for his activities drew Olmsted to a historical investigation of the city, an analysis of its growth, and a projection of its development. Olmsted perceived the need to project comprehensive plans for cities, if cities were expected to serve enlarging populations. He examined the history of the city in order to find from his analysis a rationale for comprehensive planning. This effort is apparent in the explication of his plan for the Eastern Parkway district in Brooklyn. Olmsted's exposition of city development was not so much a history of city growth as it was a theory of the origin and morphological evolution of the city. It was unique and may have been the first such analysis.

A fundamental assumption behind Olmsted's historiography is the notion of an ascending, upward development of civilization. In analyzing the history of the city and in defending the city against its detractors, Olmsted claimed that city growth has been accomplished in progressive stages marked by a law of improvement. There is, Olmsted said, "a common spontaneous movement . . . the Genius of Civilization," by which civilization instinctively preserves itself.[2] This is a dynamic process consisting of the unpremeditated, unconscious forces by which society strives for internal accommodation. Through an evolutionary development society brings its organization and forms into harmony with its needs and functions. As a microcosm and a reflection of civilization the city also undergoes internal, progressive changes to a higher level. The very fact of the continuing urbanization of society is itself a manifestation of the evolution of human progress.[3]

The commercial advantages of the town make it an attractive locus for a labor force of varying, specialized skills. Because of the internal forces city life generates, Olmsted held, it becomes an agency of human progress. Forecasting the continuing and accelerating urbanization of the

world's population, Olmsted asserted that "the further progress of civilization is to depend mainly upon the influences by which men's minds
and characters will be affected while living in large towns."[4]

While holding to a belief in continuing progress Olmsted was very
much aware that the cities had attracted too many people too quickly and
that industrial and commercial activity had brought slums, physical and
mental irritations, air pollution, and traffic and communication problems.
From stage to stage of development, at no point in the history of the city
had there been a satisfactory correspondence of function and form. Yet,
said Olmsted, there is a "law of improvement," unconsciously operating
to reconcile function with form.[5] The law operates within the city by
virtue of internal conflicts, but it also affects the city by virtue of the
forces of the encompassing civilization. Responses may be delayed and
improvements held back, but continued pressures force response.[6]

Olmsted argued that the historic course of the city is hardly affected
in any substantial, permanent way by legislation or the decisions of city
officials responding only to public opinion.[7] If local public opinion does
not bring rational action through municipal agencies, there are forces
acting indirectly which do bring change. Usually, the changes which come
to the city are "commonly determined by a discovery or an invention, for
example, made by some one having no personal interest or direct part"
in the city.[8] Olmsted gave the following examples: the progress of sanitary
engineering had mitigated devastations from plagues and lengthened the
life span of the city inhabitant; the railroads had made the influx of people
to cities easy; the invention of the telegraph had facilitated the development of commerce in the city.[9] "When currents of such exterior sources
have once been established, the local defects of a city, with reference to
them, are apt sooner or later, at more or less cost, to be remedied."[10]

Olmsted claimed that no one knows how outside causes are capable
of affecting the public opinion of individual cities in such a manner that
they motivate a "similitude" in all cosmopolitan cities.

> Notwithstanding the great differences of origin and historical development, of early
> social circumstances, of climate, of back-country conditions, and of resources of
> wealth and products to be dealt with . . . schools, churches, hospitals, courts, police,
> jails, methods of fire protection, methods in politics, in benevolence and almsgiving,
> in journalism, in banking and exchange, are rapidly growing to be closely alike in San
> Francisco and in Boston.[11]

A Theory of City Growth

The ostensible purpose of Olmsted's review of the evolution of the city
was to analyze the functional layout of street patterns. He divided the

"advance of civilization" into five stages. In four of the five stages or epochs Olmsted sketched the development of the city in western civilization from ancient times to the middle of the nineteenth century; in the fifth stage he projected a planned, suburban community in Brooklyn, New York, joined to the New York metropolitan area and its parks by a network of parkways. For each period Olmsted gave a brief analysis of the cultural level of society, the predominant functions of the town, the density of the town population, and the street structures characteristic of the stage and functions of the town. By this method Olmsted illustrated the need to accommodate the street patterns of growing towns and cities to changing functions. His contention was that existing street arrangements for European and American cities (which he claimed were derived from European patterns) were wholly incompatible with the requirements of the contemporary city. Olmsted stated, "nearly all the old European towns of importance, from which we have received the fashion of our present street arrangements, were formed either to strengthen or to resist a purpose involving the destruction of life and the plunder of merchandise."[12]

Since the purposes for which towns were originally planned have been superseded by other purposes, there has ensued a slow historical process of accommodation to fit new requirements. Olmsted held that American towns were undergoing the same slow, struggling accommodation: one in which form (i.e., the street system) must be accommodated to function (i.e., servicing the great metropolitan, commercial cities).[13]

The first stage began with the semi-nomadic primitive, herding society. Living quarters were temporary huts scattered about an entrenched camp, connected by carelessly formed trails which were sometimes improved with flat stones to keep walkers from sinking in mud. In hilly areas rough stone steps were sometimes laid for footing. No provision was made for wheeled traffic among the houses. Only the exigencies of defense provoked the widening of a few pathways to provide for wheeled traffic and these were not further improved, Olmsted claimed, until well into the fifteenth century.

The requirements of defense in early European society led to the construction of town walls. To reduce the labor costs and to permit ease of defense the walls were not unnecessarily extended. This resulted in such a compactness of the town that it left no provision for an increase in population. The demand for housing facilities led to encroachment on the remaining interstitial open spaces in the town and the addition to original structures of upper stories which overhung the narrow streets. The increase of town density and the attendant inconveniences pushed both poor and noble beyond the town wall into the suburbs: the first having recourse to temporary shelters or hovels, the second to protected strongholds for family and retainers. Both classes desired to be in close vicinity to the protection of the town's wall and fighting forces. As these suburbs increased in density, and since they lacked any planned relationship internally or in relation to the town, the street layout underwent the same desultory development as in the original town. As the protective wall of the town was extended to encompass the suburb, it continued to act as a limitation, again enforcing the process of compacting the town population.

The paramount governmental feature of each of these towns, Olmsted held, no matter what its form, was a "military despotism" which subordinated "the life, property, health and comfort of the great body of their people" to a direct and stringent control.[14] Olmsted viewed the earliest town as a garrison with the population housed in a barrack, "with only such halls and passages in it, from door to door, as would be necessary to turn it in to sleep and feed, and turn it out, to get its rations."[15] This underlying characteristic still persisted in the latter half of the nineteenth century.

As society advanced within the time frame of what Olmsted called the first stage of development there was an increase in social stability and personal safety. This allowed the upper strata of feudal society living in towns, who were possessed by "a strong reactionary ambition," to cast off their responsibilities to society and to depart from the town to seek greater independence, seclusion, out-of-door recreation (i.e., the chase, jousts, and tournaments) in an isolated, park-like, manorial environment.[16] Since early manor life was self-sufficient and the demands for articles of luxury limited, the few items of finery which the household wanted were bought from travelling merchants. As the trade of even the largest towns at this point was still restricted, the old town street system continued to serve adequately.

Olmsted's first stage closed during the fifteenth century with the opening of India, Africa, and America to commerce. These events and the general advance of civilization so fed the mercantile inclinations that an entirely new class of towns, centers of manufacturing and of trade, grew upon the sites of the old ones. The quickening of urban life attracted both rich and poor alike from their rural habitats: the first for the enjoyment of luxuries, the second for the chance of finding new opportunities which the town promised.

His second stage was an epoch that includes, roughly, the latter part of the fifteenth to the first half of the eighteenth centuries. This historical period of town development (i.e., in street arrangements) is characterized by a transition from the "serviceable foot-ways of the early middle ages, to the unserviceable wagon-ways."[17] For illustration Olmsted used the description of street life and conditions of London.[18] This was the London of narrow streets choked by heavy, horse-drawn wagons. Not only were most streets too narrow for two-way traffic, but the filth cast from the houses combined with the dung of the horses and the street mud made pedestrian traffic uncomfortable. Added to this was the danger to the man on foot of being run down or crushed against the building walls by the wagons or coaches. With the increased density of the town's population and the enlargement of trade, the street system of the growing towns was incapable of meeting the traffic requirements.[19]

The London Olmsted described still contained open and green areas to which inhabitants could resort, yet the greater part of the town's residents lived under such sordid conditions that they continually suffered epidemics, plagues, and fires. Olmsted noted that the administration of the City of London, Parliament, and Crown unsuccessfully attempted to halt the growing incidence of disease, pauperism, crime, and disorders by discouraging the influx of migrants by law.[20] The legislation failed to halt the tide and aided only the interests of the rich.

It was London's Great Fire of 1666 that destroyed a large part of London and offered the opportunity for the architect Christopher Wren to produce a comprehensive plan for the rebuilding of much of the town. Olmsted's praise for Wren's plan was unstinting. Had Wren been allowed to implement his design for London, according to Olmsted, the envisioned street system for the accommodation and flow of traffic would have provided London advantages existing in no large town in seventeenth-century Europe. The main streets were intended to be straight and so wide that several wagons abreast could have been driven from end to end of the city. Wren had also proposed parallel and intersecting streets and intermediate lanes of varying widths to interrelate with the main channel streets into a comprehensive street plan for London. Olmsted used the incident to criticize both contemporary and earlier obstructionists to comprehensive city planning. Although, he said, Wren's plan had the approval of the King himself, the incredible short-sightedness of the merchants and real estate owners halted its implementation. "These obstinately refused to give themselves any concern about the sacrifice of general inconvenience or the future advantages to their city, which it was shown that a disregard of Wren's suggestions would involve, but proceeded at once, as fast as possible, without any concert of action, to build anew, each man for himself, upon the ruins of his old warehouse."[21] Olmsted did not refrain from using the Wren incident as a lesson. In his view, had the property owners acted in concert instead of in a short-sighted, laissez-faire manner, Wren would have anticipated their requirements, relieved the city of the overwhelming expense and inconvenience of street alteration subsequently required, and saved millions of the city residents from poverty and disease.[22]

Olmsted noted that in the period following the Great Fire London's trade underwent an enormous growth while nothing was done for a century to alleviate the consequent crowding, inconvenient confinement, and turbulence. Little advance was achieved in relieving the distress of commercial or residential requirements by an alteration of the city's street system. The lag between form and function reached the point where "the merchants generally could no longer avoid the conviction that their prosperity was seriously checked by the inadequacy of the thoroughfares of the town for the duty required of them."[23] Only towards the latter part of the eighteenth century, in the ensuing third stage, was Parliament induced to embark upon a series of street and sanitary improvements that would, in the course of fifty years, effect significant changes in London's morphology.

It was the economic motives of a small sector of the society rather than the humanitarian impulse to relieve the increase of disease, pauperism, and crime that resulted in an entry into a third stage of advancement.[24]

The period from the latter half of the eighteenth century until approximately 1850 marks Olmsted's third stage of change and city growth. During this period the preeminence of the mercantile and entrepreneurial sector of London society enabled them to push measures through a reluctant Parliament and the city government of London that effected improvements in the city streets. These were largely for their own benefit.

New streets were constructed and the old streets were reconstructed. A center channel was provided for horses and wheeled traffic; flanking raised pedestrian walkways were separated from the road by curbs. Gutters and sewers were added. Efforts were made to straighten, widen, and grade the narrow winding lanes so that goods might be transported directly from one section of the city to another. What Wren had so comprehensively proposed earlier for the reconstruction of London, the grandsons of the indifferent merchants were haphazardly attempting to accomplish.

A few cities, such as St. Petersburg, Philadelphia, and some of the free cities of Germany had already improved their streets in somewhat the same manner as London. However, there still remained a general neglect in providing for the general welfare of an increasing urban population. In assessing the failure of cities to correct their structural deficiencies and to anticipate their future requirements Olmsted attempted to alert his contemporaries. In his analysis he claimed that in periods of rapid economic and social change the theory and form of city governments adhere to traditional values and forms. The antiquated modes are operationally ineffective in administering the varied requirements and conditions of an enlarging population and the broadening scope of its functions. Olmsted accused the city administrators of a calculated use of obsolete structures to neglect the general welfare. The general failure of municipal governments to respond to the new conditions of the whole corporation does not prevent, however, the energetic businessmen from carrying into effect improvements which will be of benefit to them. Olmsted held it as a general rule that "improvements have come in most cities, when they have come at all, chiefly through the influence of individual energy, interested in behalf of special mercantile or speculative enterprises, by which the supineness of the elected and paid representatives of the common interests of the citizens has been overborne."[25]

The Fourth Stage: The Nineteenth-Century City

With the close of the third stage Olmsted reached the contemporary city of the nineteenth century in his morphological analysis of the development of cities.

At this point in his analysis, at the threshold of the mounting realization of the need for change in the street systems of the great towns, Olmsted interposed between the third and fourth stages of his history of the city a defense of the contemporary city and a rationale for comprehensive city planning.

Contrary to the anti-city view that generally prevailed in the nineteenth century, Olmsted set about to show that, notwithstanding the inconveniences and dangers manifested in epidemics, fires, mendicants, criminals, unruly mobs, high morbidity and mortality rates, and shortness of life which were believed to be characteristic of the metropolis, there had been a sharp decline in these inconveniences and dangers coincident with a continued and rapid increase in population. The fears and assumptions which might have been true for the medieval and the eighteenth-century cities were entirely fallacious for the growing cities of the latter half of the nineteenth century. Urban population increased with the continued improvement of city living.

Since the eighteenth century the incremental development of science and technology had affected cities profoundly. Along with inventions in transportation, communication, and road construction, there had been a reduction of many of the disabilities which formerly plagued cities. Olmsted noted that "Even in Mohammedan Cairo, chiefly through the action of French engineers, the length of life of each inhabitant has, on the average, been doubled."[26] But these improvements affecting the cities came as an indirect benefit. The main thrust was channeled toward the improvement of national and worldwide productive and commercial activity. In 1868 Olmsted predicted that the United States was at the threshold of an unprecedented commercial development. "We seem to be just preparing to enter upon a new chapter of commercial and social progress, in which a comprehension of the advantages that arise from combination and cooperation will be the rule among merchants, and not, as heretofore, the exception."[27] This meant for Olmsted that the accelerated growth of great towns which had already occurred was only a foretaste of the "vastly greater enlargement" yet to come.[28]

In his assessment of the trends affecting structural requirements of the fourth-stage contemporary metropolis, Olmsted discerned the following: the separation of business and domestic life, the recreative requirements (i.e., physical and psychic restoration) of city dwellers, and the changing character of vehicles.

As it affects the morphology of the city, the first is the most important of the three. With the intense development of commercial activity in the earlier epoch, cities became compacted into commercial and manufacturing cores, incorporating both workplace and residence. It was the common practice to unite business and residence under the same roof. This tended toward a concentration of population in the business centers of towns. In the latter part of the eighteenth century a few who found the conditions of the city onerous, but desired the privileges of the city, separated themselves from the congested business centers and moved, Olmsted recounted, to those sections in or immediately outside the city where they could enjoy the "luxuries" of privacy, clean air, space, and abundant vegetation. This outward movement was inaugurated by the businessmen of the European cities in a desultory manner and by individual private action. With the separation of family life from business activity there was a population drift away from town centers leading to the spatial enlargement of the city and suburbanization.[29] In her social history of London, Dorothy George noted that "the eighteenth century was a stage in the transition from medieval conditions. Space and air first became a luxury of the rich and the demand for it gradually spread from class to class."[30] She wrote that the outward movement was introduced by the merchants of the City who were moving into new houses of the more pleasant streets and squares of west London. The merchant's custom of separating his business and domestic life by removing his family from the house and quarter of the town in which he worked seems still to have been an innovation to London at the turn of the nineteenth century.[31]

There were two forces, centrifugal and centripetal, causing the spatial enlargement of the city. As the commercial activities of the contemporary city quicken, they attract and hold an increased population living in and around the commercial and manufacturing centers. This has the effect of compacting the population and enlarging the spatial area forming the core of the city. At the same time the departure of the rich for open areas in and beyond the core results in the spread of the city. By the nineteenth century this process was prevalent in the major European and American cities and promised to continue unabated. The tendency of separating residence from shop had the effect of segmenting as well as enlarging the city. In his analysis of the trend, Olmsted wrote,

> Those parts of the town which are to any considerable extent occupied by the great agencies of commerce, or which, for any reason, are especially fitted for their occupation, are therefore sure to be more and more exclusively given up to them, and, although we cannot anticipate all the subdivisions of a rapidly increasing town with confidence, we may safely assume that the general division of all the parts of every considerable town, under the two great classifications of commercial and domestic . . . will not only continue, but will become more and more distinct.[32]

The change in the structural pattern of the city consequent upon the separation of residence and work had an unpremeditated impact. According to Olmsted it meliorated the evils of the city. It reduced mortality, morbidity, and crime rates, immunized the community from plagues and sweeping fires, and improved the life span and general health of the inhabitants. For illustration of this thesis Olmsted compared statistically the average age at death of Liverpudlians with that of Londoners. The mortality rate was considerably higher in Liverpool than London. Olmsted attributed this to the greater density and compactness of the living quarters of the poor in Liverpool as compared with the greater spread of London's residential area. He pointed out that a similar situation existed in Brooklyn (1868) when one compared death rates of the residents of the compact and the diffused sections of the city. He adduced that the welfare of the community is better protected when the morphology of the city allows large spaces open to sunlight and clean air.[33]

But the expansion of the city made it increasingly difficult for residents, especially those living about the commercial core, to have recourse to sunlight, clean air, and the refreshing pleasure of rural scenery. Walking to the suburbs became onerous. Since an inexpensive, convenient system of transportation was as yet unavailable to most city dwellers, easy access to distant suburbs in search of relief from pollution, noise, tension, and confinement was difficult. The alternative which Olmsted offered for relief from the tensions caused by the "intense intellectual activity, which prevails equally in the library, the work shop and the counting room" was the urban park.[34] But here, too, he cited the inconveniences, even dangers, of driving or walking to the park. Since the streets in the residential sections were constructed for the heaviest commercial traffic, precisely as were those streets formed for use in the commercial sections of the town, they afforded little pleasure for driving and their heavy traffic made them hazardous to life and limb for walkers. In addition those who would walk to the park in the season when relief from the heat would be most welcome were deterred from it because they would suffer the direct heat of the sun and the reflected heat of the flagstones.[35]

The problem was still the failure of the form of the street layout of the contemporary city to keep pace with its functions. The thoroughfares were narrow and ill-paved. There were no special truck routes and no limited access, suitably paved streets leading to dwelling houses. The surveys of the street systems of most major cities of the period describe conditions of chaotic congestion.[36]

Aware of inventions and refinements that foreshadow inexpensive, convenient means of vehicular transportation, Olmsted indicated that the promise would be nullified without equally refined street systems and paving adapted to handle the vehicles. He illustrated this problem by referring to a then recently-invented light, spring-supported, horse-drawn carriage. The carriages could be used and enjoyed only on roads expressly prepared for them, such as those Olmsted required to be constructed in his parks. But they were unfit to be used on streets adapted for heavy wagons employed in commercial traffic.[37]

Olmsted set forth the developments and propensities of the city in the period contemporary with him. In the ineluctable tendency of form to match function the city had become, if not altogether wholesome, an improved as well as a vital arena. But there is always a lag in the process. Many of the major cities of Europe and America contained, or were at the threshold of establishing, parks of a public or a semi-public nature available to their inhabitants. For Olmsted a central constituent of a city in the fourth stage of development was a large-scale park or pleasure ground. But, with reference to street systems, Olmsted knew of only two instances of cities which had advanced into the fourth epoch of development; and these were not perfect examples, he averred. His first example was the Avenue of the Empress (Avenue de l'Impératrice, now Avenue Foch) in Paris. It connects a palace and a pleasure ground within the city with a large park far out in the suburbs of Paris. It has a planted border; it is lined with detached residences. However, the avenue is so wide that Olmsted considered it to be an intermediate pleasure ground rather than part of the general street pattern of the city. The other and better example was Berlin's Linden Avenue (Unter den Linden). Unter den Linden also passes from a palace and grounds through Berlin to a great rural park on the opposite side of the city. Public buildings, art galleries, museums, the finest private houses, and hotels have been built upon it. While the avenue conveniently serves the ordinary purposes of a street, it is distinguished by a center mall with turf and trees which separates the wagon ways. On the mall there is a shaded walk and a bridle road. However, as Olmsted pointed out, these do not serve all the requirements of the community as ordinary business streets.[38]

In Olmsted's historical analysis civilization had reached the fourth stage in its progress, but, in terms of morphology, most contemporary cities were only at the threshold of the fourth stage. Science and advancing technology provided the means to alleviate the dysfunctions which plagued the city. Olmsted asserted that modern science had beyond all question determined many of the causes of the special evils by which men were afflicted in towns, and placed means in our hands for guarding against them.[39]

> One thing seems to be certain, that the gain hitherto can be justly ascribed in very small part to the direct action on the part of those responsible for the good management of the common interests of their several populations. Neither humanity nor the progress of invention and discovery, nor the advancement of science has had much to do with it. It can not even, in any great degree, be ascribed to the direct action of the law of supply and demand.[40]

Olmsted held that modern towns were fashioned to meet the demands of commerce and industry. He wrote,

> As these demands successively arise and their pressure is felt, street is added to street, building to building; railroads, canals and docks are introduced; sewers, water-pipes and gas lights are pushed out here and there, and thus, not only the extent but the direction of the town's growth is in a large degree controlled by natural laws, the acts of government following much more than leading, directing or resisting the movements of supply and demand.[41]

The vastly greater growth of cities which Olmsted projected in 1868 posed the question "whether as the enlargement of towns goes on the law of improvement is such that we may reasonably hope that life in them will continue to grow better, more orderly, more healthy?"[42] To leave the improvement of towns to unpremeditated, haphazard drift of natural laws or to wait for street improvements on the belated arbitrary decisions of merchants would only lead to the aggravation of the evils occurring in rapidly enlarging towns. An attitude of laissez-faire or indifference to the health and welfare of town inhabitants and the refusal of merchants, real estate speculators, and town officials to effect the reconstruction of towns had taken their toll not only in human welfare but in profits as well. Even in the New World, Olmsted pointed out, "where great towns by the hundred are springing into existence, no care is taken to avoid bad plans. The most brutal Pagans to whom we have sent our missionaries have never shown greater indifference to the sufferings of others than is exhibited in the plans of some of our most promising cities, for which men now living in them are responsible."[43]

Would solutions for the problems of the city come if society continued to maintain a laissez-faire attitude or is it possible to completely rely upon the "genius of civilization," the force or forces which constitutes the social impetus by which society advances? Olmsted asserted that "we are by no means justified in adopting such a conclusion."[44] It is rather "the duty of each generation living in these towns to give some consideration, in its plans, to the requirements of a larger body of people than it has itself to deal with directly."[45] To wait for nature's unconscious method of improving society would seriously endanger the progress of civilization in health, virtue, and happiness.[46] The present generation, Olmsted urged, should not only directly apply itself to reforming its cities, but also "should not be allowed to go on heaping up difficulties and expenses for its successors, for want of a little comprehensive and businesslike foresight and study."[47]

Though only two cities had advanced in their street plans to the fourth stage, and these imperfectly, Olmsted now proposed to leap into the fifth stage. In the fifth and final stage art and science are unified to produce a comprehensive plan for the metropolis.

Albert Fein asserts that Olmsted and Vaux used as their paradigm the utopian model set forth by the French "prophet," Charles Fourier. Fein states that Olmsted and Vaux "argued" that the parkway plan contributed to a sixth historic stage in the progress towards the realization of Fourier's ladder of historic stages. The authors of the Brooklyn report make no such argument. They do not mention a sixth stage.[48]

The Fifth Stage: The Parkway Plan

The fifth stage, the "Parkway" plan of street design, was authorized by the commissioners of Prospect Park, Brooklyn. The ostensible purpose of the report was to offer a system of road approaches to Prospect Park so that the people of Brooklyn "living at the greatest distance from the park" could easily reach the park.[49] What the landscape architects undertook, however, was a comprehensive survey resulting in a plan which would "affect the substantial and permanent interests of the citizens of Brooklyn, and of the metropolis at large."[50] They projected nothing less than an extensive system of elaborate boulevards radiating from Prospect Park in Brooklyn to various sections of Long Island, and interweaving with similar parkways leading both into the parks of New York City and northward to the outer reaches of the metropolis. Within the metropolitan park and parkway systems, Olmsted integrated the Eastern Parkway district of Brooklyn, a residential suburb intended to provide "spacious and healthful accommodations for a population of 500,000."[51]

The parkway itself incorporated the requirements Olmsted deemed necessary to unite form and function in the city street in his fifth stage. As depicted by Olmsted the parkway system would be interlaced in such a fashion that every part of the city would be within easy walking distance of some part of the parkway network. The parkways would be landscaped in an interesting fashion so that walkers and riders traveling to or from the park or business places would gain a substantial recreative benefit.[52] Olmsted set no rigid design pattern for these boulevards. They might vary in breadth from two hundred to five hundred feet. Typically, he preferred that they radiate irregularly from the park following the contours of the land. He suggested, for example, that the Brooklyn Park Commissioners consider extending Prospect Park by constructing a spacious parkway from the park through the Ridgewood area of Brooklyn to Williamsburgh. By purchasing the ground inexpensively before streets were laid and houses built Olmsted would still be able to introduce a broad boulevard "that would make frequent curves and considerable inequalities of surface desirable."[53] If, however, the city was laid out in the gridiron pattern that Olmsted so vehemently and unceasingly deplored, then there was no alternative save formal parkways. New York, Brooklyn, San Francisco, and Chicago, Olmsted complained, conformed to the grid system of streets.[54]

In his plan for the Brooklyn suburb the main artery, Eastern Parkway, was of formal design. The parkway was to measure two hundred ten feet in its total width. The parkway consisted of three separate, distinct roads and four walks. The central roadway for through traffic was to be sixty-five feet wide. It was to be macadamized and Olmsted intended it to be used exclusively for pleasure driving just as were his park roads. On each side Olmsted provided a mall thirty-five feet wide which was to be curbed, sodded, and flagged. The malls were to be planted with double rows of shade trees. In time the trees would form a green "tunnel" during the hot summer months to protect the walkways and pedestrians from the heat of the sun.[55] On either side of the central roadway and the malls parallel service roads were provided for local traffic; each was twenty-five feet in width and was to be paved with Belgian stone. These streets were to be used for heavy commercial and other vehicles as access roads

Figure 9. General Plan for Prospect Park, Brooklyn, 1870
(Courtesy National Park Service
Frederick Law Olmsted National Historic Site)

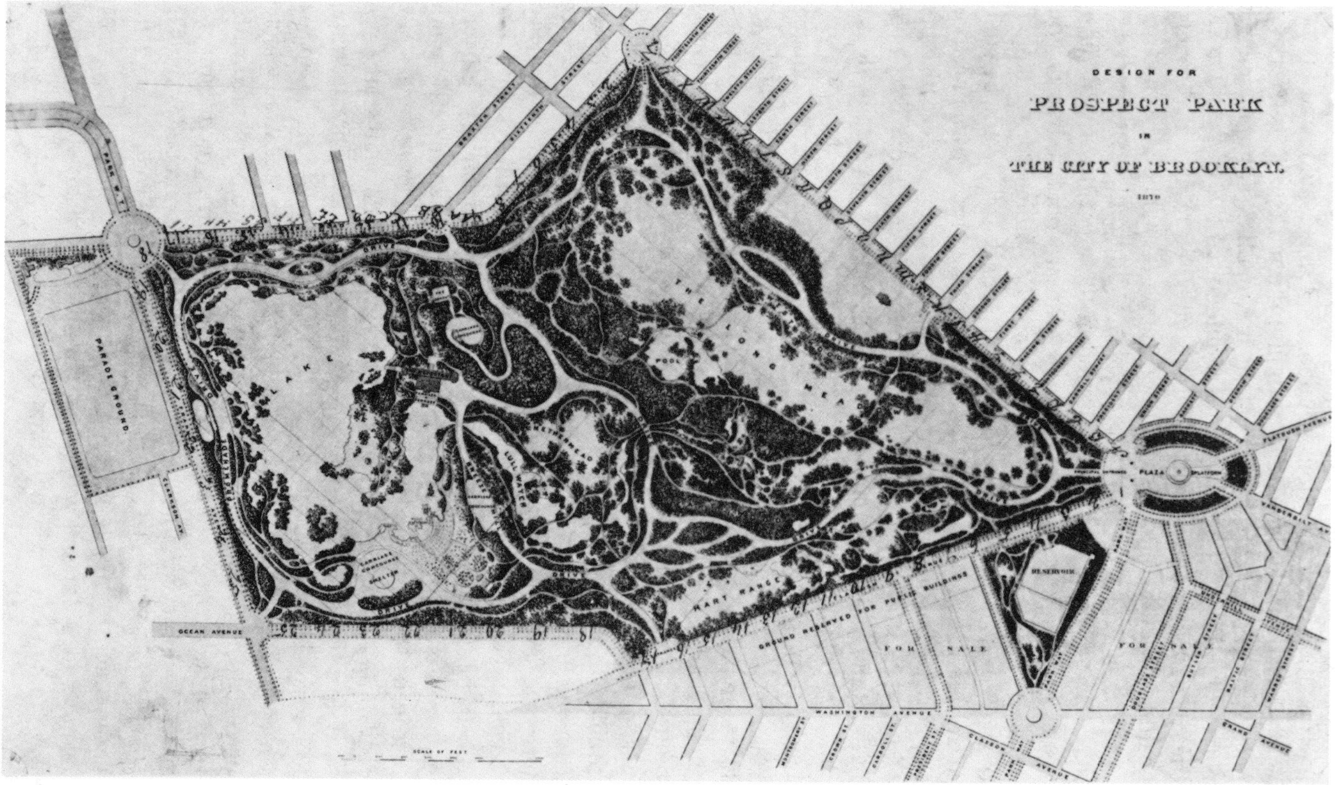

to approach the houses lining the parkway. On each side of the parkway, fronting the house lots, Olmsted located a tree-fringed walk.[56]

The parkway would serve its required ends by "giving access for the purposes of ordinary traffic to all the houses that front upon it, offering a special road for driving and riding without turning commercial vehicles from the right of way, and furnishing ample public walks, with room for seats, and with borders of turf in which trees may grow of the most stately character."[57] It would contain six rows of trees, and a space of two hundred and sixty feet from building front to building front; the parkway would constitute a perfect barrier to the progress of fire.[58]

The nuclear parkway of his suburban development in Brooklyn was the Eastern Parkway. In the original design of 1868 it was to extend eastward from the entrance of Prospect Park to the boundary of Brooklyn (then at the village of New Lots). Olmsted projected the continuance of the parkway system northward from the park entrance to the upper East River Bridge at Astoria or Ravenswood to provide a direct drive to Central Park in Manhattan joining the two parks. He envisioned a connecting system of "similar sylvan roads" leading northward to the upper end of the island of Manhattan.[59] The Fort Hamilton Parkway would originate at the park and terminate at a marine promenade overlooking the Narrows and the New York Bay. Ocean Parkway would similarly originate at the park and traverse Long Island to the seaside at Coney Island. Intervening boulevards would lead to Canarsie, Rockaway, and Jamaica.[60] While the street system which Olmsted contemplated was never fully accomplished, such parkways as Eastern Parkway and Ocean Parkway, constructed to Olmsted's design, are still in use, and excessively so, by New York motorists.[61]

Olmsted had hoped that the two thousand acres of land in the New York City and Brooklyn metropolitan area which had been reserved for parks by 1870 would be interwoven with a system of parkways. The Central Park Commissioners directed the construction of a number of broad thoroughfares in upper Manhattan which were related to Central Park. However, the New York City reform administration, guided by Andrew H. Green, the comptroller of the Board of Central Park and later of New York City, aborted Olmsted's plan for a metropolitan parkway system.[62] Even Olmsted's early attempt to widen Fifth Avenue from Madison Square to the entrance of Central Park to accommodate the anticipated traffic to the park was negated. An example of an Olmsted-designed street constructed in Manhattan is Riverside Drive. While it possesses some of the characteristics of the parkway, it was intended as an adjunct to Olmsted's Riverside Park rather than a thoroughfare.

Had Olmsted been afforded the opportunity to formulate the parkway system he projected in 1868, the

> arrangement would enable a carriage to be driven on the half of a summer's day through the most interesting parts both of the cities of Brooklyn and New York, through their most attractive and characteristic suburbs, and through both their great parks; having a long stretch of the noble Hudson, with the Palisades in the middle distance, and the Shawangunk range of mountains in the background, in view at one end, and the broad Atlantic with its foaming breakers rolling on the beach, at the other.
>
> The whole might be taken in a circuit without twice crossing the same ground, and would form a grand municipal promenade, hardly surpassed in the world either for extent or continuity of interest.[63]

Olmsted believed his system of metropolitan parkways manifested the essential characteristics of use and beauty. As extensions of the parks they would beautify the city; provide pleasant, comfortable means of recreational driving and walking; make access to the parks easier for all; and give commercial traffic an ease of maneuver. In a period when "no one in New York had a good word for its thoroughfares," its intracity communications were decidedly limited, and the inhabitants of the congested tenement districts were immobilized to their neighborhood blocks, Olmsted's parkways offered a system of interconnecting trunklines.[64] In the case where intracity travel was difficult, expensive, and "rapid transit" a euphemism, his new concept in roadways would unify the community by providing a "continuous and connecting thread" for the metropolis.[65]

Central to Olmsted's vision of the fifth-stage metropolis was the large urban park. Easy access to the park was the pivotal point upon which he conditioned his parkway system. In reference to Manhattan, in 1858, the City had hardly reached the southern borders of the park when the construction of Central Park was begun. However, he correctly predicted that it would not be long before the enlarging city would engulf the park and that it would become a central common to the city. He believed this to be true not only of New York, but in any case in which a park is located near a city. Thus for the sake of economy, convenience, and unity, at the time when a new park area was determined, Olmsted advised that new parkways between the park and the distant parts of the city, existing and anticipated, should be planned.[66]

As early as 1866 in the report on Prospect Park Olmsted projected the joining of the Brooklyn park with Central Park in Manhattan. With the elaboration of this notion in his report of 1868 Olmsted delineated as part of his fifth stage the original conception of a metropolitan *system* of parks. In its fully fashioned conception the park system would consist of a group of coordinated park areas, each park possessing a unique excellence or function, strategically distributed within a municipality or a large urban region, and united by a system of attenuated park strips (i.e., parkways).[67]

Within the range of his parks and parkway system Olmsted included plans for residential suburbs which would incorporate the conveniences of the city with the advantages of the country.

Although formal in design, his plan for the Eastern Parkway subdivision in Brooklyn is an example of such planning. Another example is Olmsted's work in the Boston area. While it is but an approximation to his ideal fifth stage, embodying a network of parks, a parkway system, and suburbs, Olmsted provided an example of his conception of comprehensive planning in his report to the Department of Parks of Boston (1887).[68] With existing broad avenues and the construction of new ones according to the parkway model, he developed the plans for a parkway system that brought into relationship a series of public grounds in metropolitan Boston. From the Commons and the Public Gardens at the center of Boston his route traversed Commonwealth Avenue to Chestnut Hill Reservoir. From the Reservoir the way followed Beacon Street back towards Commonwealth Avenue and turned into the Back Bay Fens. The course lay through the Fens, the Jamaica Pond grounds, skirting the Arnold Arboretum, and into Franklin Park (see fig. 10). From Franklin Park there ensued a long open stretch along Columbia Road and Boston Street offering views of the ocean at Dorchester Bay and leading into South Boston and the Marine Park at Boston Harbor. The total course was about twenty-four miles and hardly required the viewer to retrace a step.[69]

Much of the metropolitan park system of Greater Boston, particularly those parts which Olmsted had a hand in designing, fell into the area of metropolitan Boston which was undergoing rapid suburban development. The Back Bay, Roxbury, West Roxbury, Dorchester, Brookline, and Jamaica Plains sections were within easy reach of some part of Olmsted's system. With the rapid expansion of street railways, water and sewerage lines, and steam railroads from the compact business-industrial center of Boston to the sparsely settled outer edges, a propitious condition existed for the comprehensive planning of a variety of suburban communities that would combine urban conveniences with rural village beauty. Olmsted had but limited opportunities in the Boston metropolis to design the kind of suburban community in which he could demonstrate the unification of art and science in order to achieve the enjoyment of wholesome forms of domestic life.[70] In Roxbury, West Roxbury, and Dorchester suburban development was especially extensive, but, as Sam Bass Warner points out, the deficiencies of these suburbs resulted in their decay.[71] The degeneration of these suburbs might have been avoided had Olmsted been en-

Figure 10. General Plan for Franklin Park, Boston, 1885
(Courtesy National Park Service
Frederick Law Olmsted National Historic Site)

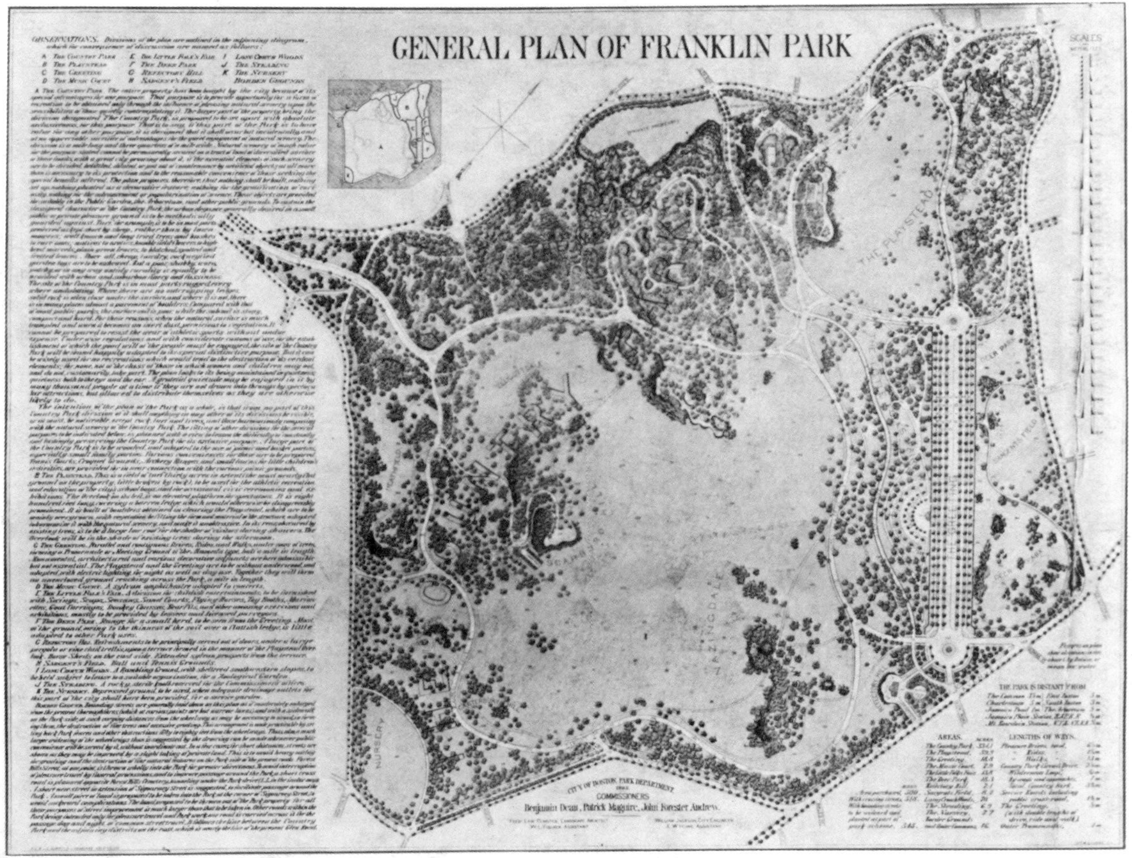

gaged to use his genius to formulate a comprehensive plan for the Greater Boston region.

Suburbs: A Special Opportunity

Olmsted observed that as cities predictably enlarged in space and in population density there was a tendency for the great agencies of commerce and related occupations and trades to group compactly together to obtain the advantages and the economy of close and direct intercommunications with each other. The sordid conditions which prevailed in the sections of the city preempted by commerce prompted those with means to remove their residences from their places of work to suburbs where they sought a more healthful and congenial environment for family life. By 1868, when Olmsted and Vaux formulated their Eastern Parkway plan for Brooklyn, Olmsted noted that the tendency had become pervasive even among families of moderate means. He safely assumed "that the general division of all the parts of every considerable town, under the two great classifications of commercial and domestic . . . will not only continue, but will become more and more distinct."[72] As the cities attracted more and more people, a concurrent countertide developed. Large numbers of families, formerly domiciled in the congested, commercial sections of the cities, left for residential suburbs in and near the cities. Olmsted perceived these two currents as parts of one process of metropolitanization.[73]

Admitting that existing travel arrangements were still inconvenient and expensive, Olmsted nevertheless saw few obstacles to prevent the indefinite extension of intra- and inter-urban, suburban commuting. With the continued improvement of horse-drawn vehicles, street railways, or other "cheap and enjoyable method of conveyance" for short travel, the pleasures of middle-class suburbs would be easily accessible.[74] Moreover, as railroads improved, "all the important stations will become centres or sub-centres of towns, and all the minor stations suburbs."[75] The rapidity of technological advances and communication facilities which he was witnessing made Olmsted confident that the rural beauty of the suburban community and the advantages offered in the city would be united into an organic whole.[76]

In discerning the trend of the metropolis to become differentiated into commercial and residential districts Olmsted saw the opportunity to apply his ideas of comprehensive planning to the development of residential subdivisions and suburbs. In the uncongested parts of the city and in outlying areas he could utilize the advantage of relatively cheaper, unused land. The principal advantage was that in the open, undeveloped sections, he was not required to contend with an established street pattern. He could create *de novo* a residential neighborhood or community which would embody completely his own ideas of planning.

By 1860 Olmsted was already knowledgeable enough to assert his ideas in relation to a projected suburban development in the old Washington Heights district of New York City.[77] The problem with which Olmsted was asked to contend was the creation and maintenance of a rural, residential suburb on the northern heights of Manhattan. In his plan he was concerned to show that the preservation of the metropolitan residential suburb as an attractive place to live required the guarantee of tranquility, seclusion, and freedom from street turmoils.[78] At the same time the residents of the community would require the advantages of the social and cultural institutions, regular and punctual services, and the use of the talents of the professional and the non-professional occupations— all habitually available to the city dweller.[79] To provide these, however, the quiet, privacy, and character of any residential neighborhood would be undermined by the invasion of all manner of shops, stores, cheap tenements, boarding houses, and taverns filling the district with noise, smoke, bustle, and vehicular congestion.[80] Without some kind of restrictions, every street, no matter how narrow or steep, would become a business thoroughfare. Since zoning ordinances were not available to him, Olmsted declared that only a controlling comprehensive plan for the subdivision would prevent its destruction as a residential neighborhood. Olmsted stated that it is the failure to initiate such planning that resulted in deterioration of other residential districts along the East River in Manhattan, on the heights of Clifton and New Brighton on Staten Island, New York, and in the suburbs of Brooklyn, Jersey City, Philadelphia and Boston.[81]

Of fundamental significance to such a plan is the street pattern, which must be adapted to the contours of the natural surface, that is to say, in a curvilinear fashion. Olmsted offered a series of rules relating to the layout of the subdivision streets which would preclude their use as business thoroughfares.[82] In the absence of zoning legislation he used the street system as a functional check to preclude commercial encroachment. To preserve the integrity of the neighborhood, Olmsted devised a street system to discourage the location of commercial activities which depend upon easy access to them. The shops and stores would remain on the periphery of the subdivision on the main city thoroughfares from which deliveries and calls might be made.[83]

In 1868 Olmsted, with his partner Calvert Vaux, made two significant efforts in planning suburbs which reached implementation.[84] The first of these was in Brooklyn in connection with the parkways radiating from Prospect Park. This was accomplished for a public authority. The second was the suburban village of Riverside, Illinois, just outside Chicago. In this case the sponsor was a private developer, The Riverside Improvement Company.

Olmsted devised the Brooklyn subdivision to complement the city street system of his fifth stage of evolution.

When Olmsted submitted his plan to the Brooklyn Park Commission in 1868, he believed that the lower part of Manhattan would become, over the years, an increasingly compacted commercial center. This development would leave little room for habitation within the commercial area, and would thus push, Olmsted thought, the residential locations northward above Central Park. He supposed, too, that the residential district would be surrounded by warehouses, factories, and trading houses. The result would be a highly compacted residential area, intersected by streets primarily providing communication and transportation facilities for commerce. Under these circumstances, Olmsted said, "the city of New York is, in regard to building space, in the condition of a walled town."[85] He saw in Brooklyn the opportunity to develop a suburban residential area to service New York City. For Olmsted Brooklyn "must be considered as a division merely of the port of New York. . . . Brooklyn is New York outside the walls."[86] As an element of the New York port Olmsted recognized the commercial relationship of the Brooklyn shore facing Manhattan. He assumed that it would be used for shipping, mercantile, and manufacturing purposes. But to the east of this district Olmsted denoted an elevated stretch of ground which he supposed offered no advantages for any commercial purposes, where there was "ample room for an extension of the habitation part of the metropolis upon a plan fully adapted to the most intelligent requirements of modern town life."[87]

Olmsted assessed his residential site in terms of the following factors: convenience to the New York port, health and recreative factors, proximity to shops and public buildings needed for local requirements, prevailing winds, elevation, the formation of the ground with reference to sanitary conditions, adjacency to the newly planned Prospect Park, and a location which offered a view of the ocean, but precluded (he thought) its enclosure "on all sides by commerce, as the habitable part of New York island soon will be."[88] The area Olmsted chose for his residential community is the Eastern Parkway District in Brooklyn.

In advocating his plan for Brooklyn as a bedroom suburb for New York City, Olmsted pointed out that improved methods of transportation made possible a

> departure from the old-fashioned compactness of towns. . . . The unwholesome fashion of packing dwelling-houses closely in blocks grew . . . out of the defensive re-

quirements of old towns; it may possibly be necessary to continue it under certain
circumstances . . . on the island of New York, but where there is no necessary boundary, either natural or artificial, to the space which is to be occupied by buildings, as
is the case with Brooklyn, it is, to say the least, unwise to persist in arrangements
which will permanently prevent any indulgence of this kind.[89]

Olmsted stipulated in this plan that the house lots would be 100 feet
wide and 225 feet deep—the full depth between two streets. The New
York state law creating the Eastern Parkway District required each house
in the District to be set back thirty feet from the street line to the house
front. To preclude the occupation of the rear streets by inferior houses
Olmsted extended the design over two blocks of ground on each side of
Eastern Parkway. The outermost boulevards, running parallel with the
parkway, were only slightly less spacious in design than the parkway.
They were of a width of 100 feet with sidewalks 20 feet wide and shaded
by a double row of trees. Between the parkway and the secondary boulevards Olmsted provided intervening stable streets, each 35 feet wide.
Houses would be arranged throughout back-to-back with a stable street
between them.[90]

The plan for the district is on formal lines, calling for broad, straight,
tree-lined boulevards. This is a contrast to Olmsted's mode of design.
Where the opportunity permitted, Olmsted followed the principles of the
romantic aesthetic as best integrating with his functionalism. He could
not do so in his Brooklyn plan because of the preexisting street design.
His plan required implementation by reconstruction of existing streets.
To meet specifications the parkways and the parallel boulevards required
widening and the intervening stable lanes required narrowing. To achieve
this it became necessary for the New York State legislature to enact implementing legislation.[91] This was accomplished in May, 1868—a few
months following the publication of Olmsted's plan. The law was unique.
It provided for the street changes; it prohibited, under the state's police
power, the establishment of any "manufactory, trade, business, or calling,
which may be in any wise dangerous, noxious, or offensive, to the neigh-
boring inhabitants"; but more significantly it also contained one of the
early legislative attempts to control the integrity of a neighborhood from
the *aesthetic* point of view.[92]

Section three of the law states:

No buildings or other erections, except porches, piazzas, fences, fountains, and stat-
uary, shall remain or be at any time placed upon any of the lots fronting upon either
of the said streets so to be widened, within thirty feet from the line or sides of the
said several streets respectively. The intervening spaces of land on each side of the
said several streets shall be used for courtyards only, and may be planted with trees
and shrubbery, and otherwise ornamented, at the discretion of the respective owners
or occupants thereof.[93]

The law further placed a control upon the stable lanes to the effect that no building fronting upon these narrow lanes could be used "for any purpose other than a stable, carriage house, conservatory for plants, or green-house."[94]

Here was an early attempt to zone a district on aesthetic grounds through use of the state's police powers. The law preceded the Prussian City Planning or Building Line Statute of 1875.[95] However, the time was not yet ripe in the United States to use police power to regulate and control the use of private property on aesthetic grounds without a reasonable reference to the safety, health, morals, and general welfare of the public. That part of the statute forbidding owners of lots on a street from building within thirty feet of the street—unless compensation were provided—was declared unconstitutional.[96]

Unable to use organic design in his parkway neighborhood, Olmsted resorted to zoning by legislation to preserve the residential character of his avenues. He must have considered this method half-safe, at best.[97] However, he advocated the control of residential districts through zoning. He aimed at alleviating the population congestion of high density areas. For health, safety, the preservation of high quality (and high land value) residential districts, and aesthetics Olmsted wanted "suburban neighborhoods where each family abode stands fifty or a hundred feet or more apart from all others, and at some distance from the public road."[98] To achieve this kind of control he pleaded for a building law similar to that of "Old Rome."[99]

The plan for the Eastern Parkway District not only brought Olmsted recognition as a city planner, it evoked support for comprehensive planning to guide the growth of all cities. In commenting upon the parkway plan during its construction the *New York Times* noted:

> We believe that to Mr. Frederick Law Olmstead, [*sic*] is to be credited the first successful application, in part, at least, of the idea that the growth of American cities can be judiciously guided; and that we need not necessarily sit patiently by, and see the most beautiful portions of them overrun by various occupants whom it is very difficult and very expensive to dislodge. Mr. Olmsted, has frequently had occasion to point out that in Brooklyn a special opportunity was offered, by early improvements, to determine beforehand that certain very beautiful quarters of the city should be taken up by first class residences, and be owned and occupied by men whose dwellings and grounds would be continually made more and more attractive.[100]

Though the plan for the Brooklyn subdivision was for Olmsted an expression of the fifth stage in the evolution of the morphology of the city, it only partially represented the organic expression of the romantic aesthetic. Olmsted needed the artist's freedom to work with the natural contours of the earth without the hindrance of a predetermined form. He, with Vaux, found this opportunity when they were hired to formulate a design for a suburban community at Riverside, near Chicago (see fig. 11). It is in such well-planned communities, springing up in close relation to large cities, that, Olmsted declared, are to be found "the most attractive, the most refined and the most soundly wholesome forms of domestic life, and the best application of the arts of civilization to which mankind has yet attained."[101] They offered pure air, verdure, privacy, and relief from the disconcerting noise, pollution, and mental strain associated with city life. In Olmsted's view residential suburbs supplemented the cities; great cities cannot exist without great suburbs. He did not consider suburban life to be retrogressive. By incorporating the refinements of civilization which characterize the city with the rural environment of the suburb, he held that civilization evidenced an advance toward a higher quality of life.[102] City and suburb are necessary components in the organic metropolis.

Through the artistry of the design for Riverside Olmsted was trying to achieve a beautiful physical environment that would provide all the advantages and comforts to be found in the large cities. He noted that many of the residential neighborhoods growing up in and around large towns were "little better than rude over-dressed villages, or fragmentary half-made towns."[103] Their development was haphazard since it was carried out by land speculators whose motives were to portion out the land into building lots in such a way as to exploit the area for profit. Olmsted's notion of suburban development was the antithesis of this. He used similar aesthetic principles in planning suburbs that he applied to park-planning.

Beginning with a comprehensive plan for the use of land, he urgently stressed the desirability of well-constructed sidewalks and wide, paved roads rather than the usual gravel roads which seasonally became quagmires. He urged that his residential developments must be accoutered with every facility and service which made the city attractive. Public laundries, bakeries, and recreational activities; daily and early deliveries of foods; door-to-door distribution of newspapers and magazines; provision for daily street cleaning; construction of sewer, water, and gas systems; rapid and convenient in- and out-of-town transportation and communication facilities must be included. All this was to be easily available to all the inhabitants of the community. Living near the commerce and culture of the city in a healthy rural environment with these conveniences would illustrate and demonstrate the advance of civilization.[104]

Just as the physical aspects of the urban park are the aesthetic vehicle to encourage a social purpose, so with the suburb. The ideal physical environment was to be the means to encourage the expression of an ideal social behavior. The ideal Olmsted sought to attain was an integrated

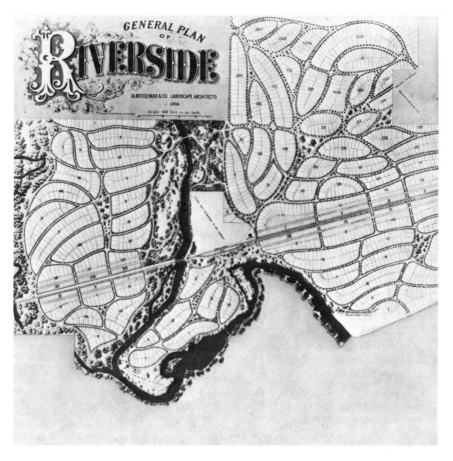

Figure 11.   General Plan for Community at Riverside, Illinois, 1869
(Courtesy National Park Service
Frederick Law Olmsted National Historic Site)

society embodying the sense of *Gemeinschaft*. The families of the community would have a private as well as a communal side to their existence.
Riverside was planned to allow the fullest expression of both sides. Olmsted
explained that there are two aspects of suburban habitation that ensure
success:

> [F]irst, that of the domiciliation of men by families, each family being well provided
> for in regard to its domestic in-door and out-door private life; second, that of the
> harmonious association and co-operation of men in a community, and in the intimate
> relationship and constant intercourse, and inter-dependence between families. Each
> has its charm, and the charm of both should be aided and acknowledged by all means
> in the general plan of every suburb.[105]

In presenting the Riverside plan, Olmsted stated that domesticity was
the essential quality of a suburb—the emphasis was on the idea of habitation. He specifically rejected the suggestion of the owners of the property that the tract be designed as a park with building lots divided by
imaginary property lines; the owners had apparently advertised the sale
of their property this way in their prospectus. Olmsted insisted upon the
individuation of building lots by obvious, clearly marked, agreeable di-
visions between private grounds and between private and public grounds;
property demarcations should on no account be imaginary lines.[106] He
did not intend to create a residential park at Riverside. In his aborted
subdivision devised in 1865 for the College of California at Berkeley
Olmsted used the model of the residential park which he had learned
from Llewellyan Park, New Jersey.[107] Olmsted abandoned the prototype
of the residential park when he formulated the plan for the Riverside
suburb.

In stating his reasons Olmsted explained that the essential qualifi-
cation for a park, as he defined a park, is range. It especially invites
"movement on all sides" to the observer.[108] All buildings and artificial
constructions must be subordinated to this idea of range. In the domestic
suburb, on the contrary, everything that favors movement should be subordinated. Hence, the controlling ideal for a park cannot be successfully
reconciled with the planned suburb on the same ground. Besides, Olmsted
pointed out to the owners, while the ground conditions at Riverside were
good for a suburb, most of the property was not good for a park.[109] His
general plan for the suburb only meant to suggest the interior arrangements for the private grounds.[110] It did not intend to intrude into the
privacy of individual owners probably because Olmsted believed each
house and its ground ought to reflect the personality of its owner. Olmsted
expressed just this sentiment in this observation: "I think, with Ruskin,
it is a pity that every man's house cannot be really his own, and that he

cannot make all that is true, beautiful, and good in his own character, tastes, pursuits, and history, manifest in it."[111]

In addition Olmsted urged an emphatic line of separation between property in common and the private properties of families because a home should be a retreat, free from any public observation and securing the privacy of its inhabitants. He was especially concerned that a family dwelling include a secluded out-of-door apartment so that the women and girls might enjoy air and sunlight while engaged in activities which might embarrass them should they be publicly observed.[112]

In contrast to the sense of alienation which characterizes the *Gesellschaft* atmosphere of the city, Olmsted viewed the suburban neighborhood as the embodiment of the fellowship of the *Gemeinschaft* association.[113] While insisting upon the privacy of the home and its grounds, Olmsted was concerned, as well, that the design of the suburb nourish harmony, cooperation, intimacy, and interdependence among its inhabitants. If he meant his suburban community to be a social model, Olmsted was, in turn, following models he had stored up in the course of his own experience.

The sentimental recollection of the kindness and neighborliness Olmsted experienced in his childhood in the Connecticut villages where he attended school or visited relatives emerges in the physical design of his suburbs. Olmsted's art was suffused with the scenery of New England. His parks are ideal formulations of the region's pastures and woodlands and his suburbs are ideal creations of its towns and villages. The "ruralistic beauty of a loosely built New England village" is the pattern which he avowedly followed.[114]

Certainly the park at Birkenhead, near Liverpool, England, and the suburb adjacent to the park had a profound effect upon Olmsted.[115] During his travels in England in 1850 Olmsted had observed the park and town which had been designed by the landscape gardener, Joseph Paxton. Olmsted noted that the park and the town, laid out on worthless land, had "become of priceless value."[116] It seemed to him to be the only town that he ever saw "that has been really built at all in accordance with the advanced science, taste, and enterprising spirit that are supposed to distinguish the nineteenth century. . . . Certainly, in what I have noticed, it is a model town, and may be held up as an example, not only to philanthropists and men of taste, but to speculators and men of business."[117]

Olmsted's experience with the German settlement at New Braunfels in Texas must also have influenced his conception of community. When he came upon the village in his travels, he was delighted with its communal life. Upon entering the village he was struck by the friendliness, neatness, and conveniences of the German community. This was in sharp

contrast to the inhospitable receptions he met among the desultory, un-
kempt habitations and settlements that he found prevailing along his route
of travel in the South and West.

Olmsted was deeply impressed by the spirit of community and the
Gemütlichkeit he found in the village.[118] The communal pattern of settlement, transplanted from the villages of Germany, was similar to that of
the early New England towns with an in-town house and garden plot and
hundreds of small farms belonging to the townspeople scattered over the
outlying neighborhood.[119] He was so impressed by the German settlement—a free labor community in the midst of a slave-holding society—
with its agricultural, mechanics', music, political, and horticultural societies, its schools, and its newspapers, that he gave its inhabitants his
highest accolade—they were like New Englanders.[120]

Olmsted wanted to re-create in his suburb the warm, cooperative,
communal unity he had found in the New England village and New Braunfels, Texas. To inspire the sense of community among the residents he
recommended to the owners of the Riverside property that some of the
best property be appropriated for public grounds to be used informally as
village-greens, commons, and playgrounds, "rather than of enclosed and
defended parks or gardens."[121] He was attempting to provide the physical
environment in which the integrity of the family would be insured and in
which face-to-face communal association would prevail. How deeply he
felt in this respect can be realized from the following extract from his
preliminary study:

> On the public side . . . the fact that the families dwelling within a suburb enjoy much
> in common, and all the more enjoy it because it is in common, the grand fact, in
> short, that they are christians [*sic*], loving one another, should be everywhere manifest
> in the completeness, and choiceness, and beauty of the means they possess of coming
> together, of being together, and especially of recreating and enjoying them together on
> common ground, and under common shades.[122]

The Riverside plan includes but transcends the residual elements of
Olmsted's early experience. In its unity of art and science in the romantic
mode, Riverside proved to be a landmark in planning. Christopher Tunnard considers Riverside to be an exposition of the planning of a whole
community using the theory of the romantic aesthetic at its best in shaping
the human environment. He declares that suburban planning became
more scientific in the attempt to improve the big urban centers and their
surroundings.[123]

There is no doubt that Riverside introduced a seminal idea into the
development of city planning in the United States. Walter Creese has even
gone beyond this in suggesting that the planned community at Riverside

has had an impact upon city planning at the international level through its influence upon Ebenezer Howard and the Garden City movement. As a court stenographer for the architectural firm of Ely and Burnham in Chicago, the young Britisher had the opportunity to visit and observe the new suburban development at Riverside. Creese notes the similarities between Howard's Garden City and Olmsted's suburb and suggests a direct relationship.[124]

In 1876 Olmsted was again given the opportunity to plan a suburb in the New York metropolitan region. The Board of the Department of Public Parks of New York City commissioned Olmsted and civil engineer J. James R. Croes to prepare a comprehensive plan for Manhattan above 155th Street and the district newly annexed from Westchester County in 1874. The latter—designated the twenty-third and the twenty-fourth wards—comprised the area north of the Harlem River to the Westchester County Line, in short, the Bronx. It was an enterprise of some magnitude.

The first report by Olmsted and Croes consists of two parts. The first part declared the need for a comprehensive plan that will serve the requirements of every legitimate sector of the New York metropolis. In a devastating critique of the existing rigid rectangular block system, adopted in New York City in 1811, Olmsted detailed the deficiencies and the resulting ineptitudes of its use. He pointed out that in the effort to make all parts of the metropolis equally convenient for all uses the rigid adherence to the rectilinear pattern of street layout had been wasteful and extravagant.[125] In a plea for the functional differentiation of parts within the organic metropolis, Olmsted asked for the consideration of an alternative system of streets which would heed differing topographical conditions of the district as they relate to the varied functions to be pursued in the metropolis.[126]

The second part of the report applies explicitly to "that part of the Twenty-fourth Ward Lying West of the Riverdale Road." Here Olmsted specifically applied the principles he expounded in the first part of his report. Fusing art and technology with the geographical configuration of the district, he created a plan for the Riverdale suburb that preserves the beauty of the area, yet uses a curvilinear street pattern as the more economical and convenient layout. To accommodate to the rugged surface, broken by ledges with steep declivities on its hillsides, he suggested that the houses be grouped in a terrace arrangement.[127]

In their report for the transportation system for the two wards the planners project the use of a "cheap and enjoyable," rapid steam railroad system to convey commuters.[128] Letting the topography determine the course of the railroad bed, Olmsted and Croes designed the layout of tracks through the two wards in such a way that the roadways would pass either over or under the tracks; the two systems would never cross on a level. With aesthetics, safety, and economy in mind the designers eliminated all grade crossings in the area.[129]

In the welter of political decision-making that involved opposing factions, the larger design for the new wards was never implemented; only fragments of the plan proposed by Olmsted and Croes were adopted.[130]

Olmsted's Suburbs: A Critique

If the public park can be reckoned as an expression of Olmsted's concern for the urban lower classes, his suburbs are his salaam to the wealthy and the middle class.

To enjoy living in Olmsted's suburbs required reserves of money not available to most working-class people, certainly not to the poor living in slums. He clearly designed his suburbs for the affluent. In his design for the Brooklyn subdivision he aimed to attract the successful businessman who had become "wealthy by close attention to his specialty" in the city.[131] "With the enlargement and progress in wealth and taste of the population" of Chicago there will be, he wrote, a market demand for residences in Riverside.[132] He expected Riverdale to attract great numbers of wealthy people who wished to live graciously within the limits of New York City.[133] And the increased value of the real estate of the district would be reflected in tax returns to the city treasury.[134]

Olmsted certainly recognized the plight of the "clerk or mechanic and his young family, wishing to live modestly in a house by themselves, without servants."[135] However, Olmsted's notion of adequate housing required detached villas surrounded by space enough to allow direct exposure to sun and wind, the maintenance of trees to purify the air for reasons of health, and space to provide safety against the hazards of fire and communicable diseases. He associated tenement housing with the conditions which he observed in city slums.[136] For the low-income segment of society to purchase the kind of homes Olmsted thought adequate was hardly possible. Nor could they buy into his suburbs. The excellence of his planning increased the land values in the suburbs and in the vicinity of the parks. Olmsted seemed to make a point of emphasizing this consequence.

In any case the cost of commuting would have made suburban residence too expensive in most instances for the working class. Only the middle class and the rich could enjoy the aesthetic condition of Olmsted's suburbs.

The Aesthetics of Street Layouts in Suburbs

Olmsted viewed the history of the city in terms of the evolution of street patterns. For him the street system was the skeletal structure of the city and the suburb. The streets comprised the means of uniting and defining the varied functions of the community, apprehended as a social organism. He applied the analogy of the division of labor to the plan of a city. As natural circumstances favor, individual parts of the city are devoted to the development of different kinds of activity.[137] Each section needs a pattern of streets that will serve its function. Olmsted conceded that in the commercial sections of the city a rectilinear system of streets facilitated easy transportation of goods, communication, and accessibility of the public to places of business.[138] Even in suburbs the sections demarcated for shopping and commerce are designed in the block pattern with straight streets.[139] The streets, including the parkways, serve not only as a means of uniting the community but also as a vehicle for "functional zoning."[140]

In his plans for residential subdivisions Olmsted devoted a substantial, if not the major, portion of his concern to the street layout. In the design for Riverside, for example, references to landscape effects and the architecture of houses were minimal.[141] The street pattern is fundamental to city planning, and it affects not only the form and function of the city, but the conditions of the interior of the houses as well.

In 1876, when Olmsted offered his plan for the Bronx, he had to contend with proponents for extending Manhattan's existing gridiron street pattern. New York City's street plan, adopted in 1811, required an inflexible adherence to a layout in which city blocks were no more nor less than 200 feet wide from street to street and building lots were not more nor less than 25 feet wide and 100 feet deep.[142] In its application the law imposed a street arrangement that disregarded Manhattan's topography and attempted to make all parts of the city equally convenient for all uses. Olmsted asserted that any of the blocks would as easily accommodate a blast furnace as an opera house; consolidation of two or more blocks to unite the grounds of Columbia College or to allow the construction of a great manufacturing enterprise was forbidden; insufficient space did not afford the spectator the opportunity to view a stately building from top to bottom either directly or in advantageous perspective.[143] In the cramped space of Manhattan the standard building lot required under the law made land expensive. The ground rents precluded cheap, private houses within the economic reach of the working class. The system promoted overbuilding: houses were built to occupy the entire depth of the lot for maximum use.[144] Under such conditions, Olmsted held, the house interiors were badly ventilated (even the homes of the rich were unpleasantly odorful) and allowed but little sunlight to penetrate. The practice left no space for a rear alley or yard through which supplies might be delivered and ashes, rubbish, and garbage removed. These last must be dragged through the house and removed to the street via the front of the house, which contributed to the infamously filthy state of the city streets.[145]

In planning the residential subdivision Olmsted applied principles of aesthetics derived from philosophical romanticism. The suburb, like the park, should manifest an aura antithetical to that of the city. To the rectilinearity of the streets, buildings, and blocks which characterize the physical form of the city and the tension, impersonality, and alienation which are the psychosocial symptoms of the commercial preoccupations of the city, the suburb offers the contrast of gracefully-curved lines, sylvan beauty, tranquility, and wholesome domesticity. In its respect for nature the organic congruence of the curvilinear street pattern was fundamental for Olmsted's suburb. In respect to aesthetic doctrine the objectives which Olmsted wished to achieve for park and suburb are the same, yet there is a difference in the manner in which he attained them. The park, as a work of art, took its form from the way in which the artist uses trees, rocks, and water in relation to great spaces of open pastoral landscapes.[146] Olmsted emphatically stated: "This should be clearly recognized. As neither glass, nor china, nor knives and forks, nor even table and chairs are the essential elements of a dinner, so neither bridges, towers, shelters, seats, refectories, statues, cages for birds and animals, *nor even drives and walks* are the essential elements of the Park."[147] Facilities for walking, driving, riding, resting, eating, and drinking are merely accessories which may help the users of the park enjoy the essential elements. The accessory elements are not only not necessary to the park as a work of art, they may, by obtruding, detract from its artistic value. It is otherwise with the city and the suburb. The city planner, as artist, gives form to his design through his system of streets.

In his plan for Riverdale Olmsted rejected the commonly used rectilinear pattern as uneconomical and destructive of the beauty of the natural features of the scenery. The practice, he pointed out, of establishing straight streets for the purpose of establishing equally sized building lots in a rugged terrain would be excessively costly. The uniformity thus attained would make much of the district unsuitable for building sites even if money and labor were expended on transforming the natural surface. However, if nature is respected and roads are laid out in correspondence with the local topography, adequate building sites could be economically achieved. They would vary in size and shape, but this would add to the picturesque character of the suburb. The flexibility of the curvilinear pattern would permit the preservation of the grace of the landscape.[148]

In regard to the problem of transportation Olmsted pointed out that the construction of a straight road on certain kinds of terrain is not economical, though the road may be the shortest distance between points. The orthodox doctrine accounts neither for the realities of wear and tear on transportation equipment required to negotiate steep hillsides nor the cost of pushing the road through the protrusions of a rocky ledge. The curving roadway avoids these difficulties and costs. At the same time it does the least violence to the terrain and affords the widest leeway to the planner in creating an aesthetically satisfying plan yet preserving the picturesque qualities of the area.[149]

If the rocky hillsides of Riverdale are best served by a curvilinear street pattern, what can be the justification for the Riverside suburb located on a flat, alluvial prairie? The directness of city streets and the resulting regularity of the street system of the city suggests, Olmsted said, "eagerness to press forward, without looking to the right hand or the left."[150] In the suburb speed is less important than comfort and convenience. Turf, trees, and foliage should abound. The greater space available allows a construction of streets of a width greater than that required only for the passage of vehicles and pedestrians. To achieve a picturesque suburb and to escape the monotony of the rectangularity of city streets, Olmsted recommended "the general adoption in the design of the roads of gracefully-curved lines, generous spaces, and the absence of sharp corners, the idea being to suggest and imply leisure, contemplativeness and happy tranquility."[151]

In the aesthetic theory that Olmsted employed and in his doctrine of the historic advancement of civilization in progressive stages, there are implications which suggest a basis for his repudiation of the gridiron street pattern. In the aesthetics of romantic idealism the artist must be free to participate with nature in a process in which a work of art unfolds. The laws and forms which control this process are determined by the artist as he produces: they may not be imposed or predetermined from the outside. Working within the mode of romantic aesthetics, Olmsted needed freedom from encumbrances in order to work with the natural contours of the earth. The curvilinear pattern allowed him to achieve that organic unity.

By contrast the gridiron pattern disregards nature. It is a simple means for the spatial and legal division of land. It makes the purchase and sale of land easy for real estate speculators. But Olmsted railed against its use because it reduces nature to a commodity to be bought and sold rather than cherished and preserved. By pushing its way over mountains, into swamps, and through woodlands the grid pattern disregards interesting natural features and perspectives; it abstractly and irrationally destroys the landscape. Confined within the grid, man's perception of the universe is limited to a box-like rectangle, like the blocks of New York City. For Olmsted the gridiron pattern imposed an arbitrary despotism upon nature.

A similar relationship may be seen between Olmsted's opposition to the block pattern and his doctrine of historic progression. He clearly associated the gridiron model of streets with an early historical stage in which towns were predominantly concerned with their military defenses. The invariable result was a military despotism "of the most direct and stringent character."[152] Under such governments the rulers have little consideration for the life, property, health and comfort of most of the townspeople. Olmsted held that, despite the general advance of society in other respects, the policy, custom, and fashion of laying out streets in a grid pattern, as if the town population were a garrison, had persisted.[153]

In contrast, the curvilinear form, with its freedom to flow with the earth's contours, permits the artist to integrate his design with nature. In Olmsted's view the freedom to use the curved lines in this organic sense represents the liberation of mankind. It provides the setting for the environment which inspires an appreciation of the beauty and unity of nature and the free flow of the imagination. Using the aesthetic reason, the artist, as city planner, advances civilization. He leaps into the fifth stage of the historic development of the city. Now art and science are united.

The Need for Active Planning

Olmsted described city growth as an evolutionary process in which the morphology of the city changes in response to internal social changes. Social changes cause dislocations which affect various social sectors, which then attempt to cope with the changes. As civilization advances from a lower to a higher stage, the city reflects the new social requirements in the change of its structural environment. This process is not a premeditated one; it occurs through the gathering and momentum of social forces, which were represented for Olmsted in "the law of improvement" or natural laws. But the experience of history indicates that the natural process of accommodation is incomplete as it relates to cities.[154] The results, in terms of morphological change, are desultory and partial; form and function do not achieve automatic reconciliation. Improvements, when they have occurred, do not come from the concerted action of the community or of the governments which are officially responsible; they come as isolated events undertaken by individuals or groups for their own special interests and not for the general welfare of the city. The law of improvement, through which the general progress of civilization operates, has achieved accommodation favorable to the health, virtue, and happiness of people living in cities only indirectly and imperfectly, if at all.

With the accelerating increase of the urban populations and the rapid expansion of cities occurring in the nineteenth century, Olmsted believed that the problem of accommodation had become acute. The inability or the inadequacy of natural social processes to effect needed changes in the structure of the city and the welfare of its inhabitants required an abandonment of the laissez-faire doctrine implicit in the natural law approach. Without concerted action the streets of the city have been laid out in a detached and desultory fashion favoring landowners or some other special interests who, for want of comprehensive planning, have permitted "difficulties and expenses" to mount for successive generations.[155]

Olmsted justly accused city governments of failure to remedy the inconvenience and suffering which could be economically alleviated by skillful management. In the welter of antagonistic special interests, personal greeds, and manufactured public opinions, municipal policy-making and administration are undermined. In spite of the dependence of the nation on the convenience, safety, order, and economy of life in the great cities, the meager efforts at reform are ineffective. Olmsted warned that the lag between rapid social change and effective, remedial political action was becoming ominously greater.[156] Unless effective action were taken to overcome the plight of the cities, the evils to which the city inhabitants were subject would be so aggravated as to lead to a grand catastrophe for civilization, "for our great cities stretch out their hands to all the world, and all the peoples of the world are provided through them."[157]

Olmsted asserted that what was needed was not a policy of public drift, but a rational, comprehensive plan which would anticipate the requirements of the city. Scientific studies indicated the way in which cities can, with a little comprehensive and businesslike foresight and study, improve the health, lengthen the life span, and provide conveniences for their inhabitants. Olmsted insisted that "it is the duty of each generation . . . to give some consideration, in its plans, to the requirements of a larger body of people than it has itself to deal with directly."[158]

The solution that Olmsted proposed is systematic planning "with a view to comprehensive and long-sighted public economy."[159] This meant an impartial survey by experts and professionals in every field salient to the project in view. The function of the planner requires him to integrate these studies with his own frame of reference into a comprehensive understanding. The analysis of Olmsted's planning reports showed that he was capable of evoking in his mind a remarkably complex, comprehensive apparatus of criteria, techniques, and potentialities and then of employing them to appraise the site and project under his consideration.[160]

It was not Olmsted's intention that a comprehensive city plan be dogmatic. He pointed out that the manner in which cities grow cannot be accurately predicted. Business centers and residential areas sometimes shift; they may even, in time, become interchanged.[161] In discussing his plan for the Bronx he said, "A judicious laying out of the annexed territory requires a certain effort of forecast as to what the city is to be in the future. In this respect, there is as great danger in attempting too much as in attempting too little."[162] In view of the possibilities of new types of transportation facilities, methods of building, professions and trades, discoveries in sanitary science, and perhaps even developments in political science, Olmsted thought it would be premature to determine the use of every acre of ground.[163]

Nevertheless, to leave the future of cities to be resolved by the laws of nature was unacceptable to Olmsted. When the exercise of human judgment can prevent many of the evils which beset cities and when the application of reason can result in a healthier, more comfortable, humane existence within cities, it is inexcusable that a metropolis should not have a plan. The plan should be "adapted to serve, and serve well, every legitimate interest of the wide world; not of ordinary commerce only, but of humanity, religion, art, science, and scholarship."[164]

In Olmsted's view, the city planner must discern the historic trends of the city as they unfold under natural laws. To these he makes a rational application of science and art to form an integrated plan for the welfare of the people living in the metropolis.

For Olmsted the organon by which the reform of the metropolis was to be achieved was a comprehensive plan. He might very well have applied to the city planner the same instructions he offered to scholars: "Scholars should be prepared to lead, not to follow reluctantly after, the advancing line of civilization. To be qualified as leaders they must have an intelligent appreciation of and sympathy with the real life of civilization, and this can only be acquired through a familiarity with the higher and more characteristic forms in which it is developed."[165]

8

Epilogue

Thirty-five years before the Chicago Fair of 1893 gave thrust to the City Beautiful Movement and to the modern city planning movement, Frederick Law Olmsted prepared the ground for these developments.

Far more significant than the glitter of the City Beautiful was the necessity of creating an awareness that the form of the city could be restructured or recreated by rational planning. Olmsted showed the way with his urban parks, suburbs, and his prognosis that the enlarging city needed a rational plan.

In a period which exhibited a strong anti-city attitude Olmsted took the pains to show that the city was both a reservoir of civilization and the spearhead of cultural development. He understood that the historical trend was in the direction of metropolitan expansion and that it was increasingly necessary that society cope with the problems posed by a rapidly increasing urban population. In a society characterized by an extraordinary mobility and by a vague sentimental nostalgia for "nature," Olmsted provided a rationale for creating rural parks within the city. Using the aesthetic reasons of romantic idealism, he gave his art a social purpose that indicated his keen understanding of the problems confronting an urban society whose orientation is the market place.

Olmsted's conviction that the configuration of the city could be rationally structured to serve not only the physical but the psychosocial needs of the city inhabitants flowed into and merged with the City Beautiful Movement. Indeed, Olmsted's seminal work was necessary to it.

Notes

Chapter 1

1. John W. Reps, *The Making of Urban America, A History of City Planning in the United States* (Princeton: Princeton University Press, 1965), pp. 298–99, 302.

2. Octavius Brooks Frothingham, *Transcendentalism in New England, A History* (New York: Harper & Bros., 1959), pp. 155–57.

3. Ralph Waldo Emerson, *The Complete Works of Ralph Waldo Emerson*. Edited with an Introduction by Emerson W. Emerson, Concord Edition, 12 vols. (Boston: Houghton Mifflin Co., 1904), 2:88–89.

4. Ibid., 3:215.

5. Ibid., 3:200.

6. Arthur M. Schlesinger, Jr., *Orestes A. Brownson* (Boston: Little, Brown & Co., 1939), pp. 40–41, 97. See also Vernon L. Parrington, *Main Currents in American Thought*, 2 vols. (New York: Harcourt, Brace & Co., 1954), 2:382–87.

7. Ernest Erber, "Urban Planning in Transition: An Introductory Essay" in Ernest Erber, ed., *Urban Planning in Transition* (New York: Grossman Publishers, 1970), p. xvii.

8. Fredrick Law Olmsted, *Forty Years of Landscape Architecture*, Frederick Law Olmsted, Jr. and Theodora Kimball, eds., 2 vols. (New York: G. P. Putnam's Sons, 1922), 2:25. The original impetus to establish a large-scale park in Manhattan came from the poet and the editor of the *Evening Post*, William Cullen Bryant. His efforts were notably supported by Andrew Jackson Downing, editor of the *Horticulturist* (ibid., 2:22–29; Allan Nevins, *The Evening Post* [New York: Boni & Liveright, 1922], pp. 192–201).

9. Ralph Waldo Emerson, *Journals of Ralph Waldo Emerson*, Edward W. Emerson and Waldo E. Forbes, eds., 10 vols. (Boston: Houghton Mifflin Co., 1909–1914), 3:278.

Chapter 2

1. Henry James, *Charles W. Eliot*, 2 vols. (Boston: Houghton Mifflin Co., 1932), 1:33–34.

2. Alice Felt Tyler, *Freedom's Ferment: Phases of American Social History from the Colonial Period to the Outbreak of Civil War* (New York: Harper & Bros., 1962), pp. 68–78, 95, 116–17, 121, 133, 142; Arthur M. Schlesinger, *Paths to the Present* (New York: Macmillan Co., 1949), pp. 260–63.

3. Olmsted, *Forty Years*, 1:46. For a definitive biography of Olmsted see Laura Wood Roper, *FLO, A Biography of Frederick Law Olmsted* (Baltimore: The Johns Hopkins University Press, 1973).

4. Olmsted, *Forty Years*, 1:46–47, 60–61.

5. Edward Chase Kirkland, *Men, Cities and Transportation, 1820–1900*, 2 vols. (Cambridge: Harvard University Press, 1948), 1:38–61.

6. Olmsted, *Forty Years*, 1:64. For a discussion regarding the growth of interest in natural scenery and tourism see Hans Huth, *Nature and the American: Three Centuries of Changing Attitudes* (Berkeley: University of California Press, 1957), pp. 71–128. For a treatment of the work of American landscape painters in the areas covered in Olmsted's travels see Oliver W. Larkin, *Art and Life in America* (New York: Rinehart & Co., 1949), pp. 200–13.

7. Olmsted, *Forty Years*, 1:70. Olmsted was referring to Timothy Dwight and Benjamin Silliman of Yale College, and Harriet Martineau, the English writer. The Olmsteds enjoyed the natural beauty of New England and New York so glowingly pictured by Dwight. "Neither the poet, nor the painter, can here ever be at a loss for scenery to employ the pen or the pencil," he wrote. After describing the natural scenery, neat farms, and "sprightly towns" of New England, Dwight concluded: "It will be difficult not to say, that with these exquisite varieties of beauty and grandeur the relish for landscape is filled, neither a wish for a higher perfection, nor an idea of what it is, remaining in the mind." Timothy Dwight, *Travels, in New England and New York*, 4 vols. (New Haven: Timothy Dwight, 1821–1822), Barbara Miller Solomon, ed. (Cambridge: The Belknap Press of Harvard University Press, 1969), 1:77, 259.

8. Benjamin Silliman, *Remarks Made on a Short Tour between Hartford and Quebec*, 2d ed. (New Haven, 1824), pp. 18–19.

9. Olmsted, *Forty Years*, 1:61, 69.

10. Ibid., 1:77.

11. Jarvis Means Morse, *A Neglected Period of Connecticut's History, 1818–1850* (New Haven: Yale University Press, 1933), pp. 21–23, 52, 71, 89–90, 223–32. See also Lois Kimball Mathews, *The Expansion of New England, The Spread of New England Settlement and Institutions to the Mississippi River 1620–1865* (Boston: Houghton Mifflin Co., 1909), pp. 157, 259–60.

12. Paul W. Gates, *The Farmer's Age: Agriculture, 1815–1860*, vol. 3 of The Economic History of the United States (New York: Holt, Rinehart & Winston, 1960), pp. 27–28, 269, 291.

13. Emerson, *Complete Works*, 7:383, 386, 392.

14. Gates, *Farmer's Age*, p. 292.

15. Ibid., pp. 295–302.

16. Olmsted, *Forty Years*, 1:61.

17. Ibid., 1:72–74.

18. Horace Bushnell, *An Address before the Hartford County Agricultural Society* (Hartford, 1847), pp. 20–21.

19. Olmsted, *Forty Years,* 1:81–82.

20. Roper, *FLO,* pp. 56, 62, 78, 80, 91, 107–8. It is strangely true that the Americans most closely associated with extolling farming life and nature were failures when they applied themselves to practical farming. Notwithstanding his attempts at scientific farming and improving the farming practices of Americans, Jefferson "did not have the faculty of making his acres yield him profit. . . . By 1825 he came face to face with bankruptcy." (August C. Miller, Jr., "Jefferson as an Agriculturalist," *Agricultural History* 16 (April 1942), p. 77.) For all the "exhilaration and health" Emerson says he felt digging in his garden, he had, by his own admission, neither training nor aptitude for carrying on a farm or even a large garden. (Emerson, *Complete Works,* 1:236–37, 439.) "Whoever sees my garden discovers that I must have some other garden." (Ibid., 2:221; see also 7:374, 384.) Thoreau never farmed for a living. When he needed cash he turned to the trade taught to him by his father—making pencils. Horace Greeley, whose *New York Tribune* was best known and most influential of the city papers among the rural population, regarded his weekend farm as a plaything. Greeley's great farm expert and editor, Solon Robinson, was "no practical farmer," never having farmed on an extensive scale. (H. A. Kellar, "Solon Robinson," *Indiana Historical Collections* 21, 22 (1936): pt. 2, p. 161.)

In his study of the literature related to farming in Illinois Bardolph makes the point that while many editor-publishers of farm periodicals constantly held up the farmer's life as the noblest of vocations and the farming class as the greatest children of God, they themselves were not farmers nor did they live on farms. They were more likely to be commission merchants, manufacturers of agricultural machinery, or storekeepers. (Richard Bardolph, *Agricultural Literature and the Illinois Farmer* (Urbana: University of Illinois Press, 1948), pp. 110–11, 162.) The fiascoes of the utopian agricultural communities Brook Farm and Fruitlands are well known.

21. Richard J. Purcell, *Connecticut in Transition: 1775–1818* (Middletown, Conn.: Wesleyan University Press, 1963), pp. 257–58, 261–62. Morse, *A Neglected Period,* pp. 3, 123.

22. Purcell, *Transition,* pp. 263–64. Morse, *A Neglected Period,* pp. 123–27.

23. The description of Olmsted's parents was written by Frederick Law Olmsted's wife in 1920 in a reminiscence. She had first come to know the Olmsted family in 1848. (Olmsted, *Forty Years,* 1:77, 80.)

24. Ibid., 1:47–49, 54–55, 56–57.

25. FLO to Frederick Law Olmsted, Jr., 23 December 1894. Olmsted Papers, Manuscript Division, Library of Congress. Cited hereafter as Olmsted Papers.

26. Joseph Haroutunian, *Piety versus Moralism: The Passing of New England Theology* (New York: Henry Holt & Co., 1932; reprint ed., Hamden, Conn.: Archon Books, 1964), pp. xxii, 182–83, 219, 279–80; Perry Miller, *Errand into the Wilderness* (Cambridge: Harvard University Press, 1956), pp. 196–203.

27. Haroutunian, *Piety versus Moralism,* pp. 281–82.

28. Ibid., p. 182.

29. Herbert W. Schneider, *The Puritan Mind* (New York: Henry Holt & Co., 1930), p. 222.

30. Ibid., pp. 233, 236.

31. Barbara M. Cross, *Horace Bushnell: Minister to a Changing America* (Chicago: University of Chicago Press, 1958), p. 17.

32. Ibid., p. 20.

33. Ibid., pp. 102, 146.

34. Bushnell, *An Address*, p. 18.

35. Mary A. Cheney, *Life and Letters of Horace Bushnell* (New York: Harper & Bros., 1880), p. 499.

36. Ibid., p. 209.

37. "Horace Bushnell's epoch-making book on *Christian Nurture* may have done more than any other single agency to break down the extreme individualism of the old Puritan theology of America." (Arthur Cushman McGiffert, *The Rise of Modern Religious Ideas* (New York: Macmillan Co., 1925), p. 277, n. 1.)

38. Horace Bushnell, *Views of Christian Nurture*, 2d ed. (Hartford, 1848), pp. 22–25.

39. Horace Bushnell, "Unconscious Influence," in *The American Pulpit*, Richard S. Rust, ed., 2 vols. (Worcester, 1847), 2:230–41.

40. Marsh introduced Coleridge's *Aids* to the American public in 1829 not only because he considered the *Aids* a "work of great and permanent value to any Christian community," but also because he believed that the doctrines of Locke and the Scotch metaphysicians, insofar as they influenced American Congregationalism, had an inevitably dangerous tendency to "undermine our belief in the reality of anything spiritual in the only proper sense of that word." The effect of Marsh's effort in bringing out Colerdige's *Aids* was electric and pervasive in the development of American Transcendental literature and upon the Unitarian Transcendental ministers. But it was Bushnell who gave Marsh's original intention implementation by infusing Coleridgeian concepts into Congregationalism. (Marsh, "Preliminary Essay" in Samuel Taylor Coleridge, *The Complete Works of Samuel Taylor Coleridge with an Introductory Essay upon his Philosophical and Theological Opinions*, W. G. T. Shedd, ed., 7 vols. (New York: Harper & Bros., 1853), 1:69, 73, 87–90.)

41. Charles Loring Brace, *The Life of Charles Loring Brace, Chiefly Told in His Own Letters*, Emma Brace, ed. (New York: Charles Scribner's Sons, 1894), p. 9.

42. Charles Capen McLaughlin, ed. in chief, *The Papers of Frederick Law Olmsted*, vol. 1: *The Formative Years, 1822–1852*, Charles Capen McLaughlin, ed. and Charles E. Beveridge, assoc. ed., (1977); vol. 2: *Slavery and the South*, Charles Beveridge and Charles Capen McLaughlin, eds., David Schuyler, assoc. ed. (1981); vol. 3: *Creating Central Park*, Charles Beveridge and David Schuyler, eds. (1983): 3 vols. (Baltimore and London: The Johns Hopkins University Press, 1977–), 1: chap. 5 passim.

43. FLO to Charles Loring Brace, 20 September 1847. Olmsted Papers, reprinted in McLaughlin and Beveridge, 1:299.

44. FLO to John Olmsted, 25 September 1848, Olmsted Papers. John Morell was an English clergyman who had studied under Fichte at Bonn. The influence of German idealism is reflected in his theological and philosophical writings. Morell's religious doctrines were attractive to Horace Bushnell, who had met Morell in England. (Cross, *Horace Bushnell*, p. 102.)

45. FLO to John Olmsted, 9 November 1849, Olmsted Papers. Johann Neander [David Friedrich Strauss] had been converted to Christianity from Judaism by Schleiermacher. Neander's theological works reflect the religious romanticism of Schleiermacher.

46. FLO to John Olmsted, 10 March 1850, Olmsted Papers. James Martineau was an English Unitarian minister influenced by the transcendental thought of German philosophy and its British interpreters, especially Coleridge and Carlyle. (*Encyclopaedia of Religion and Ethics,* 1916 ed., s.v. "Martineau, James.")

47. Brace, *Life of Charles Loring Brace,* p. 27.

48. FLO to Charles Loring Brace, 26 July 1847. Olmsted Papers.

49. McLaughlin and Beveridge, 1:358.

50. Ibid., pp. 296–97. See also Roper, *FLO,* pp. 52–53.

51. Ibid., pp. 326–28.

52. FLO to Frederick J. Kingsbury, 20 April 1871. Olmsted Papers.

53. FLO to Charles Loring Brace, 15 March 1887. Olmsted Papers. See also Roper, *FLO,* pp. 401–2.

54. G. Harrison Orians, "The Rise of Romanticism, 1805–1855," in *Transitions in American Literary History,* Harry H. Clark, ed. (Durham: Duke University Press, 1953), pp. 118–226.

55. Frothingham, *Transcendentalism,* pp. 52–56.

56. McLaughlin and Beveridge, 1:277.

57. *The Works of Thomas Carlyle,* Edinburgh Edition, 30 vols. (New York: Charles Scribner's Sons, 1903–1904), vol. 1: *Sartor Resartus, The Life and Opinions of Herr Teufelsdröckh,* pp. 96–97, 103–4, 146, 157.

58. Ibid., p. 175.

59. Ibid., pp. 47, 123, 146. See also Charles F. Harrold, *Carlyle and German Thought* (New Haven: Yale University Press, 1934), p. 100.

60. Carlyle, *Sartor,* 1:23, 52, 213, 215.

61. Ibid., pp. 43, 163, 175.

62. Ibid., pp. 43, 164, 173, 178, 211–12. See also Harrold, *Carlyle,* pp. 186–88.

63. Carlyle, *Sartor,* 1:173, 177.

64. McLaughlin and Beveridge, 1:272.

65. Olmsted, *Forty Years,* 1:80.

66. James T. Flexner, *That Wilder Image: The Painting of America's Native School from Thomas Cole to Winslow Homer* (Boston: Little, Brown & Co., 1962), pp. 128–29. See also Roger B. Stein, *John Ruskin and Aesthetic Thought in America, 1840–1900* (Cambridge: Harvard University Press, 1967), pp. 1–2, 32; Larkin, *Art and Life in America,* p. 204.

67. Flexner, *That Wilder Image,* pp. 68, 369; Larkin, *Art and Life in America,* pp. 204,

244, 251, 262, 350. See also David H. Dickason, *The Daring Young Men: The Story of the American Pre-Raphaelites* (Bloomington: Indiana University Press, 1953), pp. 5, 34, 49–50, 73–77, 92–93, 194–98.

68. *The Works of John Ruskin*, E. T. Cook and Alexander Wedderburn, eds., Library Edition, 39 vols. (London: George Allen, 1904–1912), 4:28–29.

69. FLO to John Olmsted, 25 September 1848. Olmsted Papers.

70. A common way of spending a social evening among Olmsted's set was to read aloud and discuss didactic literature.

71. Francis G. Townsend, *Ruskin and the Landscape Feeling: A Critical Analysis of His Thought during the Crucial Years of His Life, 1843–1856*, Illinois Studies in Language and Literature, vol. 35, no. 3 (Urbana: University of Illinois Press, 1951), p. 5 ff.

72. Ruskin, *Works*, 5:365. See also ibid., 35:16, 95, 113–18, 155–65.

73. FLO to Calvert Vaux, 1 August 1865. Olmsted Papers.

74. Olmsted, *Forty Years*, 1:108–9. Cf. with Ruskin's regard for nature from his autobiographical *Praeterita:*

> The living inhabitation of the world—the grazing and nesting in it,—the spiritual power of the air, the rocks, the waters, to be in the midst of it, and rejoice and wonder at it, and help it if I could,—happier if it needed no help of mine,—this was the essential love of *Nature* in me, this the root of all that I have usefully become, and the light of all that I have rightly learned. (Ruskin, *Works*, 35:166.)

75. Emerson, *Journals*, 4:65n; 9:319n.

76. FLO to John Olmsted, 6 October 1849. Olmsted Papers.

77. McLaughlin and Beveridge, 1:337–38. William Emerson later came to be Olmsted's legal counselor and representative. (Roper, *FLO*, p. 131.)

78. Ralph L. Rusk, *The Life of Ralph Waldo Emerson* (New York: Charles Scribner's Sons, 1949), p. 123. See also ibid., pp. 101, 106–8, 113; the Letters and the Journal of William Emerson, passim. Microfilm, Columbia University Library, New York.

79. William Emerson's knowledge of Carlyle's writings was an intimate one. Ralph Waldo often requested William's opinions on Carlyle's writings. It was William who often attended to the publishing details of Carlyle's and Ralph Waldo Emerson's works with the New York publishing houses. (*The Letters of Ralph Waldo Emerson*, Ralph L. Rusk, ed., 6 vols. (New York: Columbia University Press, 1939), vols. 1–6 passim.)

80. FLO to John Olmsted, 9 November 1849. Olmsted Papers.

81. John Hull Olmsted to Fredrick Kingsbury, 11 December 1849. Olmsted Papers.

82. Frothingham, *Transcendentalism*, pp. 153, 245.

83. John Hull Olmsted to Charles Loring Brace, December 1850. Olmsted Papers.

84. Brace, *Life and Letters*, pp. 176–77.

85. Frothingham, *Transcendentalism*, chap. 12. See also Henry Steele Commager, *Theodore Parker* (Boston: Little, Brown & Co., 1936), pp. 56, 58–60, 151–67 passim.

86. Brace, *Life and Letters*, p. 182. It was the result of a discussion on the slavery problem

between Olmsted and Parker that provoked Olmsted to embark upon his investigation of the conditions of slavery in the South. The outcome of his investigation was his three volumes, *Our Slave States*. (FLO to Letitia Brace, 22 January 1892. Olmsted Papers.) See also Roper, *FLO*, p. 84.

87. FLO to Elizabeth Baldwin Whitney, 16 December 1890. Olmsted Papers. Reprinted in Olmsted, *Forty Years*, 1:70. See also Roper, *FLO*, p. 345.

88. Albert Fein, "The American City: The Ideal and the Real" in Edgar Kaufmann, Jr., ed., *The Rise of an American Architecture* (New York, Washington, London: Praeger, 1970) pp. 51, 54–56. Fein's thesis that Philosophical Radicalism was influential in the religious, intellectual, political, and social life of nineteenth-century America is misleading. His assertion that Jeremy Bentham and the Utilitarians were the "principal source of inspiration" for the religious and social reform activities of such Protestant leaders as Bushnell and Ralph Waldo Emerson and the "men they influenced" deserves refutation. The philosophy of German idealism, directly or filtered through the writings of Thomas Carlyle and Samuel Taylor Coleridge, profoundly affected the intellection of some of the members of the Protestant ministry in both England and the United States. The German romantic philosophy was especially significant for the Boston and Concord Transcendental ministers. Despite the differences among them the Transcendentalists (both lay and religious) rejected the crude sensationalism of John Locke's epistemology—a fundamental element of Utilitarian philosophy. (William Hutchinson, *The Transcendentalist Ministers: Church Reform in the New England Renaissance* (New Haven: Yale University Press, 1959), pp. 26–30. See also Anne C. Rose, *Transcendentalism as a Social Movement, 1830–1850* (New Haven and London: Yale University Press, 1981), pp. 67–68.)
  Emerson, like his Scottish friend Carlyle, viewed Bentham's Utilitarianism with contempt. Emerson considered Utilitarianism to be a "stinking philosophy." (Emerson, *Journals*, 2:455.) He declared that he would "rather not understand God's world than understand thro' and thro' in Bentham's." (Emerson to Elizabeth Palmer Peabody, Concord, 3 August 1835, Emerson, *Letters*, Rusk, 1:450.)
  Fein's attempt to impose Bentham's ideology on Olmsted's intellectual-aesthetic development through Olmsted's association with Edwin L. Godkin is especially misleading. Godkin, a Britisher who founded *The Nation* in 1865 with Olmsted, had been a devoted disciple of Bentham's Utilitarianism. By 1873 Godkin had rejected Bentham's Philosophical Radicalism. In an essay on John Stuart Mill which appeared in *The Nation* Godkin asserted that Bentham's theory of human nature "did not nearly go far enough. It did not embrace the whole human nature or even the greater part of it. . . ." Bentham, the essay continues, "was almost entirely wanting in sympathy and imagination. . . . [H]e made little impression on English sociology . . . in part due to his narrowness of view and in part the absence of an interpreter. . . ." Godkin also accused John Stuart Mill, Bentham's erstwhile and ostensible disciple, of similarly lacking in imagination. ([Edwin L. Godkin], "John Stuart Mill," *The Nation* 412 (May 22, 1873), 350–51.) It may be inferred that Olmsted influenced Godkin rather than the reverse. To support his thesis Fein cites the study "Benthamism in England and America" by Paul A. Palmer. (Fein, "American City," pp. 80, 108.) However, Palmer states that Benthamism was disregarded or rejected as a social or political philosophy in the United States. He pointedly remarked that Godkin became an "apostate" vis-à-vis Benthamism. (*The American Political Science Review* XXXV (October, 1941), 864–67.)
  Finally, as will subsequently be elucidated, Olmsted considered his parks to be

works of art with the capacity to elicit a beneficial psychological transformation in the viewer's psyche. He believed that great works of art and great phenomena of nature enhanced the sensibilities of the spectator or auditor and produced a moral effect. He compared his parks to poetry. With such a conception of the effect of art Olmsted would have rejected Bentham's assertion that the "game of push-pin is of equal value with the arts and science of music and poetry. If the game of push-pin furnishes more pleasure, it is more valuable than either." (Jeremy Bentham, *The Rationale of Reward* (London: Robert Heward, 1830), p. 206.)

89. Emerson, *Complete Works,* 1:367.

Chapter 3

1. Olmsted was a keenly perceptive sociologist. He evinced this in his use of the organic principle in analyzing the social basis of individual habits, attitudes, values, and behavior. See his analysis of "Southern Breeding" in Frederick Law Olmsted, *A Journey in the Back Country* (New York: Mason Brothers, 1860), pp. 411–28.

2. Olmsted, *Back Country,* pp. 288–89, 292, 302.

3. Frederick Law Olmsted, *A Journey in the Seaboard Slave States with Remarks on Their Economy* (New York: Dix & Edwards, 1856), pp. 489–91.

4. Walter J. Hipple, Jr., *The Beautiful, the Sublime, and the Picturesque in Eighteenth Century British Aesthetic Theory* (Carbondale, Ill.: Southern Illinois University Press, 1957), pp. 206–8, 235–37, 308–9. Humphrey Repton, *The Art of Landscape Gardening,* John Nolen, ed. (Boston: Houghton Mifflin Co., 1907), p. 60.

5. Repton, *Landscape Gardening,* p. 167.

6. Olmsted's early literary efforts, selections from the manuscript of *Walks and Talks of an American Farmer in England,* were first published in Downing's journal. Olmsted, *Forty Years,* 1:88; Roper, *FLO,* p. 78. Downing has been credited with affecting "country life in its every aspect." (Liberty H. Bailey, *Cyclopedia of American Horticulture,* 4 vols. (New York: Macmillan Co., 1900), 1:501.) But he was also instrumental in influencing the configuration of New York City. With William Cullen Bryant and other prominent New Yorkers he had exerted great efforts to realize the introduction of a city park in Manhattan. (*Dictionary of American Biography,* 1930, s.v. "Downing, Andrew Jackson.")

7. Olmsted rarely referred in his own writings to Downing's work on landscape gardening. "Olmsted had strong reservations about many of the plans and grounds that Downing offered in his books." (McLaughlin and Beveridge, 1:76.) Though affecting a natural style of landscape gardening, Downing, according to Tatum, illustrated his conception of beauty in landscape gardening by referring to the paintings of Claude Lorraine (1600–1682). Downing referred to the paintings of Salvator Rosa (1615–1673) to illustrate a conception of the grand and picturesque. Both painters belong to the Baroque period. (George B. Tatum, *Andrew Jackson Downing, Arbiter of American Taste, 1815–1852* (Ann Arbor, Mich.: University Microfilms, 1950), p. 43.)

8. Andrew Jackson Downing, *Cottage Residences, Rural Architecture and Landscape Gardening,* with a New Introduction by Michael Hugo-Brunt, Library of Victorian Culture (Watkins Glen, N.Y.: Century House, 1967), p. 16. See also Roger B. Stein,

John Ruskin and Aesthetic Thought (Cambridge: Harvard University Press, 1967), pp. 45–56.

9. Quoted in M. H. Abrams, *The Mirror and the Lamp: Romantic Theory and the Critical Tradition* (New York: W. W. Norton & Co., 1958), p. 213.

10. Olmsted, *Forty Years,* 1:92. Olmsted's praise appears rather reluctant. Downing's work reflected the precedents of the English gardening school. Roper explains that Olmsted and his partner, Calvert Vaux, redefined their profession giving it a "scope and stature far beyond the modest elegance of its standing in Downing's time." (Roper, *FLO*, p. 144.) Olmsted and Vaux's aesthetic functional premises gave their calling a recognized professional standing. (George F. Chadwick, *The Park and the Town: Public Landscape in the 19th and 20th Centuries* [New York: Frederick A. Praeger, 1966], pp. 190, 196.)

11. FLO to Elizabeth Baldwin Whitney, 16 December 1890. Olmsted Papers, reprinted in Olmsted, *Forty Years,* 1:69.

12. Olmsted, *Forty Years,* 1:127.

13. "The Spoils of the Park," ibid., 2:123.

14. Written in a notebook about 1863 while in Mariposa, California. Olmsted Papers.

15. Fredrick Law Olmsted, *Mount Royal, Montreal* (New York: G. P. Putnam's Sons, 1881), p. 59, reprinted in *Civilizing American Cities, A Selection of Frederick Law Olmsted's Writings on the City Landscape,* S. B. Sutton, ed. (Cambridge: M.I.T. Press, 1971), p. 214. Cited hereafter as Sutton.

16. Olmsted, *Forty Years,* 2:310, reprinted in Beveridge and Schuyler, 3:304.

17. Abrams, *Mirror and the Lamp,* pp. 204–5. See also his entire section, "German Theories of Vegetable Genius," ibid., pp. 201–13.

18. Frederick Law Olmsted, undated fragment. Olmsted Papers. My italics.

19. Olmsted, *Forty Years,* 2:356, 474; Olmsted, *Mount Royal,* p. 39.

20. Olmsted, *Mount Royal,* pp. 55n, 77.

21. Olmsted, *Forty Years,* 2:421–23, 472–532.

22. Olmsted explains that he expects the improvement to be so natural that the Back Bay's "rushy glades and bushy islands will supply well-guarded seclusions" for all manner of wild water-fowl to breed but at the same time will have an educative effect for young, observing children as a kind of living museum of wildlife. (Board of Commissioners of the Department of Parks, City of Boston [Mass.] *Annual Report,* Doc. No. 5, 1880.)

23. Henry-Russell Hitchcock, Jr., *The Architecture of H. H. Richardson and His Times* (New York: Museum of Modern Art, 1936), pp. 111, 119.

24. Ibid., pp. 214–15.

25. [Frederick Law Olmsted] City of Boston, Park Department, *Notes on the Plan of Franklin Park and Related Matters* (Boston, 1886), pp. 44–45, Sutton, pp. 244–45. Warner shows that from the late 1880s the suburbanization of the Boston area had become a mass movement. (Sam Bass Warner, Jr., *Streetcar Suburbs: The Process of*

Growth in Boston, 1870–1900 (Cambridge: Harvard University Press and M.I.T. Press, 1962).)

26. Ibid., p. 45, Sutton, p. 245. In relation to Olmsted's illustration it is interesting to note an article by the editor of *The Craftsman,* an American magazine devoted to the ideals of Ruskin and William Morris. The author advocates the use of sienna for staining the shingles of a model rural bungalow because the sienna color

> comes to look like an autumn oak leave; and this, together with the rough stone of the large chimney, tends to tie the building to its surroundings and to give it the seeming of a growth rather than a creation. It is a curious fact that the principles laid down by the late lamented Frederick Law Olmsted, relative to the coloration of buildings with regard to their surroundings,—principles so capable of demonstration and so obvious,—should meet with so little recognition and that, instead of structures which seem to grow from the plain or the forest and become a part of the landscape, we have otherwise admirable architectural efforts that affront the sensitive eye. ("How to Build a Bungalow," *The Craftsman* 5 (November 1903), p. 256.)

27. Ibid.

28. Diane K. McGuire, "Early Site Planning on the West Coast: Frederick Law Olmsted's Plan for Stanford University," *Landscape Architecture* 47 (January 1957), p. 345.

29. Ibid., p. 349.

30. Ibid., p. 346.

31. Olmsted had made similar landscaping suggestions earlier in relation to the College of California at Berkeley. Olmsted, Vaux & Co., *Report upon a Projected Improvement of the Estate of the College of California at Berkeley, near Oakland* (San Francisco: Towne and Bacon, 1866), Sutton, pp. 286–87.

32. Frederick Law Olmsted, "Public Parks and the Enlargement of Towns," *Journal of Social Science,* no. 3 (1871), pp. 13, 14, 21, 24, reprinted (in part) in Sutton, pp. 65–66, 69–70, 84.

33. Wilhelm Windelband, *Renaissance, Enlightenment, Modern,* vol. 2 of *A History of Philosophy* (New York: Harper & Bros., 1958), p. 600. Lovejoy asserts that "Schiller may be described as the spiritual grandfather of German Romanticism." Arthur O. Lovejoy, "Schiller and the Genesis of German Romanticism," *Essays in the History of Ideas* (Baltimore: The John Hopkins Press, 1948), p. 220.

34. Ernst Troeltsch, *The Social Teaching of the Christian Churches,* trans. Olive Wyon, 2 vols. (New York: Harper & Bros., 1960), 2:793–94.

35. Coleridge, "Theory of Life," *Complete Works,* 1:380.

36. Ibid., 1:396.

37. Friedrich W. J. von Schelling, *The Ages of the World,* Frederick de Wolfe Bolman, Jr., trans. and ed. (New York: Columbia University Press, 1942), p. 13; Joseph Warren Beach, *The Concept of Nature in Nineteenth-Century English Poetry* (New York: Macmillan Co., 1936), pp. 99–101.

38. Friedrich W. J. von Schelling, "Darstellung meines Systems der Philosophie," *Sämmtliche Werke,* I, 4:128, quoted in Bolman, *Ages of the World,* p. 16.

39. Friedrich W. J. von Schelling, "Introduction to Idealism," Tom Davidson, trans., *Journal of Speculative Philosophy* 1 (1867), pp. 159–60.

40. Friedrich W. J. von Schelling, "Darlegung des wahren Verhaltnisses der Naturphilosophie zu der verbesserten Fichteschen Lehre," *Sämmtliche Werke*, I, 7:19, 32, 33–34, quoted in Bolman, *Ages of the World*, pp. 25–26.

41. Friedrich W. J. von Schelling, "System des transcendentalen Idealismus," *Sämmtliche Werke*, I, 3:624 f., quoted in Bolman, *Ages of the World*, p. 14.

42. Samuel Taylor Coleridge, *Biographia Literaria with Aesthetical Essays*, J. Shawcross, ed., 2 vols. (Oxford: Clarendon Press, 1907), 1:104–5.

43. Ibid., 1:lx, lxxviii. See also Beach, *Concept of Nature*, pp. 100, 319, 323, 330, 574; René Wellek, *The Late Eighteenth Century*, vol. 1 of *A History of Modern Criticism: 1750–1950*, 4 vols. (New Haven: Yale University Press, 1955). According to Wellek, "Coleridge's lecture on 'Poesy or Art' (1818), which has been used by several expositors of his aesthetics as the key to his thought, is with the exception of a few pious sentiments little more than a paraphrase of Schelling's Academy Oration of 1807." (*The Romantic Age*, vol. 2 of *A History of Modern Criticism*, p. 132. See also ibid., pp. 153–57.)

44. Harrold, *Carlyle and German Thought*, pp. 104–5, 162–63.

45. Lester C. Polk, *The Aesthetics of John Ruskin in Relation to the Aesthetics of the Romantic Era* (Urbana: University of Illinois Press, 1941), p. 11.

46. "I never speak of German art, or German philosophy, but in depreciation." (Ruskin, *Works*, 5:424.)

47. Ladd shows Ruskin's reliance upon the philosophies of Coleridge and Schelling. Henry Ladd, *The Victorian Morality of Art, An Analysis of Ruskin's Esthetic* (New York: Long & Smith, 1932), pp. 70, 330–331. See also Graham Hough, *The Last Romantics* (New York: Barnes & Noble, 1961), p. 13; Mary Dorothea Goetz, *A Study of Ruskin's Concept of the Imagination* (Washington, D.C.: Catholic University of America, 1947), pp. 82–83, 221n. For Ruskin's use of the concept of identity through the imagination of the artist see his *Works*, 4:164–65, 5:113–14.

48. Ruskin, *Works*, 4:392.

49. Ibid., 3:353–54, 362–63; 4:294–95. See also John Rosenberg, *The Darkening Glass: A Portrait of Ruskin's Genius* (New York: Columbia University Press, 1961), chap. 1; Hough, *Last Romantics*, p. 42; Goetz, *Ruskin's Concept of the Imagination*, p. 29.

50. E. D. Hirsch, Jr., *Wordsworth and Schelling, A Typological Study of Romanticism* (New Haven: Yale University Press, 1960), pp. 4–7, chap. 2.

51. Henry A. Pochman, *German Culture in America: Philosophical and Literary Influences, 1600–1900* (Madison: University of Wisconsin Press, 1957), pp. 200–203, 612–15. See also Beach, *Concept of Nature*, chaps. 11, 12, and notes thereto. Beach shows the fundamental relationship of Emerson to Coleridge and both to Schelling's thought. In a comparative analysis of their writings he demonstrates the carry-over of Schelling's philosophy into the literature of Coleridge and Emerson. According to Beach, Coleridge and Emerson follow Schelling in thought and in "almost identical phrases." (ibid., p. 323.)

52. Hans Kohn, *American Nationalism, An Interpretative Essay* (New York: Crowell-Collier, 1961), pp. 61–68.

53. Hans Kohn, *The Idea of Nationalism: A Study in Its Origin and Background* (New York: Macmillan Co., 1961), pp. 349, 391–92, 413, 428–30, 437; Wellek, *Romantic Age,* pp. 279–80. See also Windelband, *Renaissance, Enlightenment, Modern,* p. 530.

54. Kohn, *American Nationalism,* p. 68.

55. Max Weber, *The Protestant Ethic and the Spirit of Capitalism,* trans. Talcott Parsons (New York: Charles Scribner's Sons, 1958), pp. 105, 168–69.

56. "Hence it is manifest, that whatever statues are set up or pictures painted to represent God, are utterly displeasing to him, as a kind of insult to his majesty." (John Calvin, *Institutes of the Christian Religion,* Henry Beveridge, trans., 2 vols. (Grand Rapids, Mich.: Eerdmanns, 1964), 1:92, 94.)

57. R. H. Tawney, *Religion and the Rise of Capitalism* (New York: New American Library, 1954), p. 96; Parrington, *Main Currents,* 2:263–66.

58. Thomas J. Wertenbaker, *The Puritan Oligarchy* (New York: Grosset & Dunlap, 1947), p. 78.

59. Fragment from a draft of a projected work by Frederick Law Olmsted titled "Civilization in the Last Fifty Years." Probably written while Olmsted was in Mariposa Bear Valley, California, about 1863. Olmsted Papers.

60. For a discussion of the relation of idealist thought to some of the radical Unitarian ministers see Hutchinson, *Transcendentalist Ministers,* chap. 2, especially pp. 29, 51.

61. Vivian C. Hopkins, *Spires of Form: A Study of Emerson's Aesthetic Theory* (New York: Russell & Russell, 1965), pp. 134–37. The replacement of a mechanistic concept of nature by a "vitalistic and creative concept" had a parallel in the "replacement of a mechanical and formalistic aesthetic theory by an organic concept of the unfolding of form from within outward." (Alexander Kern, "The Rise of Transcendentalism, 1815–1860," in *Transitions of American Literary History,* Harry Hayden Clark, ed. (Durham: Duke University Press, 1953), pp. 292–93). For a comprehensive discussion of the change and the impact of German theories of organism upon aesthetic thought see Abrams, *Mirror and the Lamp,* pp. 201–13, 218–25.

62. Coleridge, *Biographia,* 2:232, 262.

63. Emerson, *Complete Works,* 6:290–91, 294.

64. Ibid., 2:367–69.

65. Charles R. Metzger, *Emerson and Greenough, Transcendental Pioneers of an American Esthetic* (Berkeley: University of California Press, 1954), pp. 71–79, 86; Hopkins, *Spires of Form,* pp. 89–93; F. O. Matthiessen, *American Renaissance: Art and Expression in the Age of Emerson and Whitman* (New York: Oxford University Press, 1941), p. 146.

66. Emerson, *Complete Works,* 6:290. "The beauty that is its own excuse is Puritan in its simplicity and bareness, Yankee in its insistence on fitness and utility." (Matthiessen, *American Renaissance,* p. 50.)

67. Horatio Greenough, *Form and Function, Remarks on Art, Design, and Architecture,*

Harold A. Small, ed. (Berkeley: University of California Press, 1957), p. 75. Green-ough, we may note, was knowledgeable in the literature of German idealism. He had been exposed to it in Europe where he traveled and studied sculpture. Ibid., p. 70. See also Matthiessen, *American Renaissance*, p. 140.

68. Greenough, *Form and Function*, pp. 9, 59, 127–29.

69. Emerson, *Complete Works*, 6:294.

70. Ibid.

71. Greenough, *Form and Function*, pp. 80–81.

72. Ibid., pp. 73–74, Metzger, *Emerson and Greenough*, p. 112.

73. Greenough, *Form and Function*, p. 118.

74. Abrams, *Mirror and the Lamp*, pp. 238–39, 273, 281; Emerson, *Journals*, 4:253.

75. Johann Wolfgang von Goethe, "On Truth and Probability in Works of Art," *Literary Essays*, J. E. Spingarn, comp. (New York: Harcourt, Brace & Co., 1921; reprint ed., Freeport, N.Y.: Books for Libraries Press, 1967), p. 57.

76. Greenough, *Form and Function*, p. 81. See also Metzger, *Emerson and Greenough*, pp. 29–31; Hopkins, *Spires of Form*, pp. 9, 230.

77. "To follow blindly the dictates of sense and instinctive craving, *that* is to be a brute and not a man; to deny the promptings of sense and instinctive craving, *that*, is to perish. Behold the absolute. Between these lies human life." (Greenough, *Form and Function*, pp. 110–11.)

78. In his discussion of objective theories of art Abrams observes that the objective orientation in poetry was beginning to emerge in the late eighteenth and early nine-teenth century. The objective approach "came to constitute one element of the diverse doctrines usually huddled together by historians under the heading 'Art for Art's Sake'." (Abrams, *Mirror and the Lamp*, pp. 27–28, 283, 320, 326–28.) Kant's dictum that the "beautiful is incapable of resting on the representation of its utility" gave some critics, especially the Germans, the impetus to develop the aesthetic doctrine of "art for art's sake." (Emmanuel Kant, *The Critique of Judgement*, James C. Mer-edith, trans. and ed. (Oxford: Clarendon Press, 1952), p. 69.) Kant's definition of beauty follows: "Beauty is the form of *finality* in an object, so far as perceived in it *apart from the representation of an end.*" (Ibid., p. 80.) In the United States this doctrine was expressed by Edgar Allen Poe. (Norman Foerster, *American Criticism: A Study in Literary Theory from Poe to the Present* (New York: Russell & Russell, Inc., 1962), pp. 8–10, 52. William Charvat, *The Origins of American Critical Thought, 1810–1835* (New York: A. S. Barnes & Co., 1961), pp. 13–17.)

79. Foerster, *American Criticism*, pp. 95–99; Matthiessen, *American Renaissance*, p. 25.

80. Green, a reform Democrat, had been appointed to the Board of Commissioners of Central Park in 1857. In 1858 he became president and then comptroller of the Board. He was named comptroller of New York City in 1871. He played an influential role in city and state administration and politics during the latter half of the nineteenth century. His impact upon the development of the configuration of New York City— the layout of streets, building plots, squares and parks—was substantial. He both aided and hindered the implementation of Olmsted's plans for the city. However,

Green's parsimony and his close control over money expenditures incurred Olmsted's anthema. (Seymour J. Mandelbaum, *Boss Tweed's New York* (New York: John Wiley & Sons, 1965), pp. 60–62, 86, 89, 90, 115–17; Roper, *FLO*, pp. 145, 348–53.)

81. Olmsted's frustrating lifelong battle against the encroachments and spoliation of his great artistic creation—New York City's Central Park—can be gleaned from his agonizing piece, "The Spoils of the Park," *Forty Years*, 2, chap. 10. From time to time he suffered mental or physical exhaustion from the continuing battle to preserve his first great piece of the landscape art. (Roper, *FLO*, pp. 146, 149, 358, 361.)

82. Laura Wood Roper, " 'Mr. Law' and *Putnam's Monthly Magazine:* A Note on a Phase in the Career of Frederick Law Olmsted," *American Literature* 26 (March 1954), 88–93.

83. Frederick Law Olmsted, Jr., "City Planning," *American Civic Association*, ser. 2 (June 1910), pp. 18–20.

84. Matthiessen, *American Renaissance*, p. 152.

85. Greenough, *Form and Function*, pp. 60–61, 62–63.

86. Metzger, *Emerson and Greenough*, p. 135; Stein, *Ruskin and Aesthetic Thought*, p. 13. See also Matthiessen, who is reminded that "Sullivan, who had doubtless never heard of Greenough's essays," had been anticipated in the "form follows function" thesis by Greenough. (*American Renaissance*, p. 144.)

87. Louis H. Sullivan, *The Autobiography of an Idea* (New York: Press of the American Institute of Architects, 1924), p. 322.

88. Louis H. Sullivan, *Kindergarten Chats and Other Writings* (New York: George Wittenborn, 1947), pp. 200, 241. Cf. Olmsted, *Mount Royal*, p. 59.

89. I am too wary to say that Olmsted forged the chain between the aesthetic theories of Greenough and Sullivan, but certainly Olmsted was an effective closing link between them.

90. Oscar Lovell Triggs, *The Changing Order; A Study of Democracy* (Chicago: Oscar L. Triggs Publishing Co., 1905), pp. 209–13. Italics mine. Triggs was a student and disciple of Thorstein Veblen when Veblen taught at the University of Chicago. Triggs not only equated Sullivan's aesthetic theory with those of Emerson and Walt Whitman, he also associated Sullivan with Lester Ward, John Dewey, Charles Cooley, George Herbert Mead, and Veblen—Triggs's teachers and colleagues at the University of Chicago. His writings, little known now, cover a wide range, including sociology and aesthetics. The similarity of aesthetic outlook that attracted Triggs to Olmsted and Sullivan also brought Whitman into his orbit of interest. He edited Whitman's collected writings. (Sherman Paul, *Louis Sullivan, An Architect in American Thought* [Englewood Cliffs, N.J.: Prentice Hall, 1962], 104–7.)

Chapter 4

1. FLO to Charles Loring Brace, 1851, in Brace, *Life of Charles Loring Brace*, p. 110.

2. Olmsted's friend Brace mentions the sermon in his journal entry dated 20 February 1841. Brace notes that it influenced his whole life. Ibid., pp. 7–8, 433.

3. The conception of the role of the unconscious in determining human behavior was

still new and in the process of discovery in the period in which Olmsted became aware of it. It was not until the 1870s that the notion of the unconscious as an integral part of the mind and a determinant of behavior entered common usage. This was more likely to be true of European rather than American intellectuals. See Lancelot Law Whyte, *The Unconscious before Freud* (Garden City, N.Y.: Anchor Books, 1962), pp. 146, 161.

4. Bushnell, "Unconscious Influence," 2:230–41.

5. FLO to Bertha Olmsted, 1855. Olmsted Papers; reprinted in Beveridge, McLaughlin, Schuyler, 2:341–42.

6. FLO to John Charles Olmsted, 15 May 1892. Olmsted Papers.

7. Ibid.

8. FLO to Elizabeth Baldwin Whitney, 16 December 1890. Olmsted Papers. Olmsted would have been gratified by Lewis Mumford's comment. In his introduction to Clarence Stein's book, *Toward New Towns for America,* Mumford notes the unconscious influence of Olmsted's work upon Stein's planning. He points out that Henry Wright and Stein were unconscious disciples of their own great precursor, Olmsted.

> Olmsted's complete separation of pedestrian walks from vehicular and horseback traffic by means of overpasses and underpasses, in Central Park, was certainly the major forerunner of the Radburn plan. . . . One can hardly doubt that Stein's daily walks through Central Park during his formative period encouraged him to hold to it [the separation of pedestrian from vehicular traffic] tenaciously once Radburn was built. Stein himself agreed with Mumford's analysis. (Clarence S. Stein, *Towards New Towns for America* [Cambridge: M.I.T. Press, 1966], pp. 16, 44–47.)

9. "Beautiful it is to understand and know that a Thought did never die; that as thou, the originator thereof, hast gathered it and created it from the whole Past, so thou will transmit it to the whole Future. It is thus that the heroic heart, the seeing eye of the first times, still feels and sees in us of the latest. . . . There is a living, literal *Communion of Saints,* wide as the World itself, and as the History of the World." (Carlyle, *Sartor Resartus,* 1:197.)

10. Ibid., 1:173–75, 178–79.

11. Ibid., 1:115.

12. Ibid., 1:126.

13. Ibid., 1:97, 132.

14. In his essay, "Characteristics," Carlyle said:

> Of our thinking, we might say, it is but the mere upper surface that we shape into articulate thoughts;—underneath the regions of argument and conscious discourse, lies the region of meditation; here, in its quiet mysterious depths, dwells what vital force is in us; here if aught is to be created, and not merely manufactured and communicated, must the work go on. Manufacture is intelligible, but trivial; Creation is great and cannot be understood. (*Critical and Miscellaneous Essays,* 3:4–5.)

15. Kohn, *Idea of Nationalism,* pp. 427–33, 445–46; Robert Ergang, *Herder and the Foundations of German Nationalism* (New York: Columbia University Press, 1931), p. 220;

Wellek, *The Late Eighteenth Century,* pp. 182–83, 189; ibid., 2:3; Whyte, *Unconscious before Freud,* pp. 46, 108–11; Abrams, *Mirror and the Lamp,* pp. 204–5.

16. Whyte, *Unconscious before Freud,* pp. 59–60; Abrams, *Mirror and the Lamp,* pp. 210–11, 216–17, 242.

17. The letters can be described as defensive. Olmsted wrote them to justify his aesthetic convictions and his artistic work. In the realm of the creative field of the artist Olmsted resisted the interference of his importunate, millionaire clients as well as meddling public officials. They could accept or reject the preliminary plan of his work; Olmsted would not permit interference in the formulation. This was a matter of the strongest conviction with Olmsted. If he could not teach a client to accept his projected design, he declined or resigned from a commission.

18. Olmsted's choice of words is unfortunate. In using "incomprehensive" he probably means to convey the conception of that which cannot be fully grasped or comprehended such as the process of artistic creation that results from the activity of the mysterious "deep" of the unconscious.

19. FLO to Morris K. Jesup, 31 January 1889. Olmsted Papers.

20. FLO to Board of Commissioners of the Central Park, 22 January 1861, reprinted in Beveridge and Schuyler, 3:303.

21. FLO to Dr. Edward M. Moore, 26 January 1889. Olmsted Papers.

22. FLO to Albert Wright, 1 February 1889. Olmsted Papers.

23. FLO to Board of Commissioners of the Central Park, 22 January 1861, reprinted in Beveridge and Schuyler, 3:303–4.

24. Schelling, "Ideen zu einer Philosophie der Natur," *Sämmtliche Werke,* II, 13–14, quoted in Beach, *Concept of Nature,* p. 357.

25. Quoted in Rowland Gray-Smith, *God in the Philosophy of Schelling* (Philadelphia, 1932), p. 32; John Watson, *Schelling's Transcendental Idealism, A Critical Exposition* (Chicago: S. C. Griggs & Co., 1882), chap. 7. See also Windelband, *Renaissance, Enlightenment, Modern,* pp. 607–9.

26. Abrams, *Mirror and the Lamp,* p. 210.

27. F. W. J. von Schelling, *The Philosophy of Art,* A. Johnson, trans. (London: Chapman & Hall, 1845), p. 9.

28. F. W. J. von Schelling, *On University Studies,* Norbert Guterman, ed., E. S. Morgan, trans. (Athens: Ohio University Press, 1966), p. 148.

29. Samuel Taylor Coleridge, *Shakespearean Criticism,* Thomas M. Raysor, ed. Everyman's Library, 2 vols. (London: J. M. Dent & Sons, 1960), 1:197–98; Coleridge, *Biographia Literaria,* 2:258–59. For Coleridge's emphasis on the rational activity of genius see also Margaret Sherwood, *Coleridge's Imaginative Conception of Imagination* (Wellesley, Mass.: Wellesley Press, 1960), pp. 7, 23–24.

30. Wellek, *The Romantic Age,* pp. 289–91, 313; Abrams, *Mirror and the Lamp,* pp. 211–17.

31. FLO to Charles Loring Brace, 22 February 1846. Olmsted Papers, reprinted (in part) in McLaughlin and Beveridge, 1:231.

32. Troeltsch, *Social Teaching*, 2:617.

33. Carlyle, *Sartor*, 1:178.

34. FLO to Charles Loring Brace, 21 December 1863, in Brace, *Life of Charles Loring Brace*, p. 262.

35. Schelling, *Philosophy of Art*, p. 20.

36. Coleridge, *Shakespearean Criticism*, 2:84–85, 91, 92, 218–19.

37. Samuel Taylor Coleridge, *Miscellaneous Criticism*, Thomas M. Raysor, ed. (Cambridge: Harvard University Press, 1936), pp. 164–65.

38. Carlyle, *Works*, vol. 5: *On Heroes, Hero-Worship and the Heroic in History*, pp. 80–81, 104, 106.

39. Emerson, *Complete Works*, 2:360.

40. "He must work in the spirit in which we conceive a prophet to speak, or an angel of the Lord to act." (Ibid., 7:48.)

41. Ruskin, *Works*, 4:42.

42. Ibid., 4:211.

43. Goethe, *Literary Essays*, p. 57.

44. Quoted in Gray-Smith, *God in the Philosophy of Schelling*, p. 44.

45. Ibid., p. 32. See also Watson, *Schelling's Transcendental Idealism*, chap. 7.

46. Coleridge, *Biographia Literaria*, 2:253.

47. Coleridge asserts that the mystery of genius in the fine arts consists in the artist's ability to focus his mind upon the scattered images of nature and "place these images totalized and fitted to the limits of the human mind, as to elicit from and superinduce upon, the forms themselves the moral reflexions to which they approximate, to make the external internal, the internal external, to make nature thought, and thought nature." (Ibid., 2:258.) In his analysis and summation of the creative process George Herbert Mead approximates Coleridge's formulation. Mead observes that in artistic invention the artist "discovers himself, discovers his own idea in the materials with which he is working." It is in the mind of the artist that the world achieves an organization. "He has discovered in it that unity and organization which belong to himself. He has discovered in it the sensations which are his own . . ." and in so doing identifies himself with nature, giving unity and meaning to it through his artistic creation. (George Herbert Mead, *Movements of Thought in the Nineteenth Century*, Merritt H. Moore, ed. [Chicago: University of Chicago Press, 1936], pp. 124–26.)

48. Coleridge, *Biographia Literaria*, 2:254–55.

49. Samuel Taylor Coleridge, *Letters of Samuel Taylor Coleridge*, Ernest Hartley Coleridge, ed., 2 vols. (Boston: Houghton Mifflin Co., 1895), 1:352, 2:450.

50. Emerson, *Complete Works*, 1:23; Emerson, *Journals*, 4:253.

51. I have followed Abram's discussion of "The Poem as Heterocosm" in *Mirror and the Lamp*, pp. 272–85. I have broadened the application from literary creativity to art generally and will presently apply the conception to Olmsted's landscape architecture.

52. Thomas Hobbes, *Leviathan or the Matter, Forme and Power of a Commonwealth, Ecclesiastical and Civil,* Michael Oakeshott, ed. (New York: Crowell-Collier, 1962), p. 98.

53. Olmsted, *Forty Years,* 2:239n.

54. Ibid., 2:474.

55. Olmsted, *Mount Royal,* p. 51, Sutton, p. 212.

56. FLO to Mariana Griswold Van Rensselaer, 22 May 1893. Olmsted Papers.

57. Olmsted, *Forty Years,* 2:321n.

58. Ibid., 2:430.

59. Ibid., 2:139, 275, 562.

60. Olmsted, *Mount Royal,* pp. 33–35, Sutton, pp. 207–8.

61. Carlyle, *Sartor,* 1:175. Coleridge declared that the artist "discourses to us by symbols—the *Naturgeist,* or spirit of nature." (Coleridge, *Biographia Literaria,* 2:259.) For a discussion of the importance of the symbol for Emerson see Matthiessen, *American Renaissance,* pp. 1–175 passim; Hopkins, *Spires of Form,* pp. 121–34. Wellek examines the uses of the symbol among the German writers. (*History of Modern Criticism,* 1:210–12, 249–52, 2:42–45, 76.) See also Harrold, *Carlyle and German Thought,* pp. 103–8.

62. Olmsted, *Forty Years,* 2:426; FLO to Mariana Griswold Van Rensselaer, 22 May 1893. Olmsted Papers.

63. FLO to Board of Commissioners of the Central Park, 22 January 1861, reprinted in Beveridge, Schuyler, 3:304.

64. Olmsted, *Forty Years,* 2:407–8.

65. Mead, *Movements of Thought,* pp. 124–26.

66. Frederick Law Olmsted, "The Yosemite Valley and the Mariposa Big Trees: A Preliminary Report (1865)," with an introductory note by Laura Wood Roper, *Landscape Architecture* 43 (October 1952), p. 21.

67. Olmsted, *Mount Royal,* p. 22.

68. Ibid., p. 29. See also Olmsted, "Yosemite Valley," p. 20.

69. Charles Eliot Norton to Frederick Law Olmsted, 23 October 1881. Olmsted Papers.

70. Emerson, *Complete Works,* 3:30. See also Hopkins, *Spires of Form,* pp. 147–52. Kern points out that for Emerson the product of creative thought was not complete in itself; it is the beginning. The audience must be kept in the artist's mind as well. (Kern, "Rise of Transcendentalism," p. 294.)

71. Emerson, *Complete Works,* 3:15.

72. Olmsted fully realized the commercial value of the eight hundred acres of Central Park. He accurately predicted that the park would become valuable real estate as Manhattan grew around it.

73. Roper, *FLO,* p. 435.

74. Windelband, *Renaissance, Enlightenment, Modern*, pp. 600–611, 665.

75. "It is, therefore, one of the most important tasks of education to subject man to form even in his purely physical life, and to make him aesthetic in every domain over which beauty is capable of extending her sway, since it is only out of the aesthetic, not out of the physical, state that the moral can develop." (Friedrich Schiller, *On the Aesthetic Education of Man in a Series of Letters*, Elizabeth M. Wilkinson and L. A. Willoughby, eds. and trans. (Oxford: Clarendon Press, 1967), pp. 165, 167, 169.)

76. Carlyle, *Sartor*, 1:181–83; Carlyle, *On Heroes*, 5:155–57. See also Harrold, *Carlyle and German Thought*, pp. 192–93.

77. Olmsted, *Forty Years*, 2:61, 175–76, 426. This is a recurrent theme in his writings on parks.

78. Buffalo Park Commission, *Preliminary Report*, p. 15.

79. Emerson says that the spectator gains insight into the "universal mind" through the artist. Emerson, *Complete Works*, 7:49. "The poet, as the romantic critics liked to say, repeats in the finite the creative process of the Infinite Creator, and is the agent of that Creator." (Foerster, *American Criticism*, p. 63.)

80. *New York Daily Times*, 30 June 1853, reprinted in Beveridge, McLaughlin and Schuyler, 2:177, 178.

81. Frederick Law Olmsted, *Walks and Talks of an American Farmer in England*, rev. ed. (Columbus, Ohio: Jos. H. Riley & Co., 1859), p. 276.

82. Coleridge, *Biographia Literaria*, 2:10, 105, 224.

83. Olmsted, *Forty Years*, 2:427n, 489.

84. Olmsted, *Notes on Franklin Park*, p. 42, Sutton, p. 243. It would seem that for Olmsted the artificial constructions of the city had little to offer in opportunities for aesthetic gratification.

85. Olmsted, *Forty Years*, 2:426, 489.

86. Emerson, *Complete Works*, 1:10.

87. Hopkins, *Spires of Form*, pp. 162–68. See also Matthiessen, *American Renaissance*, pp. 50–52.

88. Hough, *Last Romantics*, pp. 8–14.

89. Olmsted, Vaux & Co., "Sixth Annual Report, 1866," [Prospect Park] *Annual Reports of the Brooklyn Park Commissioners, 1861–1873* (January, 1873), p. 115, reprinted in Albert Fein, ed., *Landscape into Cityscape, Frederic Law Olmsted's Plans for Greater New York City* (Ithaca, N.Y.: Cornell University Press, 1968), pp. 124–25. Cited hereafter as Fein.

90. Olmsted, *Forty Years*, 2:474.

91. Olmsted, "Yosemite Valley," p. 20.

92. Olmsted, *Forty Years*, 2:426. See also ibid., 1:61, 175–76, 408.

93. Ibid., 2:176.

94. Buffalo Park Commission, *Preliminary Report*, pp. 16–18.

95. Friederich Schiller, *The Works of Friederich Schiller,* vol. 4: *Poems and Essays,* Household Edition (Chicago: Belford, Clarke & Co., n.d.), p. 130.

96. Olmsted, *Forty Years,* 2:435–36.

97. Coleridge, *Biographia Literaria,* 2:257.

98. Schelling, "Allgemeine Deduktion des Dynamischen Processes," *Sämmtliche Werke* I, 4:77–78, quoted in Bolman, *Ages of the World,* p. 14.

99. Olmsted, *Mount Royal,* pp. 22–23.

100. FLO to Mariana Van Rensselaer, 11 June 1893. Olmsted Papers.

101. Olmsted, *Forty Years,* 2:356.

102. Emerson, *Complete Works,* 1:43. Emerson only restates a cardinal principal of Coleridge's aesthetic theory: beauty consists of "multëity in unity" (Coleridge, "On the Principles of Genial Criticism Concerning the Fine Arts," in *Biographia Literaria,* 2:230). Unity in the sense it is used by the romantic idealists is not merely formal, but organic. The interdependent parts are necessary for the coexistence of the parts. (Coleridge, "Theory of Life" as Appendix C in *Complete Works,* 1:388–91.)

103. Olmsted, *Mount Royal,* pp. 22–24.

104. Olmsted, "Public Parks and the Enlargement of Towns," p. 24, Sutton, p. 82.

105. Olmsted, *Forty Years,* 2:249, 489.

106. Olmsted, Vaux & Co., "Sixth Annual Report, 1866," [Prospect Park] *Brooklyn Park Commissioners,* pp. 93, 94–95, Fein, pp. 98, 100–101. See also Olmsted, *Forty Years,* 2:46, 249, 250.

107. Olmsted, "Public Parks and the Enlargement of Towns," p. 24, Sutton, p. 82. Olmsted, *Forty Years,* 2:394–97. Olmsted echoed John Ruskin whom he quotes for support: "Your iron railing always means thieves outside or Bedlam inside. It *can* mean nothing else than that. If the people outside were good for anything, a hint in the way of fence would be good enough for them; but because they are violent and at enmity with you, you are forced to put the close bars and the spikes at top." (Ibid., 2:396.)

108. Olmsted, *Forty Years,* 2:252–53; Olmsted, *Mount Royal,* pp. 23–24; Olmsted, *Notes on Franklin Park,* p. 106, Sutton, pp. 259–61. In a commentary on Wordsworth poetry Pottle declares that Wordsworth "always connected deeply imaginative effects with the sense of infinity." (Frederick A. Pottle, "The Eye and the Object in the Poetry of Wordsworth," *Romanticism and Consciousness, Essays in Criticism,* Harold Bloom, ed. [New York: W. W. Norton & Co., 1970], p. 294.)

109. Olmsted, *Notes on Franklin Park,* pp. 32–36, 41, 43–44, 45–46, Sutton, pp. 236–40, 242–48. See also Frederick Law Olmsted, "The Justifying Value of a Public Park," *Journal of Social Science,* no. 12, pt. 1 (Boston: A. Williams & Co.; New York: G. P. Putnam's Sons, for the American Social Science Association, 1880), pp. 160–61. For a recent defense of the small, urban or "vest-pocket" parks see Thomas P. F. Hoving, "Thinking Big about Small Parks," *New York Times Magazine,* 10 April 1966, p. 12.

Chapter 5

1. Roper, *FLO,* p. 408.

2. F. L. Olmsted and Calvert Vaux, *Description of Design for the Central Park* (Doc. No. 17), p. 23.

3.   Ruskin, *Works,* 12:419–20.

4.   Ibid., 7:255, 8:236–37; 6:9, 20–21, 25–26. See also Ladd, *Victorian Morality,* pp. 136–37.

5.   Ruskin, *Works,* 3:626–28.

6.   Ibid., 4:171.

7.   Ibid., 3:627–28 and n. Ruskin allows a feeble exception to this primitivism; he grants to man the right to interfere in this process for the purpose of providing for his sustenance.

8.   Olmsted, *Mount Royal,* p. 33, Sutton, p. 207.

9.   Ibid., p. 34, Sutton, p. 208.

10.   Ibid., p. 43.

11.   Ibid.

12.   Olmsted, "Justifying Value of a Public Park," p. 163.

13.   Ruskin, *Works,* 4:64.

14.   Ibid., 4:210. See also Ladd, *Victorian Morality,* pp. 191–98; Hough, *The Last Romantics,* pp. 11–12, 30.

15.   Ruskin, *Works,* 4:211–12.

16.   Ibid., 4:64.

17.   Olmsted, Vaux & Co., "Sixth Annual Report, 1866" [Prospect Park], *Brooklyn Park Commissioners,* p. 101, reprinted in Fein, p. 108; Olmsted, *Forty Years,* 2:239 and n.

18.   Olmsted, *Forty Years,* 2:249, 250.

19.   Olmsted, "Public Parks and the Enlargement of Towns," p. 23, reprinted in Sutton, p. 81.

20.   Ruskin, *Works,* 3:427.

21.   Uvedale Price, *On the Picturesque, with an Essay on the Origin of Taste by Thomas Dick Lauder* (Edinburgh: Caldwell, Lloyd & Co., 1842), pp. 112–13, 115.

22.   Ibid., p. 115.

23.   Walter J. Bate, *From Classic to Romantic: Premises of Taste in Eighteenth-Century England* (New York: Harper & Bros., 1961), pp. 148–51.

24.   Price, *On the Picturesque,* pp. 105, 116.

25.   Ibid., p. 461.

26.   FLO to John Olmsted, 2 February 1845. Olmsted Papers, reprinted in McLaughlin and Beveridge, 1:203.

27.   Emerson, *Letters of R. W. Emerson,* 2:331 and n., 355; Sherman Paul, *Emerson's Angle of Vision* (Cambridge: Harvard University Press, 1952), pp. 198, 255n, 21; Henry Seidel Canby, *Thoreau* (Boston: Houghton Mifflin Co., 1939), pp. 206, 470–71. See also Matthiessen, *American Renaissance,* p. 77.

28.   Johann Georg von Zimmermann, *Solitude,* 2 vols. (London, 1798), 2:308–9.

29. Ibid., 1:61.

30. Ibid., 2:313, 315.

31. Ibid., 1:99.

32. Ibid., 1:102. The English garden was a new art form recently imported into Germany in Zimmermann's time. Ibid., 1:104.

33. Ibid., 1:5–6, 34, 50, 104–7; 2:31, 135, 144–45, 325–26.

34. Ibid., 1:132–33.

35. Ibid., 1:62–63.

36. Ruskin, *Works,* 4:173.

37. Ibid., 4:116–17.

38. *American Cyclopaedia,* 1881 ed., s.v. "Park" by Frederick Law Olmsted.

39. Olmsted, *Forty Years,* 2:407–8, 523–29.

40. Olmsted, "Public Parks and the Enlargement of Towns," p. 23, Sutton, p. 81.

41. Olmsted, *Forty Years,* 2:45.

42. Ibid., 2:218. See Henry Hope Reed and Sophia Duckworth, *Central Park, A History and a Guide* (New York: C. N. Potter, 1967).

43. Olmsted, Vaux & Co., "Sixth Annual Report, 1866," [Prospect Park], *Annual Reports of the Brooklyn Park Commissioners,* p. 98; Fein, pp. 104–5.

44. Coleridge, *Biographia Literaria,* 2:232, 262.

45. Ibid., 2:255–58.

46. Olmsted, *Mount Royal,* pp. 42, 43.

47. Olmsted, *Forty Years,* 2:145.

48. Compare with Emerson's aesthetic doctrine in Hopkins, *Spires of Form,* pp. 66–69.

49. Olmsted, *Mount Royal,* p. 43.

50. Ibid., p. 34, Sutton, p. 208.

51. Ibid., p. 37.

52. Olmsted, Vaux & Co., *Preliminary Report upon the Proposed Suburban Village at Riverside, near Chicago* (New York: Sutton, Brown & Co., 1868), pp. 7, 26–28, Sutton, pp. 295, 303–4.

53. Frederick Law Olmsted and J. James R. Croes, *I. Preliminary Report of the Landscape Architect and the Civil and Topographical Engineer, upon the Laying Out of the Twenty-third and Twenty-fourth Wards; II. Report of the Landscape Architect and the Civil and Topographical Engineer, Accompanying a Plan for Laying Out That Part of the Twenty-fourth Ward, Lying West of Riverdale Road* (New York City: Board of the Department of Public Parks, Document No. 72, 20 December 1876); J. James R. Croes and Frederick Law Olmsted, *Report of the Civil and Topographical Engineer and the Landscape Architect, Accompanying a Plan for Local Steam Transit Routes in*

the Twenty-third and Twenty-fourth Wards (New York City: Board of the Department of Public Parks, Document No. 75, 21 March 1877), Fein, pp. 349–82.

54. Olmsted, Vaux & Co., "Report of the Landscape Architects and Superintendents, 1 January 1868, "*Annual Reports of the Brooklyn Commissioners, 1861–1873* (January 1873), pp. 187–89, Fein, pp. 146–49.

55. Ibid., pp. 116, 117, 197–98, Fein, pp. 126–27, 158–60; Olmsted, *Notes on Franklin Park,* pp. 33–35, Sutton, pp. 236–41; Frederick Law Olmsted, "Report of the Landscape Architect Advisory," published as an appendix to City of Boston Department of Parks, *Thirteenth Annual Report of the Board of Commissioners of Parks for the Year 1887* (Boston, 1888), pp. 63–70 and especially the accompanying map.

56. Olmsted, *Forty Years,* 2:250–51.

57. Olmsted, *Notes on Franklin Park,* p. 107, Sutton, p. 262.

58. Olmsted, *Forty Years,* 2:214. See also Olmsted, *Mount Royal,* p. 74.

59. Olmsted asserts that to achieve "this most important purpose in the scenery of Central Park" required "much more labor and a larger expenditure than any other landscape feature of the undertaking." (Olmsted, *Forty Years,* 2:239–40n., 495.) Tunnard and Pushkarev claim that "human beings have some physiological needs which can be satisfied only by open space." (Christopher Tunnard and Boris Pushkarev, *Man-Made America: Chaos or Control? An Inquiry into Selected Problems of Design in the Urbanized Landscape* (New Haven: Yale University Press, 1963), p. 359.) The authors support Olmsted's aesthetic principles with their assertion: "Beyond the conceptual requirements, we know that a view of space in nature must give satisfaction in some of the basic ways in which any beautiful object satisfies." (Ibid., p. 363.) See their discussion on the aesthetics of open space (ibid., pp. 361–87).

60. Olmsted, *Forty Years,* 2:250–51.

61. Ibid., 2:250.

62. Ibid. See also Olmsted, *Mount Royal,* pp. 40, 61–62, Sutton, pp. 216–19 (in part).

63. Ruskin, *Works,* 4:88, 106.

64. Olmsted, *Mount Royal,* pp. 58–59, Sutton, p. 214.

65. Ibid.

66. Ibid., p. 25.

67. Ibid., p. 35, Sutton, p. 208.

68. Olmsted compares the contour of his roads to the natural course of a flowing stream. Ibid., p. 32, Sutton, pp. 205–6.

69. Ibid., p. 75.

70. Ibid., p. 74.

71. Frederick Law Olmsted to William A. Stiles, 10 March 1895, in Charles McLaughlin, "Selected Letters of Frederick Law Olmsted" (Ph.D. dissertation, Harvard University, 1960), p. 450.

72. Ibid., pp. 450–51.

73. Olmsted, Vaux & Co., "Sixth Annual Report, 1866," [Prospect Park], *Annual Reports of the Brooklyn Park Commissioners,* p. 63, Fein, p. 98.

Chapter 6

1. *American Cyclopaedia,* 1881 ed., s.v. "Park" by Frederick Law Olmsted.

2. Olmsted, Vaux & Co., "Report of the Landscape Architects and Superintendents, 1 January 1868," *Annual Reports of the Brooklyn Park Commissioners,* p. 187, Fein, pp. 146–47.

3. Ibid. See also Olmsted, "Public Parks and the Enlargement of Towns," p. 10, Sutton, p. 64.

4. Olmsted, Vaux & Co., "Report of the Landscape Architects and Superintendents, 1 January 1868, "*Annual Reports of the Brooklyn Park Commissioners,* p. 189, Fein, p. 148.

5. Olmsted, "Public Parks and the Enlargement of Towns," p. 11, Sutton, p. 65.

6. Ibid.

7. Olmsted, "Justifying Value of a Public Park," p. 163.

8. Olmsted, "Yosemite Valley," pp. 17, 20, 21.

9. Ibid.

10. Olmsted, *Forty Years,* 1:49–50.

11. Ibid., 1:50.

12. Ferdinand Tönnies, *Community and Society,* Charles P. Loomis, trans. and ed. (New York: Harper & Row, 1963), p. 119.

13. Ibid., p. 35.

14. Ibid., pp. 225–33.

15. Ibid., p. 143.

16. Ibid., p. 120. Tönnies' book, *Gemeinschaft und Gesellschaft,* was originally published in 1887.

17. Olmsted, "Public Parks and the Enlargement of Towns," p. 11, Sutton, pp. 63, 66.

18. Ibid.

19. Ibid.

20. Olmsted, *Seaboard Slave States,* pp. 504–10, 515–23, 537–40; Olmsted, *Back Country,* pp. 197–200, 216, 219, 224–25, 295, 297–98.

21. Olmsted, "Yosemite Valley," p. 20.

22. Schiller, *Aesthetic Education,* p. 33.

23. Ibid., p. 39.

24. Olmsted, "Public Parks and the Enlargement of Towns," pp. 6–7, Sutton, p. 59.

25. Olmsted was acquainted with Schiller's writings. Olmsted's biographer notes that

Olmsted had read Schiller's dramatic works (Roper, *FLO*, p. 54). It was likely that Olmsted had discussed Schiller's writings with his acquaintance and learned, German-educated neighbor, Judge William Emerson, Ralph Waldo Emerson's brother. Upon his return from Germany, where he had interviewed Goethe, William Emerson gave a series of lectures in New York on German literary figures. Morever, during his travels in the Southwest in 1854, Olmsted writes of his discussions with the German settlers of New Braunfels and Sisterdale in Texas. In his letter to the *New York Daily Times* Olmsted expressed the pleasure he enjoyed in his discussions of Schiller and Schleiermacher and Hegel with the settlers. (Beveridge, McLaughlin, and Schuyler, 2:278.)

There is further evidence of Olmsted's familiarity with Schiller's writings. Among the volumes in his library Olmsted possessed works by Schiller as well as other exponents of German ideal philosophy. I am indebted to Charles E. Beveridge, one of the editors of *The Papers of Frederick Law Olmsted*, for graciously providing me with the list of books belonging to Olmsted's library.

26. Olmsted, "Public Parks and the Enlargement of Towns," p. 10, Sutton, p. 64.

27. Ibid.

28. Olmsted, *Forty Years*, pp. 75–83.

29. Olmsted, *Seaboard Slave States*, p. 714.

30. John Stuart Mill, *Collected Works of John Stuart Mill*, vols. 2, 3: *Principles of Political Economy with Some of Their Applications to Social Philosophy*, J. M. Robson, ed. (Toronto: University of Toronto Press, 1965), 2:174.

31. Ibid., 2:130, 142–43, 173–83.

32. Olmsted, *Back Country*, p. 311. See also Mill, *Principles of Political Economy*, 2:120–22; 3:965.

33. Ibid., 2:120, 3:708.

34. Olmsted was also indebted to Mill for the support he found in Mill's position on slave labor. According to Mill "it remains certain that slavery is incompatible with any high state of the arts of life, and any great efficiency of labor." (Ibid., 2:247, 249.) Mill contended that free labor is more efficient than slave labor. This view of the slave economy of the South pervades Olmsted's analysis in the three volumes of his *Our Slave States*. (Olmsted, *Seaboard Slave States*, pp. 296–97, 490–91; Olmsted, *Back Country*, pp. 288–90 and n.)

Olmsted showed his admiration and indebtedness by dedicating to Mill *The Cotton Kingdom*, a synthesis of his trilogy on the *Slave States*. In his dedication Olmsted wrote, "I beg you to accept the dedication of this book as an indication of the honour in which your services in the cause of moral and political freedom are held in America, and as a grateful acknowledgement of personal obligations to them on the part of your obedient servant, The Author." (Frederick Law Olmsted, *The Cotton Kingdom, A Traveller's Observations on Cotton and Slavery in the American Slave States*, Arthur M. Schlesinger, ed. (New York: Alfred A. Knopf, 1962), p. lix.)

In his turn Mill favorably acknowledged Olmsted's work on slave labor in the later editions of *The Principles of Political Economy* (1865). Olmsted's analysis of slave labor was also noticed by Marx in *Capital*. (Karl Marx, *Capital, A Critique of Political*

Economy, Frederick Engels, ed., Samuel Moore and Edward Aveling, trans. The Modern Library (New York: Random House, n.d.), p. 219n.)

35. Frederick Law Olmsted, "The Beginning of Central Park: A Fragment of Autobiography (ca. 1877)" with an Introductory Note by his Son, Frederick Law Olmsted, Jr., *Landscape Architecture* 2 (July 1912), p. 152.

36. Olmsted, "Public Parks and the Enlargement of Towns," pp. 8–9, Sutton, p. 62.

37. Olmsted, "Justifying Value of a Public Park," p. 162.

38. Ibid.

39. Ibid., p. 163.

40. Ibid., p. 152.

41. Ibid., p. 163.

42. Ibid., pp. 152–53.

43. Olmsted, *Forty Years,* 2:46.

44. Ibid., 2:45, 97, 248. See also "Public Parks and the Enlargement of Towns," p. 31, reprinted in Sutton, p. 92.

45. Olmsted, *Mount Royal,* p. 22.

46. Ibid., p. 23.

47. William Wordsworth, *The Poetical Works of William Wordsworth,* E. de Selincourt, ed., 5 vols. (Oxford: Clarendon Press, 1940–1949), 2:389.

48. Buffalo Park Commission, *Preliminary Report,* p. 15; Olmsted "Yosemite Valley," p. 21; Olmsted, *Mount Royal,* p. 63, Sutton, p. 219.

49. Olmsted, *Forty Years,* 2:34–35.

50. Olmsted, *Cotton Kingdom,* p. 621. This passage is excerpted from one of the dispatches (12 January 1854) on Southern slavery which Olmsted wrote for the *New York Daily Times.* Reprinted in Beveridge, McLaughlin and Schuyler, 2:244.

51. Olmsted, "Yosemite Valley," p. 17.

52. Ibid., p. 20.

53. Ibid., pp. 20–21.

54. Olmsted extends this doctrine of the reconciliation of complementary opposites from the internal psyche to the external physical and social environments. His aim was to counteract the physical restraints, the density, and the tumult of the commercial city with the freedom, spaciousness, and repose of the park; the impersonal, self-regarding, alienating, calculating attitudes of the mass society with the soft, cooperative, communal, loving sentiments of the village life of his remembrance.

55. Friedrich von Schiller, *Naive and Sentimental Poetry and On the Sublime,* Julius A. Elias, trans. (New York: Frederick Ungar, 1966), p. 171.

56. Olmsted, *Notes on Franklin Park,* p. 106, Sutton, pp. 259–61.

57. Olmsted, *Mount Royal,* pp. 22–24.

58. Olmsted, *Notes on Franklin Park,* pp. 46–47.

59. Olmsted, *Mount Royal,* p. 22.

60. Ibid.

61. Olmsted, Vaux & Co., "Sixth Annual Report, 1866," [Prospect Park], *Brooklyn Park Commissioners,* p. 93, Fein, p. 98.

62. Olmsted, "Yosemite Valley," p. 20.

63. Schiller, *On the Aesthetic Education of Man,* p. 107. For Schiller's conception of the play drive and for comparison with Olmsted's view of recreation see pp. 95–107, 141–43, 163–69.

64. Olmsted, "Public Parks and the Enlargement of Towns," p. 24, Sutton, p. 82.

65. Olmsted, *Cotton Kingdom,* p. 620.

66. Olmsted, "Public Parks and the Enlargement of Towns," p. 22, Sutton, p. 80.

67. Olmsted, *Notes on Franklin Park,* p. 94.

68. Olmsted, "Public Parks and the Enlargement of Towns," p. 22, Sutton, p. 79.

69. Ibid., p. 17, Sutton, p. 73.

70. Olmsted, *Forty Years,* 2:407.

71. Ibid., 2:474.

72. Ibid., 2:407.

73. Ibid., 2:45.

74. Olmsted, "Public Parks and the Enlargement of Towns," p. 18, Sutton, pp. 74–75.

75. Ibid., pp. 18–19.

76. Ibid., p. 20, Sutton, p. 77.

77. Ibid.

78. Triggs, *Changing Order,* pp. 200–201.

79. Franz Neumann, *The Democratic and the Authoritarian State, Essays in Political and Legal Theory,* Herbert Marcuse, ed. (New York: Crowell-Collier, Free Press of Glencoe, 1964), pp. 271–72.

80. Olmsted had a high regard for the architecture of H. H. Richardson. Richardson created a new architectural form that signaled a unique advance in American architecture.

81. In contrast to the glittering array of formal buildings, Olmsted's emphasis was on the site of the Fair—Lake Michigan; he thought its "purely natural beauty" would be instructive to the public. (Frederick Law Olmsted to Clarence Pullen, 7 January 1891. Olmsted Papers. See also Roper, *FLO,* p. 427.) Henry Adams considered the architecture of the Chicago Fair to be "a breach of continuity—a rupture in historical sequence." (Henry Adams, *The Education of Henry Adams,* Modern Library [New York: Random House, 1931], p. 340.) After his enthusiasm for the Fair, Olmsted's friend, Charles Eliot Norton, upon reconsideration, averred that only Olmsted's land-

scape planning was praiseworthy; the buildings mirrored the ingenuity and the un-cultivated tastes of a wealthy, immature people. (Kermit Vanderbilt, *Charles Eliot Norton: Apostle of Culture in a Democracy* [Cambridge: Harvard University Press, 1959], p. 203.) Commager claims that the Fair "condemned American architecture to the imitative and the derivative for another generation." (Henry Steele Commager, *The American Mind; An Interpretation of American Thought and Character since the 1880's* [New Haven: Yale University Press, Yale Paperbound, 1959], p. 394.)

82. FLO to Daniel Burnham, 2 October 1893. Olmsted Papers.

83. FLO to William A. Stiles, 10 March 1895. Olmsted Papers.

84. Schiller, *Naive and Sentimental Poetry*, p. 106.

85. Ibid., pp. 111–12, 116.

86. Ibid., pp. 146–51.

87. Ibid., p. 153.

88. Ibid., pp. 154–55 and n.

89. Olmsted, *Mount Royal*, p. 30, Sutton, p. 204.

90. [Frederick Law Olmsted], "Country Living," a review of *The Woods and By-Ways of New England*, by Wilson Flagg and *Landscape Architecture* by H. W. S. Cleveland, in *The Nation* (22 January 1874): 64–65. In the same review Olmsted praised Cleve-land's book. In contrast to Flagg, Cleveland, a landscape architect Olmsted respected, asserted the case for rational planning to provide healthy, pleasurable conditions for country living.

91. Peter J. Schmitt, *Back to Nature; The Arcadian Myth in Urban America* (New York: Oxford University Press, 1969), pp. xviii, 188; George B. Tobey, Jr., *A History of Landscape Architecture* (New York: American Elsevier Co., 1973), pp. 18, 173.

92. For portrayals of barbarism see Olmsted's descriptions of degenerate living among whites in the South and the southwestern frontier in Olmsted, *Seaboard Slave States*, pp. 504–10, 523; Olmsted, *Journey through Texas*, pp. 382–85; Olmsted, *Back Country*, pp. 118–19 and n., 122–24. Olmsted's low regard for America's "noble savage" living in the innocence of the state of nature can be ascertained from his acid account of the Indian tribes he observed in the West. Olmsted, *Journey through Texas*, pp. 288–98.

93. Schiller, *Naive and Sentimental Poetry*, p. 175.

94. Ibid., p. 153.

Chapter 7

1. In 1868 the Commissioners of Prospect Park, Brooklyn, New York commissioned the firm of Olmsted, Vaux & Co. to plan a suburban subdivision adjacent to Prospect Park. In the same year the firm was employed by a private developer, The Riverside Improvement Company, Riverside, Illinois, to design a new town near Chicago.

2. Olmsted, "Justifying Value of a Public Park," pp. 152–53, 163.

3. Olmsted, "Public Parks and the Enlargement of Towns," pp. 4–5, 10, Sutton, pp. 56–57, 64.

4. Ibid., p. 10.

5. Olmsted, Vaux & Co., "Report of the Landscape Architects and Superintendents, 1 January 1868," *Brooklyn Park Commissioners,* p. 187, Fein, p. 147.

6. Ibid., p. 192, Fein, p. 153.

7. Olmsted, *Notes on Franklin Park,* p. 90, 92–93, Sutton, p. 252.

8. Ibid.

9. Ibid., p. 91; Olmsted, Vaux & Co., "Report of the Landscape Architects and Superintendents, 1 January 1868," *Brooklyn Park Commissioners,* p. 187, Fein, p. 147; Olmsted, "Public Parks and the Enlargement of Towns," p. 8, Sutton, p. 61.

10. Olmsted, *Notes on Franklin Park,* p. 90, Sutton, p. 250.

11. Ibid., p. 91, Sutton, p. 251.

12. Olmsted, Vaux & Co., "Report of the Landscape Architects and Superintendents, 1 January 1868," *Brooklyn Park Commissioners,* p. 178, Fein, p. 135.

13. Ibid.

14. Ibid., p. 179, Fein, p. 137.

15. Ibid.

16. Ibid., p. 180, Fein, p. 137.

17. Ibid., p. 184, Fein, p. 143.

18. While Olmsted gives no sources for his historical analysis, he seems to have derived much of his illustrative material from John Stow's *Survey of London.* He also closely followed the history of London's development described in *London,* a six-volume work edited by Charles Knight and published in 1851. See especially the following articles therein: Charles Knight, "Clean Your Honorin's Shoes," vol. 1, pp. 17–32, and "Suburban Milestones," vol. 1, pp. 248–56; J. Sanders, "The Monument," vol. 1, pp. 441–42; W. Weir, "The Building of St. Paul's," vol. 2, pp. 5–6.

19. Olmsted, Vaux & Co., "Report of the Landscape Architects and Superintendents, 1 January 1868," *Brooklyn Park Commissioners,* p. 184, Fein, p. 143.

20. Queen Elizabeth's proclamation of 1581, for example, forbade the construction of any new buildings within three miles of London except those suitable for the residence of the gentry.

21. Olmsted, Vaux & Co., "Report of the Landscape Architects and Superintendents, 1 January 1868," *Brooklyn Park Commissioners,* p. 182, Fein, p. 140.

22. There can be no doubt that in relation to New York City and concerning his own proposals for city planning Olmsted believed himself to be precisely in Wren's position. See also Olmsted, "Public Parks and the Enlargement of Towns," pp. 12–13, Sutton, p. 67.

23. Olmsted, Vaux & Co., "Report of the Landscape Architects and Superintendents, 1 January 1868," *Brooklyn Park Commissioners,* p. 183, Fein, p. 142.

24. Ibid., p. 185, Fein, p. 144. See also Jay B. Botsford, *English Society in the Eighteenth Century, as Influenced from Oversea* (New York: Macmillan Co., 1924), pp. 194–98.

25. Olmsted, Vaux & Co., "Report of the Landscape Architects and Superintendents, 1 January 1868," *Brooklyn Park Commissioners,* p. 185, Fein, p. 144.

26. Ibid., p. 186, Fein, p. 145.

27. Ibid., p. 187, Fein, p. 146.

28. Ibid., Fein, pp. 146–47.

29. Ibid., pp. 189–90, Fein, pp. 149–50.

30. M. Dorothy George, *London Life in the XVIII Century* (London: Kegan Paul, Trench, Trubner & Co., 1925), pp. 94–95.

31. Ibid. See also Botsford, *English Society,* pp. 191–94; Lewis Mumford, *The City in History: Its Origins, Its Transformations, and Its Prospects* (New York: Harcourt, Brace & World, 1961), pp. 487–89.

32. Olmsted, Vaux & Co., "Report of the Landscape Architects and Superintendents, 1 January 1868," *Brooklyn Park Commissioners,* p. 190, Fein, p. 150.

33. Ibid., p. 188, Fein, p. 147. Olmsted's analysis is partly correct. In his emphasis upon the morphology of the city he neglects (but he was not unaware of) the fact that socio-economic status combined with life style also plays a role in determining mortality, morbidity, and crime rates.

34. Ibid., p. 190, Fein, p. 150.

35. Ibid., p. 191–92, Fein, p. 152.

36. Olmsted, "Public Parks and the Enlargement of Towns," p. 14, Sutton, p. 69. For supporting evidence to Olmsted's observations for Manhattan see *Boss Tweed's New York,* pp. 12–17. See also Mumford, *City in History,* pp. 429–31; George Rogers Taylor, "The Beginnings of Mass Transportation in Urban America," *Smithsonian Journal of History,* 1 (Summer and Autumn, 1966), pp. 31–52.

37. It was not until the latter part of the nineteenth century that New York, Boston, London and Paris developed intracity transportation facilities that met in any satisfactory way the needs of their inhabitants—first with horse-drawn street cars and later both elevated and underground rapid transit services. For American cities see Mandelbaum, *Boss Tweed's New York,* pp. 102, 123–25; John Anderson Miller, *Fares Please! From Horse-Cars to Streamliners* (New York: D. Appleton-Century Co., 1941), passim; Constance McLaughlin Green, *The Rise of Urban America* (New York: Harper & Row, 1965), pp. 78, 115–17.

38. Olmsted, Vaux & Co., "Report of the Landscape Architects and Superintendents, 1 January 1868," *Brooklyn Park Commissioners,* pp. 196–97, Fein, pp. 157–58.

39. Olmsted, "Public Parks and the Enlargement of Towns," p. 10, Sutton, pp. 64–65.

40. Olmsted, Vaux & Co., "Report of the Landscape Architects and Superintendents, 1 January 1868," *Brooklyn Park Commissioners,* p. 187, Fein, p. 147.

41. Olmsted, "Justifying Value of a Public Park," p. 160.

42. Olmsted, Vaux & Co., "Report of the Landscape Architects and Superintendents, 1 January 1868," *Brooklyn Park Commissioners*, p. 187, Fein, p. 147.

43. Olmsted, "Public Parks and the Enlargement of Towns," p. 13, Sutton, p. 67.

44. Olmsted, Vaux & Co., "Report of the Landscape Architects and Superintendents, 1 January 1868," *Brooklyn Park Commissioners*, p. 188, Fein, p. 147.

45. Ibid., p. 189, Fein, pp. 148–49.

46. Olmsted, "Public Parks and the Enlargement of Towns," p. 13, Sutton, p. 68.

47. Ibid., p. 25, Sutton, p. 84.

48. Fein, "American City," pp. 86–87. During the late eighteenth and the nineteenth centuries it was not uncommon for philosophers and historians to describe the evolution of civilization in terms of laws of progress or improvement. Stages or epochs of progressive development were devices used (and still are) to mark discrete historic periods. This was characteristic of utopian thought. Examples of the use of the stage hypothesis of emergent evolution are found in the following utopians. Condorcet described ten periods of humanity's progress to achieve the ideal society. Saint Simon declared that civilization would reach its highest stage in five periods of transition. Comte prophesied that society would reach the Positivist stage in three epochs. Fichte, like Olmsted, believed that reason, as art, would finally reign in the fifth epoch of the progressive ascendency of mankind. Fourier's table of the evolution of mankind listed thirty-two stages of humanity's ascent, decline, and extinction with the eighth epoch as the age of harmony and perfection.

It is not likely that Olmsted would have chosen Fourier's model for the following reasons. The French utopian rejected cities; his phalansteries of 1600 to 1800 persons were principally agricultural and of a horticultural nature. Manufacturing in the phalanstery consisted of arts and crafts. (Nicholas V. Riasanovsky, *The Teaching of Charles Fourier* (Berkeley and Los Angeles: University of California Press, 1969) pp. 69, 196–201, see also Frank E. Manuel, *The Prophets of Paris* (Cambridge: Harvard University Press, 1962) p. 5). In contrast Olmsted was a staunch defender of the city as a center of progress, convenience, and culture; he foresaw the continuing expansion of city populations and the enlargement of the metropolis. Fourier expressed a justified, embittered, and vituperative criticism of nineteenth-century civilization—his fifth stage—and an absolute doubt and deviation from contemporary science and technology. (*The Utopian Vision of Charles Fourier, Selected Texts on Works, Love, and Passionate Attraction*) Jonathan Beecher and Richard Bienvenu, eds. & trans. (Boston: Beacon Press, 1971) pp. 95, 160, 196–99, 201. See also Riasanovsky, *The Teaching*, chap. 3; Manuel, *Prophets*, pp. 209–20.) Olmsted on the other hand commended the achievements of science and technology for improving the quality of life, especially in cities. Fourier rejected the division of labor; Olmsted viewed the specialization resulting from the division of labor as beneficial for the greater satisfaction of the needs and conveniences of society. Finally, to give the *coup de grace* to any Fourier-Olmsted connection, Olmsted, after examining the Phalanx at Red Bank, New Jersey, found Fourierism and life in the phalanx distasteful. He declared "I am not a Fourierist for myself. . . ." (FLO to Charles Loring Brace, 26 July 1852, reprinted in McLaughlin and Beveridge, 1:377.) Had he been so inclined, Olmsted might have considered the five-stage theory of a contemporary fellow American, John William Draper, a social historian, a physiologist, and a professor of chemistry at the University of New York. Draper's book, *A History of the Intellectual Development of*

Europe, designates five historic epochs—Credulity, Inquiry, Faith, Reason, Decrepitude—in Europe's social advancement. The fifth stage, Decrepitude, is an epoch of continuing progress through the organization and enhancement of intellection. (John William Draper, *A History of the Intellectual Development of Europe* [New York: Harper & Brothers, 1863].)

49. Olmsted, Vaux & Co., "Report of the Landscape Architects and Superintendents, 1 January 1868," *Brooklyn Park Commissioners,* p. 175. The leading features of the general plan had already been suggested in the Olmsted Vaux plan for Prospect Park in 1866. Olmsted, Vaux & Co., "Sixth Annual Report, 1866" [Prospect Park], *Reports of the Brooklyn Park Commissioners,* pp. 116–17, Fein, pp. 126, 132.

50. Olmsted, Vaux & Co., "Report of the Landscape Architects and Superintendents, 1 January 1868," *Brooklyn Park Commissioners,* p. 176. The planners admit that "the project in its full conception is a large one, and it is at once conceded that it does not follow, but anticipates, the demand of the public." Ibid., pp. 175–76, in Fein, p. 132.

51. Ibid., p. 198, Fein, p. 159. The plan for the Eastern Parkway suburb seems to have been included in the general parkway projection almost furtively. Olmsted writes, "Our plan, it will be observed, covers more ground than is necessarily required to be taken for the purposes which have been indicated." (Ibid.)

52. Olmsted, "Public Parks and the Enlargement of Towns," pp. 24–25, Sutton, p. 83.

53. Olmsted, Vaux & Co., "Report of the Landscape Architects and Superintendents, 1 January 1867," *Annual Reports of the Brooklyn Park Commissioners, 1861–1873* (1873), p. 142.

54. Olmsted, "Public Parks and the Enlargement of Towns," p. 24, Sutton, p. 83.

55. The tunnel effect may still be enjoyed in those stretches of the Brooklyn parkways where the trees are permitted to grow.

56. Olmsted, Vaux & Co., "Report of the Landscape Architects and Superintendents, 1 January 1868," *Brooklyn Park Commissioners,* map at p. 173.

57. Ibid., p. 197, Fein, pp. 158–59.

58. Ibid. For clarity it should be noted that at Olmsted's urging the Commissioners of Prospect Park obtained implementing zoning legislation to insure spaciousness by the maintenance of courtyards between the street front lines and the building foundations of thirty feet on each side of the parkway. See the act of the New York Legislature in reference to the "Eastern Parkway Boulevards": New York State Legislature, chap. 631, *Laws of 1868. An Act to Open and Widen Portions of Sackett, Douglass, and President Streets, and Otherwise to Alter the Commissioner's Map of the City of Brooklyn.* Passed May 6, 1868. Reprinted in *The East Parkway and Boulevards in the City of Brooklyn* (New York: Baker & Godwin, 1873), pp. 24–28. The significance of this law will be discussed presently.

59. Olmsted, Vaux & Co., "Sixth Annual Report, 1866" [Prospect Park], *Reports of the Brooklyn Park Commissioners,* p. 116, Fein, pp. 126–27.

60. *East Parkway,* pp. 6, 8.

61. The metropolitan parkway system, originally conceived in 1866 by the Olmsted, Vaux firm with their design for Prospect Park, was probably the model, with modifications,

later used by the planners in their system of connecting boulevards for the Chicago parks in 1871. See Carl W. Condit, *American Building Art: The Twentieth Century* (New York: Oxford University Press, 1961), pp. 278, 387 n. 5.

62. Olmsted, Vaux & Co., "Report of the Landscape Architects and Superintendents, 1 January 1868," *Brooklyn Park Commissioners,* pp. 200–201, Fein, p. 163. See also Olmsted, *Forty Years,* 2:189.

63. Olmsted, Vaux & Co., "Sixth Annual Report, 1866" [Prospect Park], *Reports of the Brooklyn Park Commissioners,* pp. 116–17, Fein, pp. 126–27.

64. Mandelbaum, *Boss Tweed's New York,* p. 12.

65. Frederick Law Olmsted, "Report of the Landscape Architect Advisory" published as an appendix to City of Boston Department of Parks, *Thirteenth Annual Report of the Board of Commissioners for the Year 1887* (Boston, 1888), p. 65 and map appended thereto. See also Walter Muir Whitehill, *Boston, A Topographical History* (Cambridge: Harvard University Press, Belknap Press, 1959), pp. 180–81.

66. Olmsted, "Public Parks and the Enlargement of Towns," p. 24, Sutton, p. 83.

67. Laurie D. Cox, "The Nature of State Parks and Parkways," *American Planning and Civic Annual,* Harlean James, ed. (Washington, D.C.: American Planning and Civic Association, 1948), p. 52. Although Olmsted focused his attention principally upon large parks, as a city planner he recognized the desirability of numerous, small public grounds such as squares, historic sites, unusual natural features, playgrounds for children, and other special purpose grounds evenly distributed about the city. See Olmsted, *Notes on Franklin Park,* pp. 32–33, Sutton, pp. 236–37.

68. Olmsted, "Report of the Landscape Architect Advisory," Boston Department of Parks, *Thirteenth Annual Report . . .* 1887, map appended thereto.

69. While all the grounds mentioned, such as the Boston Commons and the Public Gardens, were not products of Olmsted's artistry, he either created or advised on the plans for many elements of the system. He continued filling in and revising various aspects of the whole until 1892. His design for the Back Bay Fens and the extension of Commonwealth Avenue are particularly noteworthy pieces of work. They combine intricate engineering with aesthetics. See Whitehill, *Boston,* pp. 180–81. Olmsted's work in the Boston metropolitan area was continued and extended by his former student, Charles Eliot.

70. Jamaica Pond and the shore of Roxbury Bay contain sites of Olmsted's residential subdivisions in Greater Boston.

71. Sam Bass Warner, Jr., *Streetcar Suburbs: The Process of Growth in Boston, 1870–1900* (Cambridge: Harvard University Press, 1962), pp. 40–41 and n.

72. Olmsted, Vaux & Co., "Report of the Landscape Architects and Superintendents, 1 January 1868," *Brooklyn Park Commissioners,* p. 190, Fein, p. 150.

73. Olmsted, Vaux & Co., *Preliminary Report upon the Proposed Suburban Village at Riverside, Near Chicago* (New York: Sutton, Brown & Co., 1868), pp. 4–8, Sutton, pp. 293–95 (in part).

74. Olmsted, "Public Parks and the Enlargement of Towns," p. 9, Sutton, pp. 62–63.

75. Ibid.

76. "With the modern tendency to the concentration of population in towns there is also, at last, a tendency evident, with people who require to have the use of the advantages of towns for commercial and broadly social purposes, educational purposes, etc., to *dwell* under conditions differing from those to which, until lately, the word urban would be applied. Railways, telegraphs, telephones, and for suburbs near commercial centres, street railways, have nourished this tendency, of the results of which what we now see is but a premonitory effect." (FLO to Mariana Griswold Van Rensselaer. Olmsted Papers.) All the following studies support Olmsted's forecast of 1868. Taylor explains that improved means of urban transportation in New York City, Boston, and Philadelphia between 1830–1860 provided mobility for high- and middle-income groups. This resulted in the emergence of specialized business and residential districts and led to the division of business districts into separate sections for the performance of particular functions. (Taylor, "Beginnings of Mass Transportation.") Warner develops the effect of the extension of street railways on the process of suburban growth in Greater Boston between 1870–1900. (Warner, *Streetcar Suburbs*.) Liepmann shows how the invention of mechanical transport accelerated the process of differentiation in the contemporary London metropolitan area. (Kate K. Liepmann, *The Journey to Work: Its Significance for Industrial and Communal Life* (London: Kegan Paul & Co., 1944). See also Mumford, *City in History*, pp. 503–11.

77. Olmsted addressed his remarks to one of the commissioners. FLO to Henry Hill Elliot, 27 August 1860, in Beveridge and Schuyler, 3:259–67. Olmsted and Vaux had been appointed "Landscape Architects and designers to the Commissioners North of 155th Street." (Olmsted, *Forty Years,* 1:8.)

78. Ibid., 3:264.

79. Ibid.

80. Ibid., 3:265.

81. Ibid., 3:262.

82. "First, it [the thoroughfare] shall not lead with special directness toward town. Second, it shall have few if any public streets or roads opening into it and such as do lead into it shall be short. Third, tributary roads shall not approach it from a direction opposite the town. Fourth, there shall be at no great distance from it a road or roads running approximately parallel to it, but more directly toward the town." (Ibid., 3:265.)

83. Because of the topography of the Washington Heights area, the necessity of constructing complex access roads to each of the houses would destroy the landscape beauty of the grounds, and so Olmsted made the interesting proposal that the houses be built in a cluster pattern on a large scale terrace arrangement. Such a plan would allow a single, curvilinear approach road with a common ground beyond it. (Ibid., 3:263, 266.)

84. In 1866 Olmsted formulated a plan for a suburban neighborhood for the College of California at Berkeley, but the plan was disregarded. See Roper, *FLO,* pp. 305–9. The plan is reprinted in Sutton, pp. 264–91.

85. Olmsted, Vaux & Co., "Report of the Landscape Architects and Superintendents, 1 January 1868," *Brooklyn Park Commissioners,* p. 193, Fein, p. 153.

86. Ibid.

87. Ibid., p. 194, Fein, pp. 154–55.

88. Ibid.

89. Ibid., p. 199, Fein, pp. 161–62.

90. *East Parkway,* pp. 7, 8, 9–10; Olmsted, Vaux & Co., "Report of the Landscape Architects and Superintendents, 1 January 1868," *Brooklyn Park Commissioners,* pp. 197, 199. Olmsted depicts his neighborhood as "open, elegant, and healthy," accommodating 500,000 people living in detached residences surrounded by private gardens. Ibid., p. 198, Fein, pp. 159–61. It was meant for the wealthy. It is entirely likely that the plan for the Eastern Parkway District, like the design for Prospect Park, was formulated at the bidding of the Prospect Park Commissioner in order "to attract a taxpaying type of resident to Brooklyn." (Harold C. Syrett, *The City of Brooklyn, 1865–1898: A Political History* (New York: AMS Press, 1968), p. 49.)

91. Brooklyn did not have home rule yet. (Syrett, *City of Brooklyn,* pp. 41, 50, 51–52.)

92. *East Parkway,* p. 25.

93. Ibid.

94. Ibid.

95. Frank B. Williams, *The Law of City Planning and Zoning* (New York: Macmillan Co., 1922), pp. 210 and n. 1, 211–16, 401–5.

96. People *ex rel* Dilzer v. Calder, 89 New York Appellate Division 503 (1903). The court declared that the law "undertakes to deprive the abutting owners of the full and complete use of their property without just compensation."

97. In his letter to Elliott, Olmsted observed that there was nothing to prevent a future legislature from undoing present plans. Beveridge and Schuyler, 3:262.

98. Olmsted, "Public Parks and the Enlargement of Towns," p. 9, Sutton, pp. 62–63.

99. Ibid.; Olmsted, Vaux & Co., "Report of the Landscape Architects and Superintendents, 1 January 1868," Brooklyn Park Commissioners, p. 200, Fein, p. 162. Olmsted was probably referring to the regulations relating to the rebuilding of Rome imposed by the Emperor Nero, following the great fire of 64 A.D. In his two references to the Roman law Olmsted did not mention the name of Nero, the urban renewal expert of Rome. It might have prejudiced his case. In his Brooklyn Report Olmsted showed that he was under the mistaken notion that most Romans lived in detached villas. Most of the population of Rome lived in apartment houses which were congested, badly built fire hazards called *insulae.* See Jerome Carcopino, *Daily Life in Ancient Rome; The People and the City at the Height of the Empire,* Henry T. Rowell, ed., E. O. Lorimer, trans. (New Haven: Yale University Press, 1940), pp. 18–33.
    The account of Nero's building regulations from Tacitus *Annals* 15.43.1 follows:

    > In the part of the city not reserved for the Palace, the re-building was not at random nor uncontrolled, as after the Gallic fire. Regulations prescribed the alignment of roads, the width of streets, and the height of houses. They stood in spacious building plots and colonnades were added to the blocks of apartments so as to protect their street frontage. Nero undertook to construct these colonnades at his own expense, and to clear up all building-sites before restoring them to their owners.

Rewards were announced, in proportion to the standing and resources of individual citizens, for the completion of private houses or blocks of apartments by a given date.

A portion of all buildings had to be made without timber and of stone from Gabii or Albano, which is fireproof. Water-inspectors were appointed to ensure a better and more efficient service from the public supply, which had suffered from the tapping of unauthorized individuals. Each householder had to keep firefighting apparatus ready to hand. Party walls were forbidden, buildings must be surrounded by walls of their own. Necessity caused these measures to be accepted; they certainly added to the city's amenities. (Quoted in Donald R. Dudley, *Urbs Roma: A Source Book of Classical Texts on the City and Its Monuments.* Selected and translated with a Commentary ([London]: Phaidon Press, 1967), pp. 21–22.)

100. *New York Times,* 21 October 1872, p. 4.

101. Olmsted, *Riverside,* p. 7, Sutton, pp. 294–95.

102. Ibid.

103. Ibid.

104. Olmsted, "Public Parks and the Enlargement of Towns," pp. 9–10, Sutton, pp. 62–63. Olmsted wrote that the suburb is a place that is not fully urban, which provides the combination

of a certain degree of the conditions of health and of ruralistic beauty of a loosely built New England village with a certain degree of the material and social advantages of a Town. A village with houses set back and well apart with yards and gardens and orchards separating one from another; with broad tree-shaded streets, laid out with grace and some respect for natural topography, with sewers and side walks and macadamized wheelways and small greens and commons, all with a view to pleasing compositions of natural and artificial objects. (FLO to Mariana Griswold Van Rensselaer, 11 June 1893. Olmsted Papers.)

105. Olmsted, *Riverside,* p. 27, Sutton, p. 303.

106. Ibid., pp. 26, 27, Sutton, pp. 302–3.

107. Olmsted, *Forty Years,* 1:11. For a description of Llewellyan Park, designed in 1850, see Christopher Tunnard, *The City of Man,* 2d ed. (New York: Charles Scribner's Sons, 1970), pp. 183–87.

108. Olmsted, *Riverside,* p. 26, Sutton, p. 303.

109. Ibid.

110. Ibid., p. 27, Sutton, p. 303.

111. Frederick Law Olmsted, *Walks and Talks of an American Farmer in England,* 2 vols. (New York: George P. Putnam, 1852), 1:84. The sentiment which Olmsted reflected in this passage comes from Ruskin's discussion of domestic buildings in the *Seven Lamps of Architecture.* In his discussion Ruskin ardently favored the idea that each family own its own permanent dwelling which reflects the history of the family as a kind of monument. It is, Ruskin said, in "this spirit of honorable, proud, peaceful self-possession, this abiding wisdom of contented life" that the chief sources of great

intellectual power in all ages are to be found. (Ruskin, *Works*, 8:228. See also ibid., 8:225–28.)

112. Frederick Law Olmsted, "On Dooryard Fences in Village Streets," from a letter written to the Editor of the *American Garden*, August 1889, reprinted in *Landscape Architecture* 11 (October 1920): 13–15.

113. Both, of course, are necessarily complementary in Olmsted's organic conception of modern society.

114. FLO to Mariana Griswold Van Rensselaer, 11 June 1893. Olmsted Papers. See also Howard K. Menhinick, "Riverside Sixty Years Later," *Landscape Architecture* 22 (January 1932): 109.

115. Roper, *FLO*, p. 71.

116. Olmsted, *Walks and Talks*, 1:83.

117. Ibid. Impressed though he was, Olmsted did not use Birkenhead's street pattern as a model for his suburbs; the streets were laid out in a gridiron pattern.

118. Olmsted, *Journey through Texas*, p. 143.

119. Ibid., p. 182.

120. In a close community of not more than 3,000 persons Olmsted found "the evidence of an active intellectual life, and desire for knowledge and improvement among the masses of the people like that which distinguishes the New Englander." (Ibid., p. 179.)

121. Olmsted, *Riverside*, p. 28, Sutton, p. 304.

122. Ibid., pp. 27–28.

123. Tunnard, *City of Man*, pp. 191–95, 202. Adams praises Olmsted for his use of design in consideration of social needs and natural conditions. In so doing Olmsted gave a new direction to city planning. (Thomas Adams, *The Design of Residential Areas* (Cambridge: Harvard University Press, 1934), pp. 52, 126, 237–40.) Reviewing the contribution of the Regional Planning Association, Lubove cites Riverside as one of the new precedents in the American past that gave an example for the community planning synthesis of the RPAA. (Roy Lubove, *Community Planning in the 1920's; The Contribution of the Regional Planning Association of America* (Pittsburgh: University of Pittsburgh Press, 1963), pp. 2–3.) Gallion and Eisner declare that Olmsted's Riverside plan was a progressive innovation; the planner became an active participant in paying out the residential subdivision, taking the place of the surveyor who was only a tool of the land speculator. (Arthur B. Gallion and Simon Eisner, *The Urban Pattern; City Planning and Design*, 2d ed. (Princeton, N.J.: Van Nostrand Co., 1963), p. 117.)

124. Walter L. Creese, *The Search for Environment; The Garden City, Before and After* (New Haven: Yale University Press, 1966), pp. 2, 153. Mumford states that Olmsted's Riverside, as a fresh, bold innovation in the nineteenth century, prefigures the greenbelt towns of Ebenezer Howard. (Mumford, *City in History*, pp. 497, 516.)

125. Frederick Law Olmsted and J. James R. Croes, "(1) Preliminary Report of the Landscape Architect and the Civil and Topographical Engineer, upon the Laying Out of the Twenty-third and Twenty-fourth Wards. (2) Report of the Landscape Architect and the Civil Topographical Engineer, Accompanying a Plan for Laying Out That Part of the Twenty-fourth Ward, Lying West of the Riverdale Road," *Board of the De-*

partment of Public Parks, Document No. 72 (New York, 20 December 1876), pp. 2–10, Fein, pp. 350–58.

126. Ibid., p. 12, Fein, p. 359.

127. Ibid., p. 15, Fein, p. 363. Olmsted had made the same suggestion in 1860 for the Washington Heights area which has similar topographical characteristics. Since the surfaces at Riverdale and at Washington Heights are similar to that of Mount Royal in Montreal, Olmsted handled the problem of road grading in a similar manner.

128. Olmsted, "Public Parks and the Enlargement of Towns," p. 9, Sutton, p. 63.

129. J. James R. Croes and Frederick Law Olmsted, "Report of the Civil and Topographical Engineer and the Landscape Architect, Accompanying a Plan for Local Steam Transit Routes in the Twenty-third and Twenty-fourth Wards," *Board of the Department of Public Parks, Document No. 75* (New York, 21 March 1877), pp. 3–10, Fein, pp. 375–82. See also Schlesinger, *Rise of the City,* pp. 90–93; Allan Nevins, *The Emergence of Modern America, 1865–1878* (New York: Macmillan Co., 1927), pp. 81–82; Frederick Law Olmsted, Jr., "The Town Planning Movement in America," *Annals* 51 (January 1914), p. 172–81.

130. Mandelbaum, *Boss Tweed's New York,* pp. 115–17.

131. Olmsted, Vaux & Co., "Report of the Landscape Architects and Superintendents, 1 January 1868," *Brooklyn Board of Commissioners,* p. 198, Fein, p. 160.

132. Olmsted, *Riverside,* p. 3, Sutton, p. 292.

133. Olmsted, Croes, *Doc. 72,* pp. 16, 18, Fein, pp. 363, 365.

134. Ibid.

135. Ibid., p. 6 and n., Fein, pp. 353–54.

136. The literature analyzing slum conditions in New York City during this period corroborates Olmsted's view. The experiment with the dumbbell tenement planted on the standard New York City lot (100 feet by 25 feet) was a disaster. See Roy Lubove, *The Progressives and the Slums; Tenement House Reforms in New York City* (Pittsburgh: University of Pittsburgh Press, 1962), chap. 2; Lawrence M. Friedman, *Government and Slum Housing, A Century of Frustration* (Chicago: Rand McNally & Co., 1968), pp. 28–32.

137. Olmsted, Croes, *Doc. 72,* p. 12, Fein, p. 359.

138. Olmsted, *Notes on Franklin Park,* p. 32, Sutton, p. 236.

139. There is no intermingling of commercial and residential uses. In Riverside business activity is limited to a local shopping center near the railroad station. See Menhinick, "Riverside Sixty Years Later," p. 109. In the plan for Riverdale limited business activities are possible at the foot of the slopes of the suburb. (Olmsted and Croes, *Doc. 72,* p. 14.)

140. Mumford uses this term in describing the manner in which Venice uses its canals to differentiate its urban functions and maintain the integrity of its neighborhoods. (Mumford, *City in History,* pp. 323–25.)

141. Among the few stipulations in the Riverside plan relating to landscape and architecture were the requirements that houses be set back from the street a certain distance

and that the house owner maintain one or two trees between his house and the street line. These provisions were meant to screen from public view ugly or distasteful houses which might be built. (Olmsted, *Riverside*, p. 24, Sutton, pp. 301–2.)

142. Olmsted, Croes, *Doc. 72*, pp. 4–5, Fein, pp. 350, 352–53. The plan was actually approved in 1811. (Mandelbaum, *Boss Tweed's New York*, pp. 17, 59–61.)

143. Ibid., p. 5, Fein, p. 353.

144. Ibid., pp. 7–8, Fein, pp. 355–56.

145. Ibid., pp. 6–7, and n., Fein, p. 354, n. 2. In the Eastern Parkway suburb Olmsted provides for rear yards and alleys to handle these household chores. For attempts to overcome the pernicious attributes of the street system and the "shoestring" building lot as they relate to slum housing reform, see Mandelbaum, *Boss Tweed's New York*, pp. 162–64; Friedman, *Government and Slum Housing*, pp. 75–84.

146. "I reserve the word park for places with breadth and space enough." (FLO to Mariana Griswold Van Rensselaer, 22 May 1893. Olmsted Papers.) See also Olmsted, "Justifying Value of a Public Park," p. 151.

147. Olmsted, *Forty Years*, 2:251. Italics added.

148. Olmsted, Croes, *Doc. 72*, pp. 20–22, Fein, pp. 367–69.

149. Ibid.

150. Olmsted, *Riverside*, p. 17, Sutton, p. 300.

151. Ibid.

152. Olmsted, Vaux & Co., "Report of the Landscape Architects and Superintendents, 1 January 1868," *Brooklyn Park Commissioners*, pp. 179, 199, Fein, pp. 137, 161.

153. Ibid.

154. Olmsted used a similar rationale in regard to recreating nature. In his plan for Mount Royal in Montreal he explains that nature is often dull and needs to be idealized in order to be appreciated.

155. Olmsted, "Public Parks and the Enlargement of Towns," pp. 14, 25, Sutton, pp. 69, 84.

156. Frederick Law Olmsted, "The Beginning of Central Park: A Fragment of Autobiography," reprinted in *Landscape Architecture* 2 (July 1912): 153.

157. Ibid., pp. 153–54.

158. Olmsted, Vaux & Co., "Report of the Landscape Architects and Superintendents, 1 January 1868," *Brooklyn Park Commissioners*, p. 189, Fein, pp. 148–49.

159. Olmsted, *Notes on Franklin Park*, p. 31. See also Olmsted, "Public Parks and the Enlargement of Towns," pp. 25–26.

160. He evinced an understanding for agronomy, architecture, botany, business, camping, dendrology, engineering, entertainment (for children, convalescents, and adults), management, public health, real estate, riparian conditions, silviculture, transportation, and water supply.

161. Olmsted, *Notes on Franklin Park*, p. 32, Sutton, p. 236.

162. Olmsted, Croes, *Doc. 72,* pp. 9–10, Fein, pp. 357–58.

163. Ibid.

164. Ibid., p. 4, Fein, p. 352.

165. Olmsted, Vaux & Co., *Report upon a Projected Improvement of the Estate of the College of California at Berkeley, near Oakland* (San Francisco: Towne and Bacon, 1866), p. 4, Sutton, p. 265.

Bibliography

Articles

Bushnell, Horace. "Unconscious Influence." In *The American Pulpit*, edited by Richard S. Rust. Vol. 2, 230–41. Worcester, 1847.

Cox, Laurie D. "The Nature of State Parks and Parkways." In *American Planning and Civic Annual*, edited by Harlean James, 52. Washington, D.C.: American Planning and Civic Association, 1948.

Erber, Ernest. "Urban Planning in Transition: An Introductory Essay." In *Urban Planning in Transition*, edited by Ernest Erber, xvii. New York: Grossman Publishers, 1970.

Fein, Albert. "The American City: The Ideal and the Real." In *The Rise of an American Architecture*, edited by Edgar Kaufmann, Jr., 51, 54–56, 86–87, 108. New York, Washington, London: Praeger, 1970.

Hoving, Thomas P. F. "Thinking Big about Small Parks." *New York Times Magazine*, 10 April 1966.

"How to Build a Bungalow." *The Craftsman* (5 November 1903): 256.

Kellar, H. A. "Solon Robinson." *Indiana Historical Collections* 21, 22 (1936): 161.

Kern, Alexander. "The Rise of Transcendentalism, 1815–1860." In *Transitions in American Literary History*, edited by Harry H. Clark, 292–293. Durham: Duke University Press, 1953.

McGuire, Diane K. "Early Site Planning on the West Coast: Frederick Law Olmsted's Plan for Stanford University." *Landscape Architecture* 47 (January 1957): 345.

Menhinick, Howard K. "Riverside Sixty Years Later." *Landscape Architecture* 22 (January 1932): 109.

Miller, August C., Jr. "Jefferson as an Agriculturalist." *Agricultural History* 16 (April 1942): 77.

New York Times, 21 October 1872, p. 4.

Olmsted, Frederick Law. "Public Parks and the Enlargement of Towns." *Journal of Social Science*, no. 3 (1871): 1–36.

————. "The Justifying Value of a Public Park." *Journal of Social Science*, no. 12, pt. 1: 147–64. Boston: A. Williams & Co., New York: G. P. Putnam's Sons. For the American Social Science Association, 1880.

————. "Country Living." Review of *The Woods and Byways of New England* by Wilson Flagg and *Landscape Architecture* by H. W. S. Cleveland. *The Nation* (22 January 1874): 64–65.

————. "The Beginning of Central Park: A Fragment of Autobiography (ca. 1877)" with an Introductory Note by His Son, Frederick Law Olmsted, Jr. *Landscape Architecture* 2 (July 1912): 152.

_____. "On Dooryard Fences in Village Streets." *Landscape Architecture* 11 (October 1920): 13–15.

_____. "The Town Planning Movement in America." *Annals* 51 (January 1914): 172–81.

Orians, G. Harrison. "The Rise of Romanticism, 1805–1855." In *Transitions in American Literary History*, edited by Harry H. Clark, 118–226. Durham: Duke University Press, 1853.

Palmer, Paul A. "Benthamism in England and America." *The American Political Science Review* 35 (October 1941): 864–67.

Pottle, Frederick A. "The Eye and the Object in the Poetry of Wordsworth." In *Romanticism and Consciousness, Essays in Criticism*, edited by Harold Bloom, 294. New York: W. W. Norton & Co., 1970.

Roper, Laura Wood. "'Mr. Law' and *Putnam's Monthly Magazine:* A Note on a Phase in the Career of Frederick Law Olmsted." *American Literature* 26 (March 1954): 88–93.

Schelling, Friedrick W. J. von. "Introduction to Idealism." Translated by Tom Davidson. *Journal of Speculative Philosophy* 1 (1867): 159–60.

Taylor, George Rogers. "The Beginnings of Mass Transportation in Urban America." *Smithsonian Journal of History* 1 (Summer and Autumn 1966): 31–52.

Books

Abrams, M. H. *The Mirror and the Lamp: Romantic Theory and the Critical Tradition.* New York: W. W. Norton & Co., 1958.

Adams, Henry. *The Education of Henry Adams.* Modern Library. New York: Random House, 1931.

Adams, Thomas. *The Design of Residential Areas.* Cambridge: Harvard University Press, 1934.

Albion, Robert G. *The Rise of the New York Port, 1815–1860.* New York: Charles Scribner's Sons, 1939.

American Cyclopaedia, 1881 ed. S.v. "Parks," by Frederick Law Olmsted.

Bailey, Liberty H. *Cyclopedia of American Horticulture.* 4 vols. New York: Macmillan Co., 1900.

Bardolph, Richard. *Agricultural Literature and the Illinois Farmer.* Urbana: University of Illinois Press, 1948.

Bate, Walter J. *From Classic to Romantic: Premises of Taste in Eighteenth Century England.* New York: Harper & Bros., 1961.

Beach, Joseph Warren. *The Concept of Nature in Nineteenth-Century English Poetry.* New York: Macmillan Co., 1936.

Brace, Charles Loring. *The Life of Charles Loring Brace, Chiefly Told in His Own Letters.* Edited by Emma Brace. New York: Charles Scribner's Sons, 1894.

Bushnell, Horace. *An Address before the Hartford County Agricultural Society.* Hartford, 1847.

_____. *Views of Christian Nurture:* 2d ed. Hartford: 1848.

Calvin, John. *Institutes of the Christian Religion.* Translated by Henry Beveridge. 2 vols. Grand Rapids, Mich.: William B. Eerdmans Publishing Co., 1964.

_____. *Theological Treatises.* Translated with Introduction by J. K. S. Reid. The Library of Christian Classics. Philadelphia: Westminster Press, 1954.

Canby, Henry Seidel. *Thoreau.* Boston: Houghton Mifflin Co., 1939.

Carcopino, Jerome. *Daily Life in Ancient Rome: The People and the City at the Height of the Empire.* Edited with bibliography and notes by Henry T. Rowell. Translated by E. O. Lorimer. New Haven: Yale University Press, 1940.

Carlyle, Thomas. *Critical and Miscellaneous Essays.* 5 vols. New York: Scribner's Sons, 1900.

————. *The Works of Thomas Carlyle*. Edinburgh Edition. 30 vols. New York: Charles Scribner's Sons, 1903-1904. Vol. 1: *Sartor Resartus, The Life and Opinions of Herr Teufelsdrockh;* Vol. 5: *On Heroes, Hero-Worship and the Heroic in History.*

Charvat, William. *The Origins of American Critical Thought, 1810–1835*. New York: A. S. Barnes & Co., 1961.

Cheney, Mary A. *Life and Letters of Horace Bushnell*. New York: Harper & Bros., 1880.

Coleridge, Samuel Taylor. *The Complete Works of Samuel Taylor Coleridge*. With an Introductory Essay upon His Philosophical and Theological Opinions. Edited by W. G. T. Shedd, 7 vols. New York: Harper & Bros., 1853.

————. *Letters of Samuel Taylor Coleridge*. Edited by Ernest Hartley Coleridge. 2 vols. Boston: Houghton Mifflin Co., 1895.

————. *Biographia Literaria with Aesthetical Essays*. Edited by J. Shawcross. 2 vols. Oxford: Clarendon Press, 1907.

————. *Miscellaneous Criticism*. Edited by Thomas M. Raysor. Cambridge: Harvard University Press, 1936.

————. *Shakespearean Criticism*. Edited by Thomas M. Raysor. Everyman's Library. 2 vols. London: J. M. Dent & Sons, 1960.

Commager, Henry Steele. *The American Mind; An Interpretation of American Thought and Character since the 1880's*. New Haven: Yale University Press, 1959.

Condit, Carl W. *American Building Art: The Twentieth Century*. New York: Oxford University Press, 1961.

Dickason, David H. *The Daring Young Men: The Story of the American Pre-Raphaelites*. Bloomington: Indiana University Press, 1953.

Dictionary of American Biography, 1930. S. v. "Downing, Andrew Jackson."

Downing, Andrew Jackson. *Cottage Residences, Rural Architecture and Landscape Gardening*. New Introduction by Michael Hugo-Brunt. Library of Victorian Culture. Watkins Glen, N.Y.: Century House, 1967.

Dudley, Donald R. *Urbs Roma: A Source Book of Classical Texts on the City and Its Monuments*. Selected and translated with a Commentary. [London]: Phaidon Press, 1967.

Dwight, Timothy. *Travels, in New England and New-York*. 4 vols. New Haven: Timothy Dwight, 1821–1822. Reissued by John Harvard Library, Barbara Miller Solomon, ed., with the assistance of Patricia M. King, Vol. 1: 77, 259. Cambridge: The Belknap Press of Harvard University Press, 1969.

East Parkways and Boulevards in the City of Brooklyn. New York: Baker & Godwin, 1873.

Eisenstadt, Abraham S., ed. *American History*. 2 vols. New York: Thomas Y. Crowell Co., 1962.

Emerson, Ralph Waldo. *The Complete Works of Ralph Waldo Emerson*. Edited with an Introduction by Edward W. Emerson. Concord Edition. 12 vols. Boston: Houghton Mifflin Co., 1904.

————. *Journals of Ralph Waldo Emerson*. Edited by Edward W. Emerson and Waldo E. Forbes. 10 vols. Boston: Houghton Mifflin Co., 1909–1914.

————. *The Letters of Ralph Waldo Emerson*. Edited by Ralph L. Rusk. 6 vols. New York: Columbia University Press, 1939.

Encyclopaedia of Religion and Ethics, 1916 ed. S. v. "Martineau, James."

Ergang, Robert. *Herder and the Foundations of German Nationalism*. New York: Columbia University Press, 1931.

Fein, Albert, ed. *Landscape into Cityscape: Frederick Law Olmsted's Plans for a Greater New York City*. Ithaca, New York: Cornell University Press, 1967.

Fichte, Johann. *The Characteristics of the Present Age*. Translated by William Smith. London: John Chapman, 1847.

Flexner, James T. *That Wilder Image: The Painting of America's Native School from Thomas Cole to Winslow Homer.* Boston: Little, Brown & Co., 1962.

Foerster, Norman. *American Criticism: A Study in Literary Theory from Poe to the Present.* New York: Russell & Russell, Inc., 1962.

Friedman, Lawrence M. *Government and Slum Housing, A Century of Frustration.* Chicago: Rand McNally & Co. 1968.

Frothingham, Octavius Brooks. *Transcendentalism in New England, A History.* Introduction by Sydney E. Ahlstrom. New York: Harpers & Bros., 1959.

Gallion, Arthur B., and Simon Eisner. *The Urban Pattern: City Planning and Design.* 2d ed. Princeton, N.J.: Van Nostrand Co., 1963

Gates, Paul W. *The Farmer's Age: Agriculture, 1815–1860.* Vol. 3 of *The Economic History of the United States.* New York: Holt, Rinehart & Winston, 1960.

George, M. Dorothy. *London Life in the XVIII Century.* London: Kegan Paul, Trench, Trubner & Co., 1925.

von Goethe, Johann Wolfgang. *Literary Essays.* Compiled by J. E. Spingarn. Foreword by Viscount Haldane. New York: Harcourt, Brace & Co., 1921; reprint ed., Freeport, N.Y.: Books for Libraries Press, 1967.

Goetz, Mary Dorothea. *A Study of Ruskin's Concept of the Imagination.* Washington, D.C.: Catholic University of America, 1947.

Gray-Smith, Rowland. *God in the Philosophy of Schelling.* Philadelphia, 1933.

Green, Constance McLaughlin. *The Rise of Urban America.* New York: Harper & Row, 1965.

Greenough, Horatio. *Form and Function, Remarks on Art, Design, and Architecture.* Edited by Harold A. Small. Introduction by Erle Loran. Berkeley: University of California Press, 1957.

Haroutunian, Joseph. *Piety versus Moralism: The Passing of New England Theology.* New York: Henry Holt & Co., 1932; reprint ed., Hamden, Conn.: Archon Books, 1964.

Harrold, Charles F. *Carlyle and German Thought.* New Haven: Yale University Press, 1934.

Hipple, Walter J., Jr. *the Beautiful, the Sublime, and the Picturesque in Eighteenth Century British Aesthetic Theory.* Carbondale, Ill.: Southern Illinois University Press, 1957.

Hirsch, E. D., Jr. *Wordsworth and Schelling, A Typological Study of Romanticism.* New Haven: Yale University Press, 1960.

Hitchcock, Henry-Russell, Jr. *The Architecture of H. H. Richardson and His Times.* New York: Museum of Modern Art, 1936.

Hobbes, Thomas. *Leviathan or the Matter, Forme and Power of a Commonwealth.* Edited by Michael Oakeshott. Introduction by Richard S. Peters. New York: Crowell-Collier, 1962.

Hopkins, Vivian C. *Spires of Form: A Study of Emerson's Aesthetic Theory.* New York: Russell & Russell, 1965.

Hough, Graham. *The Last Romantics.* New York: Barnes & Noble, 1961.

Hutchinson, William R. *The Transcendentalist Ministers.* New Haven: Yale University Press, 1959.

Huth, Hans. *Nature and the American: Three Centuries of Changing Attitudes.* Berkeley: University of California Press, 1957.

James, Henry. *Charles W. Eliot.* 2 vols. Boston: Houghton Mifflin Co., 1932.

Kant, Immanuel. *The Critique of Judgement.* Translated and edited by James C. Meredith. Oxford: Clarendon Press, 1952.

Kirkland, Edward Chase. *Men, Cities and Transportation, 1820–1900.* 2 vols. Cambridge: Harvard University Press, 1948.

Kohn, Hans. *American Nationalism, An Interpretative Essay.* New York: Crowell-Collier, 1961.

――――――. *The Idea of Nationalism: A Study in Its Origins and Background.* New York: Macmillan Co., 1961.

Ladd, Henry. *Victorian Morality, An Analysis of Ruskin's Esthetic*. New York: Long & Smith, 1932.

Larkin, Oliver W. *Art and Life in America*. New York: Rinehart & Co., 1949.

Liepmann, Kate K. *The Journey to Work: Its Significance for Industrial and Communal Life*. London: Kegan Paul & Co., 1944.

Lovejoy, Arthur O. *Essays in the History of Ideas*. Baltimore: The Johns Hopkins Press, 1948.

Lubove, Roy. *The Progressives and the Slums; Tenement House Reform in New York City*. Forewords by Samuel P. Hays and Philip S. Broughton. Pittsburgh: University of Pittsburgh Press, 1962.

――――――. *Community Planning in the 1920's; The Contribution of the Regional Planning Association of America*. Pittsburgh: University of Pittsburgh Press, 1963.

McGiffert, Arthur Cushman. *The Rise of Modern Religious Ideas*. New York: Macmillan Co., 1925.

McLaughlin, Charles Capen, ed. in chief. *The Papers of Frederick Law Olmsted*. 3 vols. Baltimore and London: The Johns Hopkins University Press. Vol. 1 (1977): *The Formative Years, 1822–1852*, Charles Capen McLaughlin, ed. Charles E. Beveridge, assoc. ed. Vol. 2 (1981): *Slavery and the South, 1852–1857*. Charles E. Beveridge, Charles Capen McLaughlin, eds., David Schuyler, assoc. ed. Vol. 3 (1983): *Creating Central Park, 1857–1861*. Charles E. Beveridge, David Schuyler, eds.

――――――. "Selected Letters of Frederick Law Olmsted." Ph.D. dissertation, Harvard University, 1960.

Mandelbaum, Seymour J. *Boss Tweed's New York*. New York: John Wiley & Sons, 1965.

Marx, Karl. *Capital, A Critique of Political Economy*. Edited by Frederick Engels. Translated by Samuel Moore and Edward Aveling. The Modern Library. New York: Random House, n.d.

Mathews, Lois Kimball. *The Expansion of New England, the Spread of New England Settlement and Institutions to the Mississippi River, 1620–1865*. Boston: Houghton Mifflin Co., 1909.

Matthiessen, F. O. *American Renaissance, Art and Expression in the Age of Emerson and Whitman*. New York: Oxford University Press, 1941.

Mead, George Herbert. *Movements of Thought in the Nineteenth Century*. Edited by Merritt H. Moore. Chicago: University of Chicago Press, 1936.

Metzger, Charles R. *Emerson and Greenough, Transcendental Pioneers of an American Esthetic*. Berkeley: University of California Press, 1954.

Mill, John Stuart. *The Collected Works of John Stuart Mill*. Vols. 2, 3: *Principles of Political Economy with Some of Their Applications to Social Philosophy*. Edited by J. M. Robson. Introduction by V. W. Bladen. Toronto: University of Toronto Press, 1965.

Miller, John Anderson. *Fares Please! From Horse-Cars to Streamliners*. New York: D. Appleton-Century Co., 1941.

Morse, Jarvis Means. *A Neglected Period of Connecticut's History, 1818–1850*. New Haven: Yale University Press, 1933.

Mumford, Lewis. *The City in History; Its Origins, Its Transformations, and Its Prospects*. New York: Harcourt, Brace & World, 1961.

Neumann, Franz. *The Democratic and the Authoritarian State, Essays in Political and Legal Theory*. Edited with a Preface by Herbert Marcuse. New York: Crowell-Collier, Free Press of Glencoe, 1964.

Nevins, Allan. *The Evening Post*. New York: Boni & Liveright, 1922.

――――――. *The Emergence of Modern America, 1865–1878*. New York: Macmillan Co., 1927.

Newlin, Claude M. *The Life and Writings of Hugh Henry Brackenridge*. Princeton: Princeton University Press, 1932.

Norton, Sara, and M. A. DeWolfe Howe, eds. *Letters of Charles Eliot Norton*. 2 vols. Boston: Houghton Mifflin Co., 1916.

Olmsted, Frederick Law. *Walks and Talks of an American Farmer in England*. 2 vols. New York: George P. Putnam, 1852.

————. *Walks and Talks of an American Farmer in England*. Columbus, Ohio: Jos. H. Riley & Co., 1859.

————. *A Journey through Texas; Or, a Saddle-Trip on the Southwestern Frontier: With a Statistical Appendix*. New York: Dix, Edwards & Co., 1857.

————. *A Journey in the Back Country*. New York: Mason Bros., 1860.

————. *A Journey in the Seaboard Slave States with Remarks on Their Economy*. New York: Mason Bros., 1861.

————. *Mount Royal, Montreal*. New York: G. P. Putnam's Sons, 1881.

————. *Forty Years of Landscape Architecture*. Edited by Frederick Law Olmsted, Jr. and Theodora Kimball. 2 vols. New York: G. P. Putnam's Sons, 1922. Reissued in 1 vol., New York: Benjamin Blom, 1970.

————. *The Cotton Kingdom, A Traveller's Observations on Cotton and Slavery in the American Slave States*. Edited, with an Introduction by Arthur M. Schlesinger. New York: Alfred A. Knopf, 1962.

[Olmsted, Frederick Law]. City of Boston, Park Department. *Notes on the Plan of Franklin Park and Related Matters*. Boston, 1886.

Oswald, Walter S., Jr. "In the Footsteps of Frederick Law Olmsted." M. A. essay. Columbia University, 1948.

Parrington, Vernon L. *Main Currents in American Thought*. 2 vols. New York: Harcourt, Brace & Co., 1954.

Paul, Sherman. *Emerson's Angle of Vision: Man and Nature in American Experience*. Cambridge: Harvard University Press, 1952.

————. *Louis Sullivan, An Architect in American Thought*. Englewood Cliffs, N.J.: Prentice-Hall, Spectrum Book, 1962.

Pockmann, Henry A. *German Culture in America; Philosophical and Literary Influences, 1600–1900*. Madison: University of Wisconsin Press, 1957.

Polk, Lester C. *The Aesthetics of John Ruskin in Relation to the Aesthetics of the Romantic Era*. Urbana: University of Illinois Press, 1941.

Price, Uvedale. *On the Picturesque*. With an essay on the Origin of Taste by Thomas Dick Lauder. Edinburgh: Caldwell, Lloyd & Co., 1842.

Purcell, Richard J. *Connecticut in Transition: 1775–1818*. New ed. With a Foreword by S. Hugh Brockunier. Middletown, Conn.: Wesleyan University Press, 1963.

Reps, John W. *The Making of Urban America, A History of City Planning in the United States*. Princeton: Princeton University Press, 1965.

Repton, Humphrey. *The Art of Landscape Gardening*. Edited by John Nolen. Boston: Houghton Mifflin Co., 1907.

Riasanovsky, Nicholas V. *The Teaching of Charles Fourier*. Berkeley and Los Angeles: University of California Press, 1969.

Roper, Laura Wood. *FLO, A Biography of Frederick Law Olmsted*. Baltimore: The Johns Hopkins University Press, 1973.

Rosenberg, John. *The Darkening Glass: A Portrait of Ruskin's Genius*. New York: Columbia University Press, 1961.

Rusk, Ralph L. *The Life of Ralph Waldo Emerson*. New York: Charles Scribner's Sons, 1949.

Ruskin, John. *The Works of John Ruskin*. 39 vols. London: George Allen, 1903–1912.

von Schelling, F. W. J. *The Philosophy of Art*. Translated by A. Johnson. London: Chapman & Hall, 1845.

_____. *The Ages of the World*. Translated with Introduction and Notes by Frederick de Wolfe Bolman, Jr. New York: Columbia University Press, 1942.

_____. *On University Studies*. Edited with an Introduction by Norbert Guterman. Translated by E. S. Morgan. Athens: Ohio University Press, 1966.

Schiller, Frederick. *The Works of Frederick Schiller*. Vol. 4: *Poems and Essays*. Household Edition. Chicago: Belford, Clarke & Co., n.d.

von Schiller, Friedrich. *Naive and Sentimental Poetry and On the Sublime*. Translated, with Introduction and Notes by Julius A. Elias. New York: Frederick Ungar Publishing Co., 1966.

_____. *On the Aesthetic Education of Man in a Series of Letters*. Edited and translated with an Introduction, Commentary, and Glossary of Terms by Elizabeth M. Wilkinson and L. A. Willoughby. Oxford: Clarendon Press, 1967.

Schlesinger, Arthur M. *The Rise of the City, 1878–1898*. New York: Macmillan Co., 1933.

_____. *Orestes A. Brownson*. Boston: Little, Brown & Co., 1939.

_____. *Paths to the Present*. New York: Macmillan Co., 1949.

Schmitt, Peter J. *Back to Nature: the Arcadian Myth in Urban America*. New York: Oxford University Press, 1969.

Schneider, Herbert W. *The Puritan Mind*. New York: Henry Holt & Co., 1930.

Sherwood, Margaret. *Coleridge's Imaginative Conception of Imagination*. Wellesley, Mass.: Wellesley Press, 1960.

Silliman, Benjamin. *Remarks Made on a Short Tour between Hartford and Quebec*. 2d ed. New Haven, 1824.

Stein, Clarence S. *Towards New Towns for America*. Introduction by Lewis Mumford. Cambridge: M.I.T. Press, 1966.

Stein, Roger B. *John Ruskin and Aesthetic Thought in America, 1840–1900*. Cambridge: Harvard University Press, 1967.

Still, Bayrd, ed. *The West: Contemporary Records of American Expansion across the Continent, 1607–1890*. New York: Capricorn Books, 1961.

Sullivan, Louis H. *The Autobiography of an Idea*. Foreword by Claude Bragdon. New York: Press of the American Institute of Architects, 1924.

_____. *Kindergarten Chats and Other Writings*. New York: George Wittenborn, 1947.

Sutter, S. B. *Civilizing American Cities*. Cambridge: M.I.T. Press, 1971.

Syrett, Harold C. *The City of Brooklyn, 1865–1898: A Political History*. New York: AMS Press, 1968.

Tatum, George B. *Andrew Jackson Downing, Arbiter of American Taste, 1815–1852*. Ann Arbor, Mich.: University Microfilms, 1950.

Tobey, George B., Jr. *A History of Landscape Architecture*. New York: American Elsevier Co., 1973.

Tönnies, Ferdinand. *Community & Society (Gemeinschaft und Gesellschaft)*. Translated and edited by Charles P. Loomis. New York: Harper & Row, 1963.

Townsend, Francis G. *Ruskin and the Landscape Feeling: A Critical Analysis of His Thought during the Crucial Years of His Life, 1843–1856*. Illinois Studies in Language and Literature. Vol. 35, no. 3. Urbana: University of Illinois Press, 1951.

Triggs, Oscar Lovell. *The Changing Order: A Study of Democracy*. Chicago: Oscar L. Triggs Publishing Co., 1905.

Troeltsch, Ernest. *The Social Teaching of the Christian Churches*. Translated by Olive Wyon. Introduction by H. Richard Niebuhr. New York: Harper & Bros., 1960.

Tunnard, Christopher. *The City of Man*. 2d ed. New York: Charles Scribner's Sons, 1970.

Tunnard, Christopher, and Boris Pushkarev. *Man-Made America: Chaos or Control? An Inquiry into Selected Problems of Design in the Urbanized Landscape*. New Haven: Yale University Press, 1963.

Tunnard, Christopher, and John Hope Reed. *American Skyline*. Boston: Houghton Mifflin Co., 1955.

Tyler, Alice Felt. *Freedom's Ferment: Phases of American Social History from the Colonial Period to the Outbreak of the Civil War*. New York: Harper & Bros., 1962.

Vanderbilt, Kermit. *Charles Eliot Norton: Apostle of Culture in a Democracy*. Cambridge: Harvard University Press, 1959.

Warner, Sam Bass, Jr. *Streetcar Suburbs: The Process of Growth in Boston, 1870–1900*. Cambridge: Harvard University Press, 1962.

Watson, John. *Schelling's Transcendental Idealism, A Critical Exposition*. Chicago: S. C. Griggs & Co., 1882.

Weber, Max. *The Protestant Ethic and the Spirit of Capitalism*. Translated by Talcott Parsons. Foreword by R. H. Tawney. New York: Charles Scribner's Sons, 1958.

Wellek, René. *A History of Modern Criticism: 1750–1950*, 4 vols. Vol 1: *The Late Eighteenth Century*, Vol. 2: *The Romantic Age*. New Haven: Yale University Press, 1955.

Wertenbaker, Thomas J. *The Puritan Oligarchy*. New York: Grosset & Dunlap, 1947.

Whitehill, Walter Muir. *Boston, A Topographical History*. Cambridge: Harvard University Press, Belknap Press, 1959.

Whyte, Lancelot Law. *The Unconscious before Freud*. Garden City, N.Y.: Anchor Books, 1962.

Williams, Frank B. *The Law of City Planning and Zoning*. New York: Macmillan Co., 1922.

Windelband, Wilhelm. *A History of Philosophy*. Vol. 2: *Renaissance, Enlightenment, and Modern*. New York: Harper & Bros., 1958.

Wordsworth, William. *The Poetical Works of William Wordsworth*. Edited by E. de Selincourt. 5 vols. Oxford: Clarendon Press, 1940–1949.

Zimmerman, Johann Georg von. *Solitude*. 2 vols. London, 1798.

Reports

Croes, J. James R., and Frederick Law Olmsted. *Report of the Civil and Topographical Engineer and the Landscape Architect, Accompanying a Plan for Local Steam Transit Routes in the Twenty-third and Twenty-fourth Wards*. New York: Board of the Department of Public Parks, Document No. 75, March 21, 1877.

[Olmsted, Frederick Law]. Buffalo Park Commission. *Preliminary Report Respecting a Public Park in Buffalo and a Copy of the Act of the Legislature Authorizing Its Establishment*. Buffalo: Matthews & Warren, 1869.

————. Board of Commissioners of the Department of Parks, City of Boston (Mass.). *Annual Report*. Doc. No. 5, 1880.

————. "Report of the Landscape Architect Advisory." Published as an appendix to City of Boston Department of Parks. *Thirteenth Annual Report of the Board of Commissioners of Parks for the Year 1887*. Boston, 1888.

Olmsted, Frederick Law. "The Yosemite Valley and the Mariposa Big Trees: A Preliminary Report (1865)." Edited with an introductory note by Laura Wood Roper. *Landscape Architecture* 43 (October 1952): 12–25.

Olmsted, Frederick Law, and J. James R. Croes. *I. Preliminary Report of the Landscape Architect and the Civil and Topographical Engineer, upon the Laying Out of the Twenty-third* and *Twenty-fourth Wards; II. Report of the Landscape Architect and the Civil and Topographical Engineer, Accompanying a Plan for Laying Out that Part of the Twenty-fourth Ward, Lying West of Riverdale Road*. New York: Board of the Department of Public Parks, Document No. 72. December 20, 1876.

Olmsted, Vaux & Co. *Report upon a Projected Improvement of the Estate of the College of California at Berkeley near Oakland*. San Francisco: Towne and Bacon, 1866.

_____. "Sixth Annual Report, 1866." [Prospect Park] *Annual Reports of the Brooklyn Park Commissioners, 1861–1873*. January, 1873.

_____. "Report of the Landscape Architects and Superintendents, 1 January 1868." *Annual Reports of the Brooklyn Park Commissioners, 1861–1873*. January, 1873.

_____. *Preliminary Report upon the Proposed Suburban Village, near Chicago*. New York: Sutton, Brown & Co., 1868.

Index

Abrams, M.H., 30

Adler, Dankmar, 47

Aesthetics: aesthetic experience, 66, 94, 106, 107-9; American, development of, 42; romantic, 22. *See also* Romantic idealism, German; Transcendentalism

Agrarian myth, 4, 98

Agricultural societies, 11, 12

Agriculture, 100-101, 153n20; dehumanizing nature of, 98; mechanization of, 11, scientific, 10-11, 12, 28

Alienation, 57, 98, 109, 139

Arcadian myth, 112

Architecture, 45, 61; American, 48, 177-78n81; Beaux Arts school, 48, 91, 110; Chicago school, 47; Gothic, 43, 75; Mission (California), 33; organic functionalism, 47; Renaissance, 110; Romanesque, 33

Art, 42, 43, 45; American, 9, 47, 48-50, criticism of, 40-41; beauty in, 106; as civilizing agent, 103-4; nationalism in, 41; organic concept of, 29; as servant to needs of society, 110; as synthesizing agent, 94; unconscious in, 51-58, 70

Art for art's sake, 44, 50, 163n78

Artists: as analogon of God, 59-63; artistic ideals, 63; artist-spectator relationship, 64-73, 168n70, 169n79. *See also* Creative activity

Beauty, concept of, 22, 65, 66, 69, 75, 77-78, 79, 90, 93, 94, 105-6, 109, 111, 112, 128, 163n78, 170n102; and function, 43, 45, 66, 90; Ruskin's aesthetic doctrine of, 78

Bentham, Jeremy, 20, 25, 61, 157-58n88

Birkenhead Park (London), 139, 187n117

Boston, 31-32, 88, 129, 132, 159nn22, 25, 180n37, 183n69, 184n76. *See also* Franklin Park (Boston)

Brace, Charles Loring, 15, 17, 18, 19, 22, 23, 24, 51, 58, 59

Bronx, the, 143, 148

Brownson, Orestes A., 2

Bryant, William Cullen, 28, 151n8

Building restrictions. *See* Zoning and building restrictions

Burnham, Daniel, 48, 110, 141

Burns, Robert, 72

Bushnell, Horace, 11, 12, 15-17, 18, 19, 20, 25, 51, 53, 154n44, 157-58n88; *Views on Christian Nurture,* 16, 154n37

Calvinism, 7, 10, 14-15, 19, 20, 24, 41-42, 44, 45, 58, 67

Carlyle, Thomas, 16, 20-21, 22, 23, 25, 39, 53-54, 59, 63, 66, 98, 155n46, 156n79, 157-58n88, 165n14; *Sartor Resartus,* 20, 21, 53, 63

Central Park (New York City), 3, 4, 22, 27, 30-31, 48, 56, 59, 61, 62-63, 64, 69, 70, 71, 76, 81-85, 89, 94, 100, 102, 107-8, 127, 128, 133, 164n81, 165n8, 168n72, 173n59; aesthetic basis of design, 27

Chiaroscuro, Olmsted's use of, 89-90

Cities: as agents of human progress, 113; anti-city attitudes, 93, 119, 149; attraction of, 93; development of, 93, 95; disadvantages of, 95, 96; effects of science and technology on, 119, 123, history of, 113-48; law of improvement and, 146-47;